# ART-MAKING WITH REFUGEES
# AND SURVIVORS

*of related interest*

**A Practical Guide to Therapeutic Work
with Asylum Seekers and Refugees**
*Angelina Jalonen and Paul Cilia La Corte*
*Foreword by Jerry Clore*
ISBN 978 1 78592 073 8
eISBN 978 1 78450 334 5

**Arts Therapists, Refugees and Migrants**
Reaching Across Borders
*Edited by Ditty Dokter*
ISBN 978 1 85302 550 1
eISBN 978 1 84642 988 0

**Reading and Expressive Writing with Traumatised
Children, Young Refugees and Asylum Seekers**
Unpack My Heart with Words
Part of the Writing for Therapy or Personal Development series
*Marion Baraitser*
ISBN 978 1 84905 384 6
eISBN 978 0 85700 747 6

**Using Art Therapy with Diverse Populations**
Crossing Cultures and Abilities
*Paula Howie, Sangeeta Prasad, and Jennie Kristel*
*Foreword by Mercèdes B. ter Maat and Gaelynn P. Wolf Bordonaro*
ISBN 978 1 84905 916 9
eISBN 978 0 85700 694 3

**Art Therapy and Social Action**
Treating the World's Wounds
*Edited by Frances Kaplan*
ISBN 978 1 84310 798 9
eISBN 978 1 84642 551 6

**Trauma is Really Strange**
*Steve Haines*
*Art by Sophie Standing*
ISBN 978 1 84819 293 5
eISBN 978 0 85701 240 1

# ART-MAKING WITH REFUGEES AND SURVIVORS

*Creative and Transformative Responses to Trauma*
*After Natural Disasters, War and Other Crises*

SALLY ADNAMS JONES, PhD

Jessica Kingsley *Publishers*
London and Philadelphia

First published in 2018
by Jessica Kingsley Publishers
73 Collier Street
London N1 9BE, UK
and
400 Market Street, Suite 400
Philadelphia, PA 19106, USA

*www.jkp.com*

Copyright © Sally Adnams Jones 2018
Chapters 5, 6, 7 and 8 copyright © Jessica Kingsley Publishers 2018

Cover artwork by Nomfusi Nkani
10/12/1974–19/12/2017
In loving memory

**Library of Congress Cataloging in Publication Data**
A CIP catalog record for this book is available from the Library of Congress

**British Library Cataloguing in Publication Data**
A CIP catalogue record for this book is available from the British Library

ISBN 978 1 78592 238 1
eISBN 978 1 78450 518 9

Printed and bound in Great Britain

# CONTENTS

*Chapter 1*

# INTRODUCTION

This book explores how creativity can transform people's lives, including the healing of trauma. It proposes that programs that support creative forms of self-expression be taken much more seriously, both as a personal practice within the therapy office, the classroom and the studio, and as a funded practice within public health. In order to illustrate understandings of the link between optimal health and creativity, we have gathered stories here of the expressive arts being practiced in vulnerable communities living on the front lines of global crises. We share the voices of facilitators working directly in the field of creativity and public health, as they tell their stories of making art with survivors of some of today's major global traumas—refugees from poverty, war, ethnic genocide, fundamentalism, climate change, pandemic, tsunami and earthquake. These stories are woven together with a theoretical understanding about the nature of individual and social trauma, and the principles behind transforming trauma through the creative arts.

It is my belief that the capacities for both trauma and creativity are innate to everyone, and so this book is relevant to us all, not only for those living in hotspots of intense social emergency. By reading this book, we can all learn to bring these two concepts together, in order to live more adaptively, in a challenging world. We can learn to heal our own trauma by tapping into our own creative and generative resources. This book is therefore not only for therapists or program administrators who deal with trauma on a professional level. It is for anyone who wishes to understand the relationship between their own creativity and their own transformation more deeply, and thereby bootstrap themselves into higher levels of consciousness and joy. By resolving trauma through creative self-expression, readers can change in positive ways: develop compassion for themselves and others, connect to community, regulate their own nervous system, expand their brain integration, increase their resilience, and deepen their sense of identity and their life's meaning, thereby reaching their full potential. We will include discussion on exactly how transformation happens, as we define trauma and healing in much more depth as we proceed.

Simply put, trauma usually includes difficult changes in our circumstances (either sudden or chronic) that we cannot immediately integrate. Processing painful change, which is often accompanied by loss, can sometimes be challenging. Processing the traumatic event can stall, and we can get "stuck" when our consciousness is overwhelmed. "Stuck processing" results in trauma. Most of us will experience changes in our lives at some point, such as the loss of a loved family member, or a friend. Many of us, too, will experience the loss of other significant support structures in our lives, such as the loss of a marriage, our health, possessions, home, safety, country, employment, language or status. Change and the subsequent loss can often result in disorientation, dislocation, dispossession and disconnection—some of the more common side effects of traumatic challenges in our world today. These are pervasive experiences for many people, and not only for those who might be defined as living on the front lines of global disaster. We are, in fact, all survivors of some change-loss or another, with varying degrees of severity and complexity, so this book is addressed not only to those supporting refugees of global disaster, but also to anyone resolving change, healing trauma and wishing to expand into their full capacity by connecting to their creativity.

Fortunately, many of us will never experience the overwhelming intensity of the sudden and simultaneous loss of everything that we once understood to be ours, including our identity, meaning, relationships and possessions—all at once. This intense level of complex change that refugees experience—the loss of all intersecting support structures, often at the same time—is, fortunately, not an everyday occurrence for most of us. However, most of us will experience some trauma, spread over a lifetime, and paradoxically, this continual peristalsis of us by life can actually help us to deepen and mature, if we have support structures and understand how to move forward. However, more and more people on the planet are now experiencing macro traumas—precipitous, concurrent, multiple losses without the support structures that help them through the change. Loss and traumatic events can be deeply overwhelming without the necessary tools to process complex change.

As our planet flirts with existential crises, people find themselves more frequently on the move—escaping war, genocide, pandemic, tsunami, earthquake or climate change. These survivors may face layer upon layer of loss, including the disappearance of everything with which they once identified—their home and their possessions, their family, their role in their community, their country. Who they are, who they love, what they own and where they live and belong are sometimes lost overnight. Luckily there are some methods and practices available to help people integrate these changes, through creative actions.

The simultaneous loss of identity, meaning, relationships and possessions can at first be experienced as a deep shock, or numbness. Over time, this can be followed by pain, grief, anger, anxiety or chronic depression. To complicate matters, those who experience such depth of loss can also sometimes lose their articulation around the experience—the words to describe such a shattering experience can be hard to find. How do we process such layered trauma, so deep and wide that it includes the loss of everything once held familiar, understood and loved by us, including our words? It may be surprising to know that by accessing our creativity, on a preverbal level, words can be found, and trauma can be alleviated.

Survivors of this level of trauma can in fact come back from such intense events through visual self-expression, and in some cases, can even go on to flourish. It would be lacking in compassion to rank levels of trauma from person to person, but those of us who may be more insulated from such all-encompassing "macro" traumas can learn greatly from people who have lived through, or worked with, this end of the human-change spectrum. Human resilience and the capacity to adapt and flourish in such dire circumstances is, in fact, one of humanity's most profound, selective traits that has, in the past, contributed to the evolutionary survival of our species, especially in times of existential risk.

Although this book respectfully includes stories that describe the courageous suffering of macro traumas by some, it is realistic to suggest that this book will probably not be read by those people currently living through such extreme circumstances, as they are, by necessity, preoccupied with survival. This book will more likely be read by those who lead more stable lives—people perhaps surviving the daily "micro" traumas of "normal" life, and not dealing with such overwhelming complexities. I would like to point out, however, that although the stories in this book describe projects with vulnerable people, this book is not intended to be trauma-tourism by the more fortunate. These stories are only shared here in order for us to learn from existing projects about how the expressive arts, and acts of creativity, can help heal trauma, so that our understanding, compassion and creative curricula may deepen. This book is written not only to encourage a more positive understanding of creativity, but also as a celebration of humanity's resilience.

This book will reveal exactly how acts of creativity can help people transform through three, time-linked aspects of the self: healing "past" wounds or blockages; learning to access their "present" endurance and power; and evolving into new "future" meanings and identities. Healthy identities are now understood to be fluid (Gee, 2000), and problems arise when identities get "stuck" in less adaptive forms as life changes around us. Our identities are on a continual trajectory through life, and in order to be resilient, the internal needs to evolve in step with the external. Expressive projects can help us update ourselves, reboot and be more adaptive to external circumstances.

Although many of the selected stories here focus on visual art, all forms of the expressive arts can accomplish this same end. It is important to note that any form of expression can be transformative if it follows certain criteria. It is from people who have done this work in the field, who have tapped into their own power of creativity, either as survivor-participants or as facilitators, that we, as readers, can also learn how to do this in our own lives.

Transformation (or "transformance" as Diana Fosha (2017) calls it) can happen at many levels if we allow it, and can include several processes: healing, learning and evolving. "Healing" implies there is a past wound, blockage or pathology that is preventing us from moving forward into an expanded version of our present or possible health. "Learning" implies an understanding of "how" to heal, repeatedly, so that we can move forward every time there is a blockage. "Evolution" implies we are now deliberately aligning ourselves with this creative principle, of expanding our consciousness and future through various practices. In this book, we will explore how transformation through creativity happens in the past and present. Deliberate creative practices designed for our full future self-actualization and highest evolution will be dealt with in another book, although these principles may occasionally be alluded to here.

Creative acts come in many shapes and sizes, including writing, dance, music, image-making and performance. All these creative "forms" share certain core transformative commonalities and principles beyond the surface differences. For example, they are all "symbolic languages" representing reality through metaphorical forms—using text, voice, gesture, rhythm or image. Visual art is only one of many metaphorical forms of expression that can be employed to externalize our human experience. This book will explore visual art-making in more depth than the other forms of expressive arts, with "images" being the primary "language." Readers can therefore extrapolate how the other art forms can also be used to resolve trauma.

Art is, at its root, primarily a visual storytelling method that uses pictures rather than words to narrate, which is especially useful for accessing visceral, preverbal understandings. Images are also useful in multicultural contexts where there is no common language, as is often the case in global hotspots where people gather in response to trauma. Images are naturally and spontaneously used by all children before self-doubt sets in at the age of puberty (when the process of individuation really starts to take off into maturity), and when self-consciousness becomes acute. Art is not only for those deemed "talented" or "educated." Children instinctively "draw" stories well before they can write them, and adults can learn to "remember" how to do this. Art is an innate form of "literacy," accessible to anyone, of any age, in any culture, speaking any language. It is a truly democratic process, not reserved only for the privileged, educated or talented. It can be practiced as a grassroots activity, any time, anywhere on the planet, no matter what the ethnicity, race, gender, class or age.

To illustrate this capacity of visual art to benefit anybody who may practice it, this book shares a diversity of art projects from across the world, situated in different contexts, facing different challenges, in order to illustrate the universal applicability of healing trauma and learning through creativity. The surface variations of the projects—the medium, the topic, the geo-location or contextual challenge—disappear when we begin to see the common underlying transformative principles of creativity that are accessible to all humans anywhere.

In this book, we start our exploration by looking at some of the theory behind understanding trauma. Then we look at the actual process of how visual art heals trauma, so that readers have a shared understanding of the connection between creativity, learning and health. We then illustrate this theory with real stories shared by facilitators working with survivors of disaster in various locations around the world. Both the facilitators and the survivors have had first-hand experience of the capacity of the expressive arts to heal people from complex, intersecting trauma. Gathering these stories together has been my great privilege, and this collection is valuable in order to deepen our understanding of how lives intensify. We can apply this knowledge, both retro-actively to past trauma that has already occurred, as well as pro-actively, to build resilience for facing future trauma, so that we might self-actualize fully.

The stories in this book are moving accounts told by some of the most experienced art facilitators in the world. They are leaders who have broken new ground in their own unique ways, by exploring an emerging field of healing through the expressive arts. Apart from being artists themselves, these facilitators have multiple other identities, such as community developers, educators, cultural activists, urban alchemists, therapists, students and medical doctors. Their stories are part autobiography, part project analysis and part discussion on how art heals. These stories are richly layered and took time to come into being, as the facilitators each thought carefully about how to distill a lifetime of experience into one chapter—at first a seemingly daunting challenge. But each story-teller has succeeded beautifully. Some have chosen factual language, some extracts from journals, while others have preferred to play with richly layered metaphor to capture the complexity of their experiences with creative community art projects. My gratitude goes out to these contributors. Together we have harvested new knowledge generated on the front lines of trauma, to deepen our understanding of transformation through creativity.

The common denominator for this work seems to be a passion for restoring health and capacity through innate human creativity, both of which can flower naturally given certain circumstances. The stories in this book reflect personal, communal, cultural, political and spiritual transformations—a ripple effect of transformations out into public life, evident in these stories. As we heal ourselves, we heal our relationships, our communities, our environments and our futures. In this way, the effect of the expressive arts is felt, not only by the survivors of the particular trauma, but by all those around them. Communal creativity can have a rehabilitative impact well beyond the personal, and in some circumstances, can be felt around the world, as art pieces travel beyond the studio context, through digital sharing or by exhibition. Transformation occurs in ever widening fields of resonance (Adnams Jones, 2016).

Only in the last 50 years or so have training programs in art therapy and community art programs become available. Art education programs have been around a bit longer, although these programs sometimes emphasize technical skills only, rather than an understanding of transformation. Programs specifically focused on art-making with displaced and dispossessed people in emergency situations are still few and far between. This book therefore attempts something entirely new—we have tried here to understand exactly how transformation through creativity happens, so that we might better understand a distinctly therapeutic practice (healing the past), an educative practice (becoming aware of how to repeat this in our present circumstances) as well as an evolutionary practice (actualizing our futures through practice). Without this understanding, healing can be just a "by-product"—"covert" to the "overt" art-making—rather than a principle around which curricula are formed. It is to be hoped that a book like this can help shift educators, therapists, institutions, governments, charities and funders into greater support of creativity for public health in all situations, which include art for healing, learning and evolving.

The stories in this book are told by innovative, courageous, compassionate people, who have had deep intuitions concerning exactly what is needed as we face challenges of mass migration, over-population, climate change, resource pressure, ideological fundamentalism and pandemic. All contributors do this work because they have seen for themselves the capacity of the expressive arts to empower people, even in the most challenging of situations, towards finding new resilience, voice and vision through creative acts.

I first became interested in the natural, innate capacity of art to heal when I experienced this phenomenon for myself. I grew up in South Africa in the 1970s and 80s, when there was political unrest, pervasive uncertainty, and threatened civil war, with high levels of violence and suffering. As I did not subscribe to the political position of the apartheid government of the time, I decided as a young adult to align my life with my conscience by leaving South Africa and immigrating to a country that shared my values. I was fortunate to have the choice to move to Canada and to have the legal status and health to do this. Although I arrived with virtually no money, the move itself does imply a certain amount of privilege compared with others, who are perhaps unable to move; or are forced to move against their will; or may be denied legal status where they do live; or who may be living in "limbo," in a "no man's land" refugee camp.

However, this privilege of a "choice" to move did not make me immune to trauma. Like many migrants who experience deep change, I was impacted by a severe sense of loss, and a certain amount of deprivation, from the loss of my own culture and loved ones. I was suddenly a status-less stranger in a new land, without any relevant "past," unable to vote or find work. For a while, as I slowly adjusted to my new country, I suffered from a loss of belonging, meaning and identity, and for many years I experienced a sense of cultural isolation. Chronic long-term loss can change a person's brain chemistry (Rosenthal, 2015; Van der Kolk, 2014) and so, as a result, like many immigrants, I experienced a period of major depression. Kirmayer *et al.* (2011) suggest "the task of preventing, recognizing and appropriately treating common mental health problems in primary care is complicated for immigrants and refugees because of differences in language, culture, patterns of seeking help and ways of coping."

For me, the complex grief I experienced from the immigration process was also exacerbated by post-partum depression—the hormonal changes following two childbirths. I was offered various forms of help, including medication, which was mildly helpful, but also had some debilitating side effects. This medication was then pulled from the market due to the high volume of fatalities from liver damage. I was then given a period of talk therapy by a psychiatrist, which was helpful but did not seem to cure my grief, lack of meaning and motivation. With the understanding that antidepressant drugs can cure only about half the number of patients who try them (Vedantam, 2006), my psychiatrist then offered me electro-convulsive shock therapy treatment, which I chose not to accept. I then faced the conundrum of how to heal myself, using less invasive treatments. I took the decision to try alternative methods in order to relieve my own pain. Luckily, among other things, I found the expressive arts, which changed my life and which, over time, helped me resolve my past and come profoundly into the present, and then helped me actualize my future.

I experimented with myself as a subject, and observed the ways in which accessing my creativity transformed me. I observed that as my creativity was activated, I became alive, began to feel the joy of self-expression return, with new insights and connections. My capacity to relate to others and the world improved. I became more vocal and therefore more self-determining and self-advocating. As I accessed my imagination, I felt myself relax out of stress and begin to build new meanings for myself, which Frankl (2006), as a survivor of the Nazi death camps, suggests is the basic skill necessary for survival of any deep trauma. As I began to read more widely on the topic of the arts as a healing mechanism, I discovered that other artists, activists, educators and therapists were also beginning to discover the capacity of the arts to be a kind of medicine (London, 1989, 1992; McNiff, 1992, 1998, 2004; Malchiodi, 2006/7, 2012). There was new evidence on multiple fronts that we could heal ourselves of individual past trauma, and that we could bring social transformation to our cultures and communities (Goldbard, 2006; Naidus, 2009). Some felt we could use art for cultural evolution (Dissanayake, 1992, 2008). Fascinated by the idea that art-making could be seen as a holistic method for influencing positive change—past, present and future—I took formal PhD (doctorate) studies in how visual art transforms us through a field of resonance (Adnams Jones, 2016).

Through my own research, I was amazed to discover that, by making art, I could not only change my environment on the external level, but also change my internal environment, including my own neurology and physiology. I realized that by making art, it was possible to enliven my right brain capacities and perspectives (Edwards, 1999; McGilchrist, 2009; Pink, 2006); explore my optimal "flow" states through my creativity (Csikszentmihaly, 1990, 1996, 1997); increase my capacity to be in the present moment (Cassou, 2008; Osho, 1999); and cultivate peak experiences (Maslow, 1964). I realized that by making art, people can release their imagination (Cassou, 2008); increase their social and emotional intelligence (Goleman, 1996, 2007); imagine a future (Greene, 1995b); and fulfill their highest human need to individuate into their full potential (Maslow, 1968). There is, in fact, no down side or negative side effect to practicing the arts, only expansion into further human potential. What had begun for me as a process of self-medicating had become a process of self-actualizing through my creativity.

I then discovered that this personal practice could be expanded to include groups of people, in safe, collective communities. After teaching art in this way for some time, and after researching this process with two different indigenous communities in order to better understand cross-cultural creative practices, I then wished to document the principles behind this socially transformative process. This book is one result of a creative collaboration with others.

So why is this book important right now? Many are feeling that our planet is under threat from over-population, pollution and polarization, with possible future species extinction. This awareness can result in existential trauma for some. The good news is that at the same time as we discover that we "need" to change the way we do business, we are also discovering that we "can." New neurological research reveals that the human brain is "plastic," and that we can "learn" to change throughout our lives (McGilchrist, 2009) depending on our genetics, conditioning, experiences and determination. We are beginning to understand that creativity affects, and is affected by, our brain plasticity. Creativity is essential to both our immediate well-being, and our future existence.

Perhaps the most insidious threat to our creativity, which in itself is creating subtle internal trauma (McGilchrist, 2009), is the mounting pressure in our world, and within ourselves, to shift constantly into the left-hemisphere of the brain. We live in a world that is beginning to favor the power of logic, efficiencies and bottom-line numbers (or left-brain activity), over creativity and imagination (or right-brain activity)—although I use this "hemispheric division" loosely, more as a metaphor here. Dividing our capacities into two separate hemispheres is a reductive over-simplification, but I do this here to avoid more complex analysis of our brain function. There are already books that successfully do that (McGilchrist, 2009). Simply put, our education systems have, in the past, emphasized and valued some of our capacities over others, and some symbolic languages over others (for example, numbers and words over images, rhythm or gesture), setting up a "hierarchy" of only a few of our many innate intelligences and literacies. IQ tests have in the past generally valued and measured "left-brain" activities over "right," and careers that reflect the use of these capacities have become valued monetarily. Our schooling has shifted to reflect our values, therefore institutionalizing a limited cognitive activity to favoring logic, rote learning and short-term memory of facts over imagination and somatic knowing. Today's schooling is often market driven, training children for "jobs" rather than aiming for a creative education with balanced growth, and the long-term development of our full creative capacities. As imaginations become devalued, we are slowly starving ourselves of half our capacities.

The irony is that, at the same time this kind of pervasive "left-brain chauvinism" leads to cuts in the arts and the general devaluing of our "creatives," global pressures are simultaneously mounting, forcing humans to adapt and change more rapidly and more frequently than ever before. The arts are needed more than ever to help us with processing change, arriving at creative solutions, learning about difference and building social and emotional intelligence. Yet they are being cut from our schools and communities on an unprecedented scale. As we become more and more focused on power, money, goals and device screens, rather than on imagination, books, performances and exhibitions, and as we become more and more isolated in apartment blocks, we are generally reducing our active engagement in the arts. We are now living in a crisis of intimacy. So how do we develop the communal and creative skills necessary to change this? One way is to resurrect communal, creative practice.

As our societies move rapidly from the industrial age into the information age, many will experience change and loss such as technological expansion, human redundancy, divorce, stress and corresponding changes in health. The planet, too, is experiencing complex change at this time, such as population growth, food scarcity and climate warming. Consequently, social trauma is being experienced on an unprecedented scale, including the loss of control over environments, job security, relationships and futures. Some hotspot communities are experiencing war, genocide and natural disasters like famine, flood, drought, tsunami and earthquake.

Ultimately, none of us is insulated from the challenges of the cycle of change-loss-growth. Logic, money, power and education cannot insure against it. However, there are existing practices that can help us before, during and after change so that we do not get stuck in trauma. The expressive arts are emerging as a tried-and-true methodology that can help us not only process past trauma, but adapt and flourish into new futures, thanks to those pioneering this modality on the front lines of global crises today.

The art projects described in this book are located in places undergoing some intense challenges and consequently some of the stories may be a little disturbing. However, this book is intended to be a positive read. Even though it takes readers on a journey through the challenging situations of others, it is not intended to be pain voyeurism. The book explores people's dignity and courage, and shares exactly how art-making can and has been therapeutic even in the most challenging of situations. This is a very positive book for an evolving humanity that offers practical examples and applications for a transformative creativity.

I hope that the stories gathered here will be helpful to individuals struggling with change on whatever level, who might be wondering what modality to turn to for help. I hope this book will help artists and teachers who want to deepen their own studio work into a more transformative kind of practice. I hope it will help administrators to advocate for the continued presence of creative practices in public education and health. I hope this book will be helpful to community developers who may want to include art-making as a method for envisioning new futures. I especially hope this book will be helpful to those wishing to procure funding for regenerative change-projects in both rural or inner city environments, or wherever confluences of people might be gathering. Finally, I hope this book will be helpful to counseling professionals, who may wish to embed the expressive arts more deeply into their practices.

I am perennially grateful and excited by the possibilities of creativity and the expressive arts, and it is my hope that by gathering these stories, valuable experiences may be shared with all those interested in moving beyond art's decorative aesthetic, and its market commodification, into a more transformative practice of conscious creativity. It is my hope that creativity might be taken more seriously as a dignified transformative methodology for adults, adolescents and children alike, from all walks of life, who are willing to tap into their own innate human creativity, which is the source of both their power and their evolution. May this book reach all those who need it, for their health, happiness and transformation.

*Chapter 2*

# MAPPING PERSONAL AND SOCIO-POLITICAL TRAUMA, INCLUDING CURRENT GLOBAL MIGRATION PATTERNS

Let's begin by exploring how trauma arises, and then we will look at how migration patterns reflect and affect personal trauma.

All sentient life, of which humans are a part, is defined by the fact that it has "sensations," or feelings—subjective experiences on the inside, as a response to stimuli from the outside. Multicellular organisms, including our own human body, have developed a nervous system, so that our bodies can "talk" to us through nerve endings that send chemical signals to our brains. This allows us to "read" our environment, by experiencing the biofeedback of both pleasure and pain. Somatic sensations can therefore guide us, in order to keep us safe. Pleasure indicates our need to move towards that which is "good" for us, and pain indicates our need to move away from that which is "bad" for us. Pleasure and pain can of course be interpreted in a more sophisticated way as guides at various levels, but simply put here, both pleasure and pain are both non-verbal, neurological messaging systems, conditioning us to either repeat or change our circumstances.

Feelings of pleasure and pain usually peak and pass like a wave, and the wave's duration can be short and sudden, or long and chronic. Let's focus just on pain for a moment, as it is pain that can become "stuck" or "traumatic." Feelings of pain are on a spectrum, and can intensify from simple discomfort, to annoyance, to pain, to agony—either emotionally or physically. This intensification does not necessarily create trauma; for example, the wave of childbirth agony passes, and few are traumatized by it afterwards. We will look at the nature of how pain becomes trauma in much more depth here, but for now, let's first look at how trauma arises socially, in the current world situation of biological and political "systems" in which we live. Then we will narrow our focus down to look at personal trauma, which is often nested within the macro trauma of the bigger political and biological determinants of "change."

Just as pain does not in and of itself cause trauma, neither does "change." Change is actually an essential aspect of evolution. It is more the rate of change within an environment that can be problematic, or the lack of support we might feel during the change. Historically, if change has been too rapid, aggressive or complex, species have become extinct, as their physical biology and mental conditioning are unable to adapt rapidly enough in order to evolve and survive. When change is too rapid, or too slow, species can become vulnerable. Grizzly bears, for example, are presently struggling to adapt to the rapid rate of change in their territories, with newly built highways cutting through customary breeding grounds and resources. Coral reefs are struggling to survive in water temperatures that have changed too rapidly for them to adapt, leading to bleaching and death. Adaptation to change is an essential skill for survival of any traumatic event, as we have noted with animals at risk. But adaptation takes "time" and "learning," both critical aspects for survival.

So, in the big contextual picture, it is the rate of change in an environment that can be traumatizing and it is "learning" that helps the adaptation. Our foremost learning is from our mothers, about what nourishes us. Organic life usually has to procure food—energy from outside itself—to stay alive. We need to gather energy for fuel through consumption, in order to produce, as well as reproduce. This energy exchange system requires resources, and many species, including humans, are prepared to fight or migrate in order to keep resources coming their way.

Sometimes resources in one area can become scarce, and movement from a resource-scarce context to resource-rich context can occur—a natural phenomenon of migration that has happened ever since organic life first evolved the ability to be mobile. These movements towards energetic resources and away from disturbances are driven by the pleasure-pain principle, towards safety, comfort and bounty, and away from danger, distress and scarcity. There are many examples of mobile forms of organic life creating routes that follow seasonal fluctuations in resources, some half way around the world, such as the monarch butterfly or the trumpeter swan. In and of themselves, these migrations are not generally traumatic. They build strength and resilience over time. In fact, migration can be viewed generally as an act of adaptability as it allows for species to successfully change locations and to strengthen and increase the herd.

Although humans migrate naturally, first moving from the rift valley in Africa and out across the world, sometimes we have been unable to move, due to low energy, during times of famine, winter, drought or plague. The loss of the weak, the young and the old does serve to strengthen the genetics of any species. As the weak are left behind, resources are conserved for the stronger breeding animals. Humans, however, have moved beyond this pattern of "survival of only the fittest." We have developed compassion, whereby we take care of our weak and vulnerable. In stable countries, we have also developed tax systems for example, that can redistribute resources to the infirm. We have developed educational programs and compassionate institutions that assist the vulnerable to survive. The projects in this book reflect this compassion, of facilitators developing programs and institutions in order to support vulnerable members to become more resilient to change.

As our institutions and technology have improved, including agriculture, engineering and medicine, humans have become very successful, increasing our survival rates, both at childbirth and into old age. The global population has therefore exploded, even in resource-poor locations. And over the centuries, as we have changed from hunter gatherers into farmers, and then moved into the industrial and information ages, migrations towards resources have become blocked due to land ownership and borders becoming ever more fixed. Over time, populations have become no longer free to simply migrate to other areas in search of energy resources. In response to increased human numbers, pressures build, and resources become more defended through aggressive action. There are ever more complex legalities around border controls, requiring passports and citizenship in order to access or protect resources.

Humans are complex, social creatures who need more than physical resources to thrive. We also require stable support structures, and a sense of belonging—to a family, a community, an ethnicity and a country. Like the old adage says, "Man cannot live by bread alone." We also require identity and meaning in order to flourish. As social, pack animals, we need psychic structures to survive and thrive, through ongoing micro and macro traumas. We are perhaps the only animal prepared to fight to protect not only our resources and territory, but also our psychic structures or "beliefs," such as ethnic ideologies or religious fundamentalisms.

Despite new understandings that healthy identities are fluid (Gee, 2000), and that trauma occurs when we get "stuck," humans seem to build ever-more entrenched identities, beliefs and meanings, and our capacity to protect these physical and psychic structures seems to grow in more and more sophisticated ways. However, these support structures can occasionally fall precipitously away, due to war, climate change, pandemic, tsunami, earthquake or famine. During periods of rapid change to our identities and resources, the big question is, how do people find new meanings (Frankl, 2006)? Luckily, we humans are remarkably adaptable, a quality that has greatly contributed to our success and the explosion of our species.

Unlike the rhino or tiger, humans are essentially creative and have multiple forms of intelligence. We have developed certain mechanisms, a kind of multi-literate capacity for expressing ourselves, that other animals do not have. We have, for example, devised various languages, including text, numbers and images, as ways to transmit, learn and replicate knowledge. Because of our talent for literacy, we can "learn" to document knowledge and process change faster than most other creatures.

Humans have developed organizations that actually help us to facilitate deliberate change. Unlike other creatures, we have sophisticated educational and therapeutic institutions, where "learning to change" becomes both the process and the goal. The fields of education and psychology have developed processes to maximize this adaptive learning, and within both systems, the making of art is one of these adaptive models—through either art education or art therapy. Both routes share similar "learning" and "healing" scaffolding—

how to develop deliberately and consciously into our full potential, which makes us more resilient, depending on how the art-making is facilitated. When we draw on both these fields and practice art consciously for our own evolution, we transform ourselves.

Our capacity for literacy and self-expression can be viewed as an evolutionary asset, within a geo-political context of continual change. Let's take a closer look now at the nature of "personal" trauma, so that we can better understand what it means to "transform" it through art. I use the word "transform" deliberately, as it includes both the adaptive processes of "healing" (the central focus of psychology); "learning" (the central focus of education); and "evolving" (one of the central foci of consciousness studies, science, biology and also ancient spirituality).

Our understanding of the nature of personal trauma has deepened over time. Although pain has always existed wherever there is feeling, any "theory" concerning emotional pain and how to work with trauma has been developed only very recently, in the past century. In the early 1900s, Pierre Janet explored "stress" and how people could "dissociate" from it. He called it an "illness," where people were not fully alive or present. Freud explored "hysteria" and "repression" caused by stress. Funded studies of stress, however, only began in depth with survivors of the Holocaust and the Vietnam war, when it was first understood that those who had experienced "stress," now also called "trauma," were no longer thought of as "morally weak" or "sick," as they once were, but rather as injured and in need of healing. We first learned about emotional pain, trauma, resilience and adaptability from the experience of survivors, and we continue in this tradition today, with this book.

In 1994, the American Psychological Association (APA) officially defined trauma as "post-traumatic stress disorder," or PTSD, resulting from "an event that involved actual or threatened death or serious injury, or a threat to the physical integrity of self or others, and which involved fear, helplessness, or horror" (Joseph, 2012). However, this definition was limited, framing trauma as occurring only in helpless people. This is currently thought to be far too restrictive. Certainly, it is not a very empowering view. Many therapists now prefer the view that *all* life events have the potential to be "perceived" as traumatic (or not), and the extent of the trauma is influenced by two things: people's support systems, and their vulnerability (Joseph, 2012). Events can be viewed as "potentially" traumatic by some and not by others, and therefore events can affect us differently. It is important to note that our "resilience," "perception" and our "support" determines the amount of trauma we experience.

> These days, the American Psychological Association defines trauma as an emotional response to a terrible event like an accident, rape or natural disaster. Immediately after the event, shock and denial are typical. Longer term reactions include unpredictable emotions, flashbacks, strained relationships and even physical symptoms like headaches or nausea. While these feelings are normal, some people have difficulty moving on with their lives. (American Psychological Association, 2017)

Many therapists today accept this more inclusive definition, of pain becoming "stuck" somehow, or taking longer to process in the vulnerable, and so the understanding of "vulnerability" continues to broaden. Vulnerability is a quality that is now much more acceptable than it once was. Present understandings of trauma include not only survivors of war, such as refugees, but also survivors of abuse, such as emotional, sexual or violent assault, as well as survivors of residential schools and cultural genocide. The Center for Nonviolence and Social Justice suggests that trauma refers to experiences that are emotionally or physically painful and distressing, including separation and discrimination, and that, for some groups of people, trauma can occur frequently, becoming part of the common human experience:

> In addition to terrifying events such as violence and assault, we suggest that relatively more subtle and insidious forms of trauma—such as discrimination, racism, oppression and poverty—are pervasive, and when experienced chronically have a cumulative impact that can be fundamentally life altering. Particular forms of trauma…are directly related to chronic fear and anxiety with serious long-term effects on health and other life outcomes. (Center for Nonviolence and Social Justice, 2014)

Trauma occurs when we get stuck in "hyper-arousal" (vigilance, over-reactivity or nightmares) or in "hypo-arousal" (numbing out, isolation or depression). Medical researcher Bessel Van der Kolk, who has studied trauma for 40 years, suggests (2014) that trauma can disturb hormones, circuits, sensorimotor systems, what we think about and how we think it. Van der Kolk says "all traumatized people get stuck in the past. They are attached to an unsurmountable obstacle" (2017). Minds are contaminated and hijacked by the only significant thing—their fixation on the past incident. They feel disconnected and are afraid to feel their feelings. The present seems bleak. They cannot concentrate or pay attention to right now; they do not feel fully alive, and have little sense of meaning. Because they are stuck in certain maladapted patterns of thought and physiology, they cannot accumulate new experiences from which to learn more adaptive responses to life. They experience a failure of interpersonal safety and reciprocity. They feel worthless and ashamed. Many of those in the art projects featured in this book have experienced this kind of trauma.

Some doctors (for example, Anda *et al.*, 2006) have assessed trauma not only as a result of adult life, but also as a background to the development of the young. They now believe insecure attachment to the initial caregiver and accumulated adverse childhood experiences (known as ACEs) can be considered traumatic, as they affect the developing brain quite significantly before it is resilient. ACEs are linked to social and health outcomes in adulthood. One study (Anda *et al.*, 2006) looked at inventories of insidious types of childhood traumas. These included: early separation from parental figures; physical, sexual or emotional abuse; physical or emotional neglect; whether a mother was treated violently; whether there was household substance abuse; mental illness; parental divorce; or the incarceration of a household member. The study concluded that childhood experiences, both positive and negative, have a tremendous impact on future attachment, violence, victimization, perpetration and lifelong health and opportunity. As such, early developmental experiences are now understood to be an important public health issue, and many of the stories featured in this book are about children. The younger the child, the more impact the trauma can have.

So to be clear, trauma is not just a "fleeting" pain wave moving through the body. Whether acute or chronic, trauma is a pattern of response that becomes "stuck" in our physiology and implicit memory, especially in the early, preverbal years, due to the combination of the intensity of the painful moment/s and the arousal of the nervous system, whereby the event becomes part of our later response to life. Responses to perceived danger can become wired into our nervous systems, through a hyper-reactive amygdala, which tends to keep our systems in the fight-and-flight response longer than is necessary, or arouses the sympathetic nervous response more quickly than it ought. Arousal becomes chronic and easily triggered, and the wear and tear on human bodies through the perpetual "activation" of cortisol and adrenalin becomes detrimental. Stress hormones are designed for short-term activation of bodies during actual danger, and are detrimental to thoughts and internal organs when chronically released over the long term, due to "perceived" dangers, or patterned, hard-wired responses. We can re-enact subconscious patterns and responses due to this arousal, with neuronal pathways wiring together over time. Trauma can therefore also be enacted forward into the next generation, through memory, physiology and subconscious patterning.

When we are stuck in a subjective experience, we can lose our ability to find language around the event. This means we cannot create the narrative that might help us get some distance from the original event by becoming the observer of it, or the witness of ourselves and our responses. If we have been scared speechless, and can't find the words to describe what happened, we cannot organize our experiences or find a sense of linear history—the before, during and after. We can lose our sense of self, when the event and the associations around it are buried deep in the implicit memory. But as Peter Levine, the founder of Somatic Experiencing, suggests (2010), trauma is a fact of life, but it doesn't have to be a life sentence. Researchers Richard Tedeschi and Lawrence Calhoun have extensively pioneered the idea that transformation can and does occur post-traumatically. They call it "post-traumatic growth":

> A central theme of the life challenges that are the focus here is their seismic nature. Much like earthquakes can impact the physical environment, traumatic circumstances, characterized by their unusual, uncontrollable, potentially irreversible and threatening qualities, can produce an upheaval in trauma survivors' major assumptions about the world, their place in it and how they make sense of their daily

lives. In reconsidering these assumptions, there are the seeds for new perspectives on all these matters and a sense that valuable—although painful—lessons have been learned. (Tedeschi and Calhoun, 2004)

The expressive arts, including visual art, are a helpful intervention that can assist people to move from "stuckness" into post-traumatic growth, by bringing the "implicit" into the "explicit," the unconscious into conscious. The expressive arts help trauma survivors find the preverbal images, and then the words. They can help soothe arousal, change neuronal patterning, process emotions, develop opportunities for witnessing the self and its responses, and therefore break cycles of personal, social or inter-generational trauma. Through the use of "memory work" and "family of origin work," art can help break patterns, release grief and enable survivors to let go of limiting perspectives, so that "managed change" can happen slowly and safely. Art can help to integrate the trauma that has occurred in our brains and bodies, either from chronic, long-term exposure or early arousal; or from an overwhelming sudden event, which has resulted in psychic freeze-up. "Healing" is psychic "movement," integration and resolution.

Luckily, art too can be considered to be a change-event, over time—one which can drip feed or "titrate" safe change at a rate that can be integrated, in a slow, healthy and manageable way, as we make new neuronal connections. When offered with supportive facilitation in safe places, art is a gentle and sustainable way to explore and investigate issues that have been psychically blocked off, by arousing our creativity instead of our amygdala. Creativity can be soothing, involving repetitive gestures (such as the arm and hand movements required for painting, carving or needlework) that soothe the amygdala, induce slower brainwaves and balance brain hemispheres, thus helping us come down from hyper-vigilance, come up from hypo-arousal, and into an open frame of mind, able to draw on our own history. Careful arts programming includes witnessed biographical narrative that is "paced" and "dosed" at a speed that is optimal for integration. Original trauma can be reframed into a new story with more adaptive responses and perceptions. Compassionate witnessing of this process can then aid in resolving the trauma. We will explore this process in more depth throughout the book.

As we have seen, change itself is simply a neutral process intrinsic to the universe, which can be sudden or slow, large or small, intense or gentle, detrimental or helpful, and which can affect our physiologies and psyches. The only question is, can we observe the disruption to our habituation, integrate the change and then adapt healthily to the new situation? Change can actually be delivered in structured, manageable doses in order to relieve the hyper- or hypo-arousal and the "intensity" that people call pain. People can then create new, more adaptive memories, beliefs and wiring. In this way, without pathologising or diagnosing people's experiences, art transforms through a "naturopathic" or "homeopathic" model of safe intervention in small doses, rather than an "allopathic" or suppression model of intervention that does not treat symptoms but just blocks the pain messages.

Today, it is understood that there are small traumas such as losing a job, failing an exam, losing a tooth or being sued. Most people learn how to cope with these events. But there are also major traumas, like rape, witnessing a murder, being in a war or migrating, from which some people find it hard to recover. These may take much longer to titrate, heal and understand. The question around trauma is, can we cope with the event or not, by restoring a measure of control, even if it's only control of something like an art work?

Some of these major traumas can be both personal and political, as people can always be considered to be members of a social and political system—we are always members of a family, an ethnic group, a gender, a race, a religion, a political system. Our group memberships and identities impact our lives and our destinies and are part of our psychic structures, which shore up our identities, meanings and beliefs. Let's take a look at some possible socio-political traumas that can deeply affect individual trauma.

One of the largest global issues today is the movement of people referred to as "migrants" (those who are on the move for reasons discussed above, resources and safety, as well as repressive ideologies). The United Nations (UN) (2016, p.9) suggests the world is currently experiencing the most extreme migrations of people since World War Two. There are many reasons for this phenomenon: "Conflict, poverty, inequality and lack of decent jobs are among the reasons that compel people to leave their homes in search of better futures for themselves and their families" (United Nations, 2016, p.2). Modern transportation has made it easier, cheaper and faster for people to move, and there are many entrepreneurs who are willing to move people, legally or illegally.

The number of migrants around the world continues to rise. A migrant can be defined as a person who is living in a country other than their country of birth (United Nations, 2015, p.4). Many people are leaving their countries of origin, which are challenged on various levels, to seek a better life for themselves and their families somewhere else. There is often significant circumstantial pressure in the country of origin in order for people to start such a migratory journey, which can involve further risk, vulnerability and complex, comorbid traumas (including loss of language, culture, relationship, belonging, identity, status, income and meaning) in the belief that a measure of security, safety and a higher standard of living can eventually be gained. For some, this trade-off journey can also involve physical deprivation such as hunger, thirst and lack of sleep, or exposure to emotional, physical or sexual violence. One example is the group of 20,000 young orphan children known as the Lost Boys, who banded together to escape the horrors of the Sudanese civil war, by embarking on a challenging journey of up to two years in search of safety. They endured many layered traumas and hardships, including the risk of forced conscription into child armies, and the witnessing of the slaughter and rape of family and friends.

It is important to distinguish here that there is a distinction between "migrants" and "refugees." Without reducing people and their trauma to cold statistics and theories, refugees are a specific "subset" of migrants. The World Health Organization (2016) further defines a refugee as "someone who fears being persecuted for reasons of race, religion, nationality, membership of a particular social group or political opinion. A refugee is outside the country of his or her nationality, and is unable or unwilling to be protected by that country." This is a different experience from someone wishing to immigrate legally with a visa and a container of household possessions to another country as a legal immigrant. Without denying that this kind of migration certainly involves trauma, risk and loss, refugees experience these things at a much more overwhelming and complex level. We will meet some of these courageous migrants in our stories later, in some of the major refugee camps of the world.

Many migrants, and particularly refugees, are dislocated not by choice, but by force of circumstance well beyond their control, and it is often this loss of control that forms part of the trauma. It seems that vulnerability is inversely related to the amount of control one has over one's life, and is one of the causal factors as to whether pain becomes trauma. In 2014, the subset of migrants known as refugees— those with extreme vulnerability and with very little control—reached a staggering 60 million. According to the United Nations Refugee Agency (2016), one in every 122 humans is now either a refugee, internally displaced within their own country of origin, or seeking asylum. If this was the population of a country, it would be the world's 24th biggest country. The number of refugees worldwide represents about 8 percent of all international migrants (United Nations, 2016, p.9, quoting the United Nations High Commissioner for Refugees, 2015). This is the highest level since World War Two. Tragically, according to the UN, half the world's refugees are children. Displacement and dispossession can now be viewed as two further and significant adverse childhood experiences not yet officially listed.

In the past five years, according to the United Nations High Commissioner for Refugees (2015), at least 15 conflicts, including civil war, ethnic cleansing and genocide, have erupted or been re-ignited. Conflicts such as these result in corridors of moving people. Refugees from Tunisia, Algeria, Senegal, Ivory Coast, Somalia, Kenya, the Sudan region, Eritrea and Nigeria are also fleeing drought in Sub-Saharan Africa through Libya. North Africa is the main portal to Italy, France, Germany and Britain for these refugees. Climate refugees from low-lying areas prone to flooding such as Bangladesh have moved to India, while many Indians have moved to Arab countries, such as Oman and the Emirates, to escape poverty and find employment (*New York Times*, 2015). One of the chapters in this book, contributed by Max Levi Frieder, describes art projects currently helping some of these refugees in camps in India, Israel, Palestine, Greece, Syria and the infamous "Calais Jungle" in France.

Another major phenomenon currently creating global distress is the spread of the Human Immunodeficiency Virus (HIV), which continues unchecked, mostly in Sub-Saharan Africa, along these refugee corridors. This as-yet-incurable virus is carried from person to person, from city to city, often along trade routes. The HIV pandemic not only affects the health of individuals, households and communities, but also negatively impacts the development and economic growth of many African nations. Disease is part of the intersecting traumas found in some of the poorest countries.

> Many of the countries hardest hit by HIV also suffer from other infectious diseases, food insecurity, and other serious problems. Despite advances in our scientific understanding of HIV and its prevention and treatment, as well as years of significant effort by the global health community and leading government and civil society organizations, most people living with HIV, or at risk for HIV, do not have access to prevention, care, and treatment, and there is still no cure. (AIDS.gov, 2017)

Statistics (AIDS.gov, 2017) reveal that, in 2015, approximately 36.7 million people worldwide were living with HIV or Acquired Immune Deficiency Syndrome (AIDS), and that in that year an estimated 2.1 million individuals became newly infected. An estimated 35 million people have already died from AIDS-related illnesses since the start of the pandemic (AIDS.gov, 2017). The vast majority of people living with HIV/AIDS are in Africa, with an estimated 25.6 million people being HIV positive. Currently only 60 percent know their status. The remaining 40 percent (over 14 million people) still need to access HIV testing services. However, the good news is that the number of people accessing effective treatment, known as anti-retroviral therapy (ART), is now increasing. Although this is not a cure, people with HIV can now enjoy a longer life and reduce the risk of transmitting the virus to others.

Trauma among HIV survivors can include loss of health, loss of income, loss of family members, complex grief, and depression. Groups of people living with a pandemic are also particularly vulnerable to other diseases, such as tuberculosis (TB) and pneumonia. There are many side effects for communities facing these kinds of health challenges, including poverty, due to the loss of so many breadwinners; a rise in the number of orphans and child-headed households; and an increase in the number of grandparents raising grandchildren. Tightly knit villages and urban communities can lose their structures and support systems. However, art can be very helpful in these areas. One of the contributors to this book, Dr Carol Hofmeyr, has been working in such a community facing this struggle for nearly two decades, and her story will illustrate how art is an effective agent for change in communities that are impacted by the complex trauma of living with a pandemic.

It is important to point out that while some organizations working with art in these traumatized neighborhoods employ specifically trained art therapists for their outreach, not all transformative art programs are built on formal "therapeutic" models. The art programs featured in this book, while having a deeply therapeutic effect, are in some ways grassroots "transformation" projects, consisting of programs of informal art learning and healing. Some are public-health based, such as the Keiskamma Trust in South Africa, which offers art in the context of the HIV/AIDS pandemic. Some are community-development based, such as the story shared in this book by Lily Yeh with her Barefoot Artists organization, which offers art in earthquake, genocide, refugee and urban contexts. Some of the featured art projects are contemplation based, such as the Butterfly Garden project in Sri Lanka, shared here by Paul Hogan, which offered various arts in a post-civil war and a post-tsunami context. Some grew out of street art and moved into contexts of poverty and civil war, such as Artolution, which now works within refugee camps. Some are renaissance based, including the preservation and resurrection of dying culture and traditions, such as projects with indigenous people living in neo-colonial countries, which is the story I share. Community art projects lend themselves to a variety of models, in both formal and informal settings, using multifaceted ways of helping participants heal, learn and integrate.

As a reader, you may be thinking, I am neither a migrant nor a refugee. I am neither hungry, dispossessed nor dislocated. I am neither suffering from post-traumatic stress disorder nor HIV/AIDS.

So what has art got to do with me—my healing, my learning and my transformation? As trauma is a fact of life, most people have suffered some loss, depression, grief, anxiety, hyper-arousal or addiction, even though we are taught from an early age to minimize our own "first world" problems, such as loneliness, the loss of a marriage or job, our health or a move. Maybe we have suffered from "different worlds colliding," such as conflicting identities, misogyny, homophobia or racism, where there is condemnation of diversity. Whichever world we are from—first, second or third—art can help us process very subtle levels of wounding that occur every day in our society.

Whether we are in a refugee camp in the Middle East or in a summer camp in Manhattan, the way to transform through any of the expressive arts is to access our creative capacities, and tell our story to someone who holds that story respectfully and then "witnesses" or mirrors it back to us. Let's look now in more detail at how art is a kind of visual truth and reconciliation process for all of us, whether we live in Aleppo, London or Los Angeles.

# Chapter 3

# HOW CREATIVITY AND THE EXPRESSIVE ARTS TRANSFORM INDIVIDUAL TRAUMA

So what is art and what is its purpose? On the surface, visual art is simply an "object"—it is a drawing, a painting or a sculpture, perhaps with a number of marks or colors on it, often exhibiting an aesthetic awareness of the principles of design. But these apparently simple "objects" can accrue a deeper meaning. Feige (2010) suggests art is a practical, reflexive practice that "changes our understandings, our ways of seeing, hearing and behaving, our ways of narrating aspects of our lives" (p.139). Tolstoy (1942) defined art as a human activity whereby "one man [*sic*] consciously, by means of certain external signs, hands on to others feelings he has lived through" (p.123).

Art is more than a simple object. Together, the artist and their audience create an opportunity to resonate with feelings transmitted through the art work. Both the creator and their viewers share an "experience" mediated through the art (Alexander, 1987). Art can sometimes therefore be understood both as a noun (it is an object with a field of meaning) and as a verb (it is an activity that includes a shift in consciousness). It is therefore a kind of gerund, or transformative "product process."

From the very beginning, art has served significant purposes. In Paleolithic times, marks were made on cave walls for many shamanic purposes, such as to alter states of consciousness; to manifest visions; to codify information; to strengthen social ties; and to unite goals. From early on, art has also served as a calming action in times of insecurity and uncertainty, in times of famine and flood. In other words, art has been a way to work with information, anxiety and the unknown, in all its forms (Dissanayake, 1992, 2008; Steif, 2010).

As man moved out of caves, and formed socially cohesive tribes, Arnheim (1966) says "Art served to make the gods visible and rulers immortal, to exert magic powers, to give praise, to tell about the past, or to unite a crowd by a common rhythm" (p.350). Prior to the invention of the camera, art was central to our documentation processes, as well as more complex social messaging. Fleming (2010) lists other functions as "cultural heritage, personal growth, training in functional skills, development of creativity and imagination, understanding of the human condition, problem solving, and the development of empathy" (p.59).

Arnheim (1966) notes that art is "the quality that makes the difference between witnessing or performing things, and being touched by them, shaken by them, changed by the forces that are inherent" (p.342). This implies a level of power intrinsic within the art that can be harnessed by those who are aware of it. The ability of art to "move" people has been recognized over the centuries by various religious institutions and political leaders who used this power for their own ends. In Europe, for example, as humans became more "civilized" over the centuries, art began to serve significant religious purposes, by representing Greek and Roman deities. The notion in the West of art being in the service of religion culminated in the Middle Ages, when art was used by the Roman Catholic Church to tell Bible stories to non-readers, and thus entrench the church's power by making converts out of the illiterate masses. Art could garner allegiance through storytelling.

During the first dawning of the "modern" era with the Renaissance, "perspective" literally came into focus for the first time, and art began to include wider, more secular themes, such as nature, love and the beauty of the human body. At this time, the production of art was still considered to be exclusively the domain of male "geniuses," who generally trained in guilds and who were believed to be "career" Artists with a capital A (Battersby, 1989; Korsmeyer, 2012). Art was not yet considered to be a practice for the common citizen, and certainly not as a leisure activity, a hobby or a healing methodology. However, over the centuries, art slowly became democratized, and has become more accessible to non-church-goers, non-guild members, non-professionals, non-geniuses and non-males.

As we can see, art has served many functions over the millennia. Pure embellishment has rarely been one of them. In the past hundred years, in particular, art deepened its democratic reach, and began to include more secular purposes—for aesthetic, educational, propagandist, leisure and expressive reasons. Art has also moved from the notion of "fine" art to the business of selling, and the creation of a digital, visual culture, including profit for both individuals and institutions. But, significantly to this book, in the past fifty years or so, art has begun to serve deliberate growth, learning and therapeutic purposes for the deliberate evolution of our consciousness. Although art has always had these properties, it has only very recently been acknowledged as having them.

Jung was one of the first therapists (Jung, 1971, 2014) in the West to recognize art's healing capacity. He was influenced by ancient Eastern practices, such as yoga and meditative mandala-making (Moacanin, 2003). He also pioneered archetypal dream work, which explored the unconscious (Jung, 1959, 1966) through image-making. His *Red Book* (Jung, 2009) is a great example of his own work in this area. Later, others followed in his footsteps. Traditionally, in education, for example, art was recognized as philosophical growth (Read, 1943, 1951, 1960, 1967) and creative expression and development (Lowenfeld and Brittain, 1987); and in psychology as perceptive development (Arnheim, 1966) and the final stage of five in the self-actualizing process of adulthood (Maslow, 1954; May, 1994) and as healing (McNiff, 1992, 2004). Most recently, art as a deliberately "transformative" practice has been explored by London (1992), Adnams Jones (2016) and others.

No other animal makes art, so why do humans engage in this peculiar activity? Early in the 20th century, educationalist John Dewey alluded to art as a force within us (Alexander, 1987; Dewey, 1934/2005), which he called an "impulsion," a natural inclination of the human to interact with its environment, and thereby exert more control and influence over it. This creative "impulsion" produced works of art that, in turn, changed us. As artists transformed their materials into objects, they transformed themselves, thereby shaping their inner and outer worlds consecutively with each stroke of the brush, needle, hammer or chisel (Dewey, 1934/2005, p.79). Later, Greene (1995b) understood art as an "envisioning" activity. She focused on the "possible" through art, rather than on the "necessary," in order to create new consciousness. She considered art to be a way to create imaginative breakthroughs, and contradictions of established ideas. She felt that consciousness had an "imaginative" phase, and that imagination, more than any other capacity, could break through the "inertia of habit." Art became a way to revise our thinking.

Contemporary art educators such as Elliot Eisner (2002) focus on art as "cognitive" expansion, including "skills enhancement" and "sensory refinement," while other contemporary scholars focus more on "aesthetics as an adaptation"—where learning through art is understood to be a kind of cultural adaptation, a natural side effect of our evolutionary biology (Dissanayake, 2008; Dutton, 2009). London (1989, 1992) looks at art-making as cultural transformation, rather than for the production of "novel aesthetic amenities" or "distinguished entertainments" (1992, p.9), and McNiff understands art to be "medicine" (1992).

At the core of all these slightly different contemporary under-standings of art's purpose is both a learning and a healing process. Art can now be seen as a practice for change (Naidus, 2009), social engagement (Goldbard, 2006), public health (White, 2009) and empowerment (Adnams Jones, 2016). I prefer to integrate all these meanings and simply refer to "transformation" (Adnams Jones, 2016).

So how do we "transform" through art? Art is the telling of one's story through a visual medium, which is the central transformative focus of this book. Arnheim (1966) describes this process as the external manifestation of the internal—the "physical manifestation of psychical processes" (p.63). Images are a way to capture preverbal understandings, a way to intercept and externalize the "oral-visual interior," as Stafford (1994) calls it. London (1989) asks, "how can we come before life with no intermediaries and bear witness to our own experience? … We can tell our own story if we can be candid, simple, and unflinching. This is the ground of art" (p.54).

Gaztambide-Fernandez (2013) suggests that the arts "refine, cul-tivate, transform, enhance, impact and even teach" (p.213). By making "metaphors" about reality through creative acts, we can "art-iculate" experiences, before we even have the words. Images are powerful ways to communicate directly from the subconscious, making conscious the unconscious material held in our implicit memory, which forms our patterns of thinking and response. Being both preverbal, and non-verbal, images are especially helpful forms of self-expression in locations where language is silenced—where voices may be repressed by those in power; or during the shock phase immediately following deep trauma, when there can sometimes be no mental access to words. Images are a kind of universal language understood by all ages, genders and ethnicities.

In this view, we "learn" as we "heal," and we "heal" as we "learn," and by doing creative activities deliberately, we "evolve" into new capacities. Provencal and Gabora (2007) suggest that there is "convincing evidence of the relationship between the creation of art and the therapeutic transformation of the self." They refer to the film *Art Has Many Faces*, which states there is a "magic power of the image" that serves to reaffirm the age-old saying that "a picture is worth a thousand words" (quoted in Provencal and Gabora, 2007, p.255). The power of images lies in their ability to "access places that talk cannot reach" (p.255). The act of art-making is a trajectory. There is a natural movement from the preverbal, to the verbal, to the transverbal, as broader, deeper, more inclusive consciousness occurs, with shifts on the inside, on a brain-material and somatic physiological level, which is reflected through the expression of artifacts.

So, we see here that the creation of visual metaphor—including images, words, numbers and gestures—can change us bodily. Likewise, our bodies can change our culture, as we visually represent reality in ways that otherwise cannot be grasped or represented. Huston Smith (1976) suggests that anything beyond or outside a person's level of consciousness "can only be discussed or thought about by using symbols, and these symbols can only be finally understood upon transformation to that higher level itself" (as quoted in Wilber, 1996, p.48). In other words, images "bootstrap" our consciousness into higher orders. Creations of metaphors or symbols help move us towards deeper understandings and wider, more inclusive perspectives, more organized and complex thinking (Lakoff and Johnson, 1980). Art moves us into deeper articulations of our realities.

So how do we use this understanding of creative knowledge production to practice and facilitate transformations, and to build curricula for ourselves and others? As we will see in the following stories, there is no one way to make art that is transformative. In fact, there are several approaches, but the central component is the healing "narrative"—telling our biography through images, using recognizable objects in the art that represent the artist and their history, their context, their identity, their challenge, or their future context and their future identity. Other core practices focus on "communicating ideas"—making a political comment, or taking a stand, in order to clarify one's meaning or "position" in life, or to make social change or spread new awareness through visual memes.

Some art therapies encourage the creation of non-objective works—abstract expressions of pure energy and color through spontaneous expression. This product is then open to interpretation or analysis of the artist's energetics. Art works do not have to have recognizable objects in them to be biographical or healing. Abstract metaphor can work just as well, if analysis follows. Some facilitators use art as "memory work." Provencal and Gabora (2007) note that art "can help painful memories surface to a place where they can be faced and released" (p.256). Other, more meditational approaches to art-making tend to use "patterning"—the creation of geometric shapes such as mandalas, or repetitive, mindful, soothing gestures such as brush strokes, carving gestures or tapestry stitching to encourage rhythmic movement, which can bring practitioners out of hyper-vigilance and lead to an ecstatic mental emptiness, beyond any thought-symbols altogether. With a meditational approach, we experience ourselves in a formless, expanded sense of self, as a fractal perhaps, within larger fractals. The recent trend of adult coloring books serves this purpose, of soothing anxiety through rhythmic activity, much like eye movement desensitization reprocessing (EMDR) therapy, tapping or hemispheric balancing.

So there is no "right" way to facilitate transformation through art. But when boundaries between the self and the other are breached, art can be viewed as "heart work," "bridge-building," a "cross-border" practice or "identity" work. McNiff (1998) notes, "When we make analogies between artistic experiences and our lives, the images help us see patterns and themes…it elicits stories from us… The perceptual form evokes a corresponding sense of structure within otherwise undifferentiated life experiences" (p.102). In all these approaches, by externalizing our internal world through art, there are some central mechanisms for transformation, including unblocking our self-expression, sharing our different and unique perspectives, and finding a voice. It is the "voicing" of a central metaphor that is, in my view, one of the most transformative elements of art.

Healing and learning occur within the act of creating a storytelling object, such as a mural, totem, tapestry or poem. A metaphor is created and then "witnessed" by an audience. It is the externalizing of an experience through metaphor, into the community, that is the voicing of the story, and it is "voicing" which ultimately relieves us of the burden of carrying that experience alone. The metaphor has the potential to create intimacy. Private interior lives and identities are, in this way, translated into art, and the art stories then create a field of resonance. The image becomes an "identity," which becomes a "voice," which becomes a "discourse," which becomes a "field," which can then create change. The "others" that witness or resonate with the art then belong to a circle of meaning. In this way, the artist articulates a new meaning, is "seen" and "heard" by those who receive, empathize with or even resist the new meaning. We paint/stitch/carve/dance ourselves into "being," then into our "communities" and then into action. We bridge our interior world into the social world and into political change through art, and through this act we evolve culture and awareness into deeper, more intimate, more inclusive ways of being.

In this transformative process of creating "change" within and without us, art moves far beyond simple decoration, marketplace commodification or aesthetic metaphor. Like Frankl (2006), London (1989) suggests that art becomes transformative through "meaning-making": "By shifting our concerns from trying to make the beautiful thing, to seeking the honest and the meaningful thing…the paralyzing self-consciousness…is diminished…and we nurture our…uniquely human quest for establishing meaning in a possibly meaningful universe" (p.20).

In a world that can sometimes seem rather bleak, Rollo May (1978/1994) suggests it is the job of the artist to "struggle with the meaninglessness and silence of the world" (p.89). In this view, art becomes individually made meaning, which can then be translated into larger cultural or universal meanings. This takes enormous courage, as it requires honesty and vulnerability to dig deep into the subconscious layers of the self and make them visible. In this way, we reveal our nakedness, our possible traumas, which might appear at first glance to be individual to the artist, but which are often shared communally. In this way, we realize we are not alone. Our boundaries become porous. The personal and intimate is then revealed to be both social and political, and vice versa. By touching below the individual story, we tap into the shared human, storied experience. London (1989) says:

> When we are motivated to find increasingly complete and satisfying means to convey what is of great personal importance, and draw from both the conscious and the subconscious levels, our images naturally become more vivid, deeper, more articulate and interestingly, more universal. (p.21)

So how does art arise out of the human body to transform us? Dewey (1934/2005) was the first to write about art "impulsions"—somatic urges towards self-expression, through the medium of art, into a metaphor (on metaphor, see Kovecses, Benczes and Csabi, 2009; Lakoff and Johnson, 1980; Shusterman, 2008). The articulation of meaning is not easy for humans, and in fact is impossible without symbols or metaphors—words, images or gestures of some kind. Without these, we are trapped and isolated. But the process of using metaphor for transformation is actually very simple. London (1989) suggests that "having created a metaphor within which your meaning resides, you have made that thing called art. You did what you had to do to bear witness to the things you know. That's all" (pp.18–19).

In this deceptively simple act of continually bearing witness to what we know, the transformative process is activated. The human body/mind becomes the site of healing, learning and evolution. Transformation through art is therefore both somatic (in the body/mind complex) and semantic (has meaning in language and logic). Through the deceptively simple and childlike act of art-making, ruptures or freeze-overs can be repaired in the psyche and in society, and discernment and empathy can be developed. Arnheim (1966) notes that "images stand for referents…therefore art requires the judging of meaning, relevance and truth… The task is accomplished largely by…the capacity for feeling" (p.314).

Art is the safe and healthy "acting out" of energy and feeling into a form. Transformation occurs through catharsis. As art-makers externalize their pain, pleasure, meanings and identities into art, it transforms them by relieving intensity, tension and isolation. Art is made through actualizing an "impulsion." But the reverse is also true. "Not actualizing," or not expressing our impulsion, is "repressive" of our tension, identity and meanings. This repression creates blockages, which can complicate our adulthood with fixed responses and solidified but outmoded identities. And so we accumulate layers of trauma and patterned stress. Cutting off the normal human impulsion to express can suppress the voicing mechanism that is so transformative. Our bodies and minds are psychic containers that need to be emptied regularly of our accumulations. If we do not express outwards, intimacy becomes difficult. Trauma stays on the inside, living on within us as compulsive patterns, which can be passed on inter-generationally through acting out in destructive ways rather than constructive, creative ways.

It should be pointed out here that although the art object that is made during this act of emptying or catharsis represents someone's "story"—their identity and meanings—the art itself is neither the person who made it, nor the audience who receives it. It is a "third" entity unto itself—a membrane that holds the art-maker's subjective world which has a life of its own. As the story is remembered and externalized, turning the subjective experience into an objective experience, "distance" is achieved. Through triangulation between creator/metaphor/audience, or giver/gift/receiver, a larger flow of giving and receiving is created. Energetic movement is healing, rather like a river breaking through a man-made dam. Art can then reorganize our thoughts in new ways, and a measure of clarity can be achieved. London (1989) suggests that, by making art, "there are three worlds. The world out there, the world in here, and the world of things you make…appearing alive, but not alive" (p.42).

The art membrane, therefore, captures the outgoing story and reflects a level of objectivity, or "distanciation" from our subjective experience. In my opinion, it is this third mediated space that holds the cultural flow between artists and their audiences, enabling clarity, social cohesion and evolution. Art becomes the transition site between the "felt" and the "told," the body and the world, where the subconscious becomes conscious, and the subjective becomes objective—both visible and audible. Art becomes the culturally mediated "voice" of change, both literally and figuratively. Creativity becomes an act of evolution—bringing the new into existence, and knowing it for the first time. Body, mind and audience are involved in creating new ideas or memetic evolution. Some might also add "spirit" to this partnership (Osho, 1999). Art is therefore a generous show-and-tell behavior that is mutually beneficial, for the healing of both the individual and the world. A systems partnership at the deepest level can therefore be viewed as a transformative partnership that creates a shift in power, internally and externally. As we work with the layers of the individual psyche (Kandel, 2012), and that of others, we see the universal "oneness" in our experiences. Art-making becomes the visual democratization of the power to reveal larger patterns, to create change and to create "truths" as we surrender to the creative energies that wish to come through us.

Transformation through art-partnering also occurs at the internal, material level of our brain—the partnership between left and right hemispheres. Many parts of our brain are active during most of our daily acts, and so it would be an over-simplification to deny this complexity by neatly dividing the brain in two fractured and independent halves. But without being overly simplistic and reductive, researchers have found that the left brain is generally more focused on words and numbers, while the right brain is generally more focused on images and feelings (McGilchrist, 2009). Generally too, the left brain also tends to want to dominate our right brain, both inside us and outside us in the world, as the left brain is associated with the more "masculine" approach of "doing" rather than "being," with interests in objectivity, competitiveness, power and dominance, which tend to devalue the more subjective, softer, "feminine" aspects of the body, with its feelings and imagination, which are the more vulnerable aspects of ourselves that tend to get repressed by our needs for safety and power. As reflected in and reinforced by Descartes (1637) who said "I think, therefore I am," humans tend to create hierarchies (rational thought over intuitive feeling; the mind over the body; words and numbers over images) in order to feel safe and have order. As Schneider Adams (1994) says, "generally people are still inclined to attribute greater intellectual complexity to words than to pictures" (p.41), perhaps because there is more certainty around words than the more open-ended image. The problem of the dominance of word over image, and the left brain over the right brain, was well examined, initially as a simple binary in the 1970s in art education (Edwards, 1999) and later, with more meta complexity, in neuroscience (McGilchrist, 2009). These hierarchies come at great cost to ourselves and to our world, yet art can help mend these splits. Edwards, for example, says:

> There appear to be two modes of thinking, verbal and nonverbal, represented separately in left and right hemispheres respectively, and that our educational system, as well as science in general, tends to neglect the nonverbal form of intellect. What it comes down to is that modern society discriminates against the right hemisphere. (quoted in Hall, 2006, p.69)

McGilchrist (2009) says that "our brains not only dictate the shape of the experience we have of the world, but are likely themselves to reflect, in their structure and functioning, the nature of the universe in which they have come about" (p.460). He describes how the two hemispheres can fight for dominance. He suggests that, particularly in the West, the human brain can wound itself with this split, by shifting activity predominantly into the left hemisphere, which has evolved a narrow focus of theory, structure and mechanization over the wider focus of empathy. In some cases, he says, our left hemispheres are actually getting bigger than our right. Being interested in heirarchy and power, the left brain, which is designed to exploit the world efficiently, can sometimes devalue the right hemisphere's function, which is broader in focus with a more generous perspective on the world, and which is responsible for understanding and generating new and immediate experiences, including empathy, feelings, creativity and imagination. But no one can run well with only one leg, or fly with only one wing. The right brain is essential to our balance and happiness, as it helps us relate to others with emotional and social intelligence.

To transform ourselves therefore, the two hemispheres need to work together, in partnership, for our most optimal functioning and health. As a culture, when we devalue this creative and empathic part of ourselves, and others, we are becoming wounded in the right brain. Trauma therefore can include the repression of half of our own capacity.

To perform an act of art is therefore healing, as it is an act of shifting into balance, creative agency, the unknown and the new. It can constitute an act of overthrowing our "safe," dominant hemisphere, however temporarily. This takes courage (May, 1994) and a willingness to "feel"—often intense—discomfort (Mezirow and Associates, 1990, 2010) or ecstasy (Buber, 1958; Deecke, 2013; Osho, 1999). Adding to our cognitive and aesthetic capacities can be confusing and challenging to experience in the body. Many of us would prefer to avoid intense feelings, or "stigmatization" by others. The poet W.B. Yeats (2015), who speaks for those who make art and poetry, describes how the bankers of the world, as he calls the more left-brained of us, look at the arts as "idling," whereas he describes the arts as "hard labor." In his poem *Adam's Curse* (p.1), he suggests:

> *Better go down on your marrow bones*
> *And scrub a kitchen pavement, or break stones*
> *Like an old pauper, in all kinds of weather,*
> *For to articulate sweet sounds together,*
> *Is to work harder than all these.*

This stanza refers to the sometimes very uncomfortable act of creative "labor" that many writers and artists experience. Yet it is this very discomfort—the agony and the ecstasy, sometimes experienced ambiguously and paradoxically, at the same time—that releases and transforms us. Without a tolerance for either discomfort and ambiguity, or intense pleasure; without application and effort; without the ability to take risks and become vulnerable and tell our story either through images or words, we cannot fully self-actualize.

Many have tried to understand this uncomfortable space, often metaphorically as Yeats did, as hard labor or a curse, but many have also described this "bodying forth" as self-actualization (Maslow, 1954), a peak experience (Maslow, 1964, 1970/2014) or flow (Csikszentmihalyi, 1997). All these responses to art-making—pain and pleasure, agony and ecstasy—can co-exist at the same time as an intense, transformative paradox of integrating opposites that catapults our capacities. In a world fast becoming feeling-avoidant, and left-hemisphere dominant, creativity can be interpreted as weakness, instead of a sign of aliveness. Bearing our own intensity is transformative.

As we become more present, alive and awake to ourselves and each other, we become more aware of the intelligent creative processes that operate through and within us, and which bind us socially. With an art-practice that gently and continuously encounters the unknown and brings something into manifestation from nothing, awareness of our true nature is deepened, as surrender to the universal creative principle is practiced. By accessing our right brain, we become more present, and flow is deepened (Csikszentmihalyi, 1990, 1996, 1997). Art-making in this view becomes a practice of spiritual actualization (Osho, 1999) and an optimal way to grow knowledge of the self, the other and our universe. In this view of an art-practice, spiritual transformation occurs as the by-product of surrender to a larger creative force that wants to actualize itself within the world, through us and despite us.

I would like to emphasize that art can be produced without any need to understand these deeper processes. Benefits accrue automatically whether we realize it or not. Many artists prefer to live in the moment and be spontaneous. They prefer not to emphasize the Western, left-brained, academic approach to life including an analysis of their own practice or their product; nor might they be interested in the science of evolution, or the spiritual practices of the East that refer to "the Tao" or "Tantra," both ancient ways of describing this balancing process of opposites. However, a "conscious" awareness of the process of balancing the opposites of action and surrender— the lived oxymoron—is probably necessary for teachers, community developers, health practitioners, therapists and funders who are facilitating a transformative process for others. With awareness, we can become more deliberate about evolving consciousness, instead of leaving it up to happenstance beyond our control.

## Chapter 4

# HOW CREATIVITY AND THE EXPRESSIVE ARTS TRANSFORM SOCIAL TRAUMA

Art-making is a powerful supportive process for the individual but it is amplified when done in community. Chalmers (1984), for example, mentions that art "maintains and improves collective existence. Art, directly and indirectly, bolsters the morale of groups to create unity and social solidarity. As used by dissident groups, art creates awareness of social issues...for social change" (p.104).

Art-making can be both socially responsive and responsible. We will now look at group practice and co-creativity, and its advantages. One of the newest conversations emerging around art is that of art activism—not only for the therapeutic healing of individual trauma, but also for the socio-political exploration of pressing issues and concerns—as a community development tool, especially for those recovering from political emergency. The artists who share their stories in this book facilitate communal art for change on many levels, including the healing of personal trauma, but also for the social, political and spiritual levels of change. Our pain can be understood as contextual—our bodily response to political injustice and the failures of our social systems. When creating together, when the trauma narrative is shared, healing happens in several ways, among many. In this view, our deliberate and conscious personal transformation can also be very much understood as a political act of empowerment, in order to further evolve social justice in our world.

The stories shared in this book illustrate the rich variety of ways art transforms those co-creating together. Paul Hogan, for example, is a

Canadian who has facilitated art in Toronto and Batticaloa, Sri Lanka. In 1996, he created the Butterfly Peace Garden for young tsunami and civil war survivors—children who voluntarily came to his art garden. He worked in multiple art forms, including painting, costume-making, clowning, poetry and dance. He also used art forms grounded in the meditative and spiritual realms, using ritual and breath work (see also Chase, 2000; Santa Barbara, 2004). His art garden became a refuge for those surviving ethnic civil war and religious fundamentalism.

Lily Yeh, a Chinese-American, otherwise known as the Barefoot Artist, is an art activist featured here, who brings the resources of art to people who have been severely challenged by poverty, underemployment and global emergency. She facilitates art around the world in order to develop underserved communities, by bringing both healing and self-empowerment. She brings her group work to people who have experienced deep communal trauma, such as poverty, drugs and gang violence in inner cities; genocide survivors in Rwanda; and earthquake survivors in Haiti. She recognizes that creativity and beauty are powerful agents for both personal healing as well as social change.

Max Levi Frieder and the organization Artolution work with refugees, focusing more on young people than adults. Initially inspired by street art, Max has moved into art as psycho-social activism. There are several examples where art is now practiced among the dislocated and dispossessed, both in refugee camps and earthquake aftermaths, and in urban communities, such as the Remix Project in Toronto, the Troubadours of Hope and the Cirque du Monde, both in Haiti. These arts projects differ in their creative mediums but share a specific value: the centering of marginality and the liberation of the imagination. This approach to art-making creates spaces to engage people in groups through capacity building, particularly in the areas of self-expression, cooperation, skills education, fraternity, community building, risk taking and resilience development. These projects employ creative approaches to "transform anger into engines of change" (Shephard, 2014). The intention of such environments is to support individual healing and build hope, laughter and self-esteem, which might then later lead to community transformation through visioning, in places that have been impacted by poverty, war, natural disaster or cultural genocide.

Some, like Dr Carol Hofmeyr, who shares her work with survivors of the Human Immunodeficiency Virus (HIV)/Acquired Immune Deficiency Syndrome (AIDS) pandemic, position art and its healing capacity squarely in the arena of public health. This view suggests that governments should take more responsibility for providing group access to art-making. White (2009), for example, supports this approach, by saying, "it is time to stop arguing for the role of the arts as a useful adjunct to health services and declare that the arts sector, by the very nature of what it does, is in the business of health" (p.5). He explains that the factors that make for good health include a sense of personal and social identity, human worth, communication, participation in the making of political decisions, celebration and responsibility. He says, "the language of science alone is not enough to describe health; the languages of story, myth and poetry also disclose truth" (p.17).

Good health is defined by the World Health Organization (WHO) (1948) as a "state of complete physical, mental and social well-being and not merely the absence of disease or infirmity" (p.100). White (2009) says this moves the definition of health from the biomedical model to a social model (p.42). He cites a World Health Organization report that identifies health assets in a community as including wisdom, creativity, talent and enthusiasm, and he adds, "this definition has since become popularized to the point of symbolizing a paradigm shift" (White, 2009, p.48). Carol Hofmeyr's view is fuelled by an awareness of the wider social determinants of health. She has initiated the Keiskamma Trust Art Project in South Africa, which facilitates a dual process for people—medicine and art. She suggests that medicine makes people's bodies better, while art gives their lives meaning. Medical science, art-making and learning programs cooperate in this integrated system, a kind of bio-psycho-educative model. There is an increasing convergence of the arts with health and education due to the fact that community arts build social integration, foster emotional intelligence and motivate healthier lifestyle choices. The arts can incorporate creative health messaging and political, issue-based support for improved social cohesion, as well as opportunities for specific learning about health. Community art has the capacity to increase group awareness around many social issues, such as HIV/AIDS, but it needs to be understood as funded learning. Goldbard (2006), for example, says some community art projects can raise political awareness and can "move gatekeepers and others who wield power to respond constructively" (p.14).

The story I share here with indigenous Canadian survivors of colonialism and multi-generational trauma involves a coming together of young men who have suffered life-long racism, family abuse, foetal alcohol syndrome, residential school, cultural genocide, drug addiction and incarceration. Poverty and violence are deeply related to aspects of power and the lack of it, including the lack of control over one's life. Dissanayake (1992) believes that the reason art is transformative is because it allows us to "order, shape, and control at least a piece of the world" (p.83). This group art project focused on a method of resurrecting a dying culture and reconnecting people to their traditions as a way of overcoming isolation, building better self-esteem and healing trauma through native, traditional methods of wood carving. In these different ways, art is transformative of groups, as it activates community agency among disempowered people.

There is a growing awareness, too, of the transformative nature of the arts among peace workers. Scholars such as Huss and Cwikel (2005), for example, have successfully used art as an intervention when working with displaced, lower-income, minority groups of Bedouin women. They suggest that art helped "to illuminate the women's self-defined concerns and goals, and simultaneously moved these goals forward" (p.1). White (2009) says the arts can "alleviate stress caused by environmental factors and provide support in personal and collective trauma, such as bereavement" (p.85). Goodman (2002) says, "drama, art, dance, music and storytelling are used all over the world for peace-building, reconciliation, and trauma healing" (p.193), yet there are many hotspots of grief and loss in our world where, as yet, no art practice is available. So, it is time for both governmental funders and non-governmental organizations (NGOs) to become far more aware of the social benefits of this simple and accessible practice.

Art is transformative in so many ways, but in my humble view, at the core of all the transformative mechanisms, individual or social, it is the gaining of a "voice" that is key for people who have been disempowered through silencing. Most dispossessed, vulnerable people, especially women, children and refugees, have experienced varying measures of "de-voicing," of being unable to speak up and have their needs met due to repressive cultures that value only one perspective—usually that of the patriarchy in its many forms, including colonialism, misogyny, fundamentalism or heteronormative values. Feminist social researchers such as Ryan-Flood and Gill (2010), Alcoff and Potter (1993), Harding (1993), Stanley and Wise (1993) and Ramazonoglu (2002) have long been concerned with questions of "breaking silence" by the marginalized as an act of empowerment, and suggest that facilitating the finding of a "voice" is key. Voice usually implies an act of communication between an individual and others, the critical first step to changing any dehumanizing situation. Without the movement from images to words, to voice, to advocacy, or the trajectory from preverbal to verbal to collective activism, those who are marginalized (those who might have their diversity silenced) are often unable to motivate for themselves, because by doing so, they put themselves in danger. Hierarchies of power are built and maintained by intimidation—the silencing of voices and experiences of certain groups from public discourse. Those who control which story can be told, and by whom, control the discourse and therefore control the power. By facilitating art with grassroots groups of marginalized populations, peripheral voices can be developed and brought into the center. In this way, healing through art occurs through gaining a visual voice, within an ecology of power relationships. The individual requires the collective to support the development of agency, through witnessing and supporting the voice, visual or otherwise.

In this view, that both trauma and the healing from it are social, the individual is always understood to be part of intersecting hierarchies—a member of a class, race and gender—at all times. Finding a voice is a particularly empowering act of accessing power. Within this view, questions of who speaks for whom, and about what, are raised, as well as many important questions about power, ethics, subjectivity, epistemology and agency through a reflexive art engagement. Images can disrupt power through the dismantling of silence, both within us and outside us. Art-making in this view becomes resistance to invisibility and silencing, a way of speaking up, and showing up. Ultimately, the arts become a critical, mediated performance of waking up.

True agency lies in claiming an identity or a position, and results in an articulation of the "I am." Ryan (2001) explains Lacan's idea that "the entry into language," whether it be verbal or visual language, is the pre-condition for becoming aware of oneself as a distinct entity (p.51). Some researchers have even noted that there is a link between "voice" and "knowing," although this is not necessarily a linear progression. Belenky *et al.* (1986) are critical of assumptions that people learn in an orderly manner, especially women. The aim for these feminist scholars is to draw marginalized people into a state of constructed knowledge described as a condition of "becoming and staying aware of the working of their minds" (p.141). Art in this view can be understood as acts of knowledge construction. We can construct, deconstruct and reconstruct our knowledge through creating visual symbols and gradually telling and retelling our stories in ever more empowering ways. In this way, our stories determine who we are— our identities. The telling of the self-story through images, when practiced in community, is the telling of ourselves into "being." Art can be understood as a compelling vehicle for self-declaration. Reaching others through disclosive images, thereby creating authenticity of experience, and intimacy, brings multiple voices into a visual discourse, and these "add human-scale information and meaning to the official record by sharing first-person testimonies and the artifacts of ordinary lives" (Goldbard, 2006, p.71).

It is understood that by disclosing our stories, stereotypes are also challenged (Merryfeather, 2014). This is particularly true with taboos and stigmatized silencing. In South Africa, for example, visual art is deliberately used among those with HIV/AIDS to encourage disclosure around this very silenced and painful subject (see Kesby, 2005; Mak, 2006; Manji,1999; Mitchell, 2008, 2011; Mitchell *et al.*, 2005; Moletsane, *et al.*, 2009). Making art in groups helps support those who are courageously speaking out about an intensely stigmatized group identity, such as living with HIV/AIDS.

So how is culture moved forward collectively by people finding a visual voice and speaking out through their diverse stories that might otherwise be stigmatized and silenced? Repressive cultures tend to have a dominant narrative that excludes other more marginal narratives. Adichie (2009) warns us of the danger of a "single story." By using art-making to narrate our diverse stories into the dominant narrative, cultures can be moved from a single discourse into many discourses and perspectives, from a cultural monologue towards a dialogue and, at best, even a polylogue.

Interestingly, because art uses images instead of words, it is a medium completely suitable for polylogues, especially in locations where people share diverse languages. There are also diverse ways of interpreting images, so when looking at an image that represents a story from another culture, it is important to remember that images are not a "universal" visual language. Art does not rely on a fixed set of symbols. Interpreting images produced by and about others is not a simple "read," cross-culturally. Visual "literacy" means understanding that meanings and symbols are contextual. Images are culturally determined, interpreted and significant. London (1989) says, "much evidence is required to tease meaning from images... Certainly biographical, or better still, autobiographical information is a minimum prerequisite for any real analysis" (p.63). So, while with art there is no common "alphabet" to learn, we can often receive the meaning of an image viscerally, bypassing analysis by the cortex. Scholars such as Chalmers (1984) suggest that all visual art is essentially "tribal" (p.104) (for example, heavily local and contextual) and he advocates a multicultural or ethnological practice when looking at or interpreting another's art. In fact, "Discovering the structure and content of such forms, processes and philosophies from the indigenous point of view is preeminently an ethnographic task" (Chalmers, 1984, p.103).

The difficulty of interpreting images cross-culturally, however, should not prevent the facilitation of cross-cultural work. There are many examples of facilitators successfully using art in diverse contexts other than their own, and this book illustrates this point. In a global world, hosting programs exclusively in one's own birth culture would be unrealistic, as well as stultifying of transnational diversity. Scholars such as Huss and Cwikel (2005) successfully use art cross-culturally in Israel; Hement (2007) in Russia; and Mak (2006), Mitchell (2008), Mitchell et al. (2005) and Moletsane et al. (2009) in South Africa, among different race groups and ethnicities. All these facilitators have sensitively employed arts-based methods across racial, ethnic, gendered and economic group lines. In fact, "culture is a peculiarly successful means of promoting social cohesion, inclusion, or regeneration" (Belfiore, 2002, p.104). However, it is critical that any facilitation across diversity should be handled with the greatest sensitivity to the practices, concerns and traumas that are present in any particular context, in order to prevent further inadvertent exclusion, power abuse, colonization or traumatization.

So we see that, with this understanding, art is a cultural and contextual "echo object" (Stafford, 2007) that voices and transmits cultural experiences through locally determined metaphors. However, it is important to note that meaning-making is not the same as finding "truth." Meaning-making is always relative, and so "truth" is acknowledged to be a difficult issue. Ryan (2001) cites Foucault, who states that "truth" is often politically produced to represent and maintain power interests (p.33). With art, we are not dealing with "facts." Subjective experiences are represented, and knowledge is understood to be constructed. However, this does not discount "relative" truth, which can sometimes be more truthful than factual statistics. Ryan (2001) draws on Derrida, who claimed that truth, as a stable, coherent reality, is in fact a "fiction" (p.36), even in the sciences, as we are constantly updating our knowledge as previous paradigms become "untrue." In this view, all voicing becomes a kind of subjectively "located" storytelling, relative and fictional, but at the same time more "true" than true.

Voicing through images is a relative, critical performance. The arts are allegorical heuristics sometimes disguised as "truth," as Brodkey explains:

> One studies stories not because they are true or even because they are false, but for the same reason that people tell and listen to them, in order to learn about the terms on which others make sense of their lives; what they take into account and what they do not; what they consider worth contemplating and what they do not; what they are and are not willing to raise as problematic and unresolved in life. (quoted in Ryan, 2001, p.118)

It is therefore important for artists, art teachers, facilitators and therapists to remember that we work with storied "perspectives," open to various distortions due to interpretation, artistic license, the filter of memory, the filter of culture and values, and perhaps the "translation" problems of using a symbolic or second language. However, transformation can occur anyway, without requiring either truth with a capital T, or analysis. There is never only one truth. Nigerian feminist writer Chimamanda Ngozi Adichie (2009) suggests that if we do not reject the notion of a single story or "truth," we rob people of their diversity and dignity. For example, in the movie *The Help*, based on the novel by Kathryn Stockett (2009), the personal stories of marginalized black women from Mississippi during the 1960s are recounted, and one of the women, Aibileen, states in the movie, "No one asked me before what it be like to be me. Once I told it, I be free."

When facilitating an art project, we need to bear in mind "who" tells the story, "how" it is told and "when" or "where" it is told, as these are all questions of contextual power. Stories exist at the personal level, but they also exist at the political level as group "discourses" (Foucault, 1980) and at the intellectual level as "memes" (Dawkins, 1989) that spread like epidemics via host brains. All discourses can be understood as memes jostling for more or less power. But Berry maintains that "in order to survive our moment, we must be prepared to take a journey into a new, creative 'story'...we need an 'integral' story that will educate us, a story that will heal us, guide and discipline us" (quoted in O'Sullivan, 2002, p.4). Artists empower themselves and others into a more functional and inclusive way of living and being, through the propagation of visual memes. By creating art, a new visual discourse is started, and we can envision a new collective story, a new future, with new possibilities. Visual art is a skill that then enables multiple perspectives to gain entry into single discourses that tend to crush diversity. Schugurensky (2002) notes:

> Reflective discourse can be understood as a process in which we actively dialogue with others to better understand the meaning of experience... This in turn promotes a better understanding of issues by tapping into collective experience and knowledge and allows all participants to find their own voice in light of alternative perspectives. (p.65)

To enter the highly competitive fray of discourse-jockeying in such a loud world, silence needs to be overcome, and emerging voices, especially for women, children and minorities, need to be nurtured out of silence, within safe places, and then developed through learning certain skills. Ryan (2001) suggests, "the presence of other women allows women to build up personal authority through the telling of and listening to their stories" (p.118). However, "in overcoming silence and learning to talk to each other, women need to be presented with discourses that position them with agency, rather than with discourses that simply map their oppressions" (p.119). It is important to move people from healing to learning to activism; or from victim to survivor to warrior to evolutionary, on the unfolding progression of a transformational trajectory. Through the sharing of stories, a common experience of oppression can be recognized and then a narrative of effective resistance can emerge. A new, communal discourse and a more inclusive identity that is more functional can be authored.

I suggest that the activity of speaking out through images can be seen as a healthy way for any person to "act out," to avoid acting out in other more violent ways, or acting "in" in more depressive or repressive ways. But issues of voice are complex, and include a sensitivity towards the dangers of speaking out, especially in hotspot geographic areas. The ability to speak our truths (or not) reflects our level of safety, agency and empowerment (Gilligan, 1982; Olsen, 1978/2003). Silence has been deplored as a "symbol of passivity or powerlessness" (Gal, 1991, p.175). But due to the occurrence of silencing in intersecting ways across all levels of society, especially for the vulnerable, such as women, children and refugees, it is important to note that under certain circumstances the disclosure of a story can also be disempowering. It is critical for a facilitator to know the difference when working with groups. Ahmed (2010) discusses issues around safety, the constraints and limits to some voicing, and the possible invasiveness of art facilitation within some marginalized lives, especially in violent hotspots: "The desire to know the truth about the other can participate in, and reproduce violence, as if 'they' could provide us with what 'we' are missing" (p.xix). Feminist research, not unlike the Hippocratic Oath, requires "a commitment to not causing harm...[but] promoting good" (p.xx). She mentions that "what to do with what we are entrusted—whether we speak or keep silent—[this] remains an important question" (p.xx).

This sensitivity to revelation, declaration, intimacy and security means that not every story will be told by the participants in an art project, and natural reservation needs to be respected. Issues of voicing can sometimes include actual danger for both the facilitator and the participants. Parpart (2010) acknowledges that:

> openly voicing dissent and opposition is often dangerous and even suicidal among women (and men). Clearly, new ways of thinking about agency and voice are needed, ones that take into account the many subtle forms of agency required to cope in an increasingly dangerous world. (p.17)

Cornwall (1998) notes that "there may be aspects of women's lives and livelihoods which are especially important to conceal" (p.55). Silence itself can also be viewed as a choice for a private space to deal with trauma, regain self-esteem and a sense of empowerment in an often unpredictable world (El-Bushra, 2000; Kelly, 2000; Majob, 2004; Silber, 2005). Silence can equal safety, but it can also point to experiences that are simply so horrific they cannot be articulated. Silence and voice will co-exist in any group as a reflection of power, agency, repression and safety, revealing gender, ethnicity, class, education and age.

Art, with its ability to speak without words, can remain ambiguously "silent" while visually voicing. Parpart (2010) suggests that using symbols (the arts) is useful in these ambiguous situations. She says "symbols can disrupt and challenge the discourse of the powerful, while providing space for solace, sharing and collective empowerment" (p.23). To privilege voice over silence and secrecy as evidence of empowered agency ignores the complex mix of choice, including the choice to speak, but agency "may take surprising forms, including the judicious use of...silence" (p.25). Because both silence and voice are ubiquitous and may mean different things contextually, power relationships can be played out through their negotiation in an art project. Ward and Winstanley (2003), for example, have identified five forms of silencing: reactive silence (or the absence of response), a form of suppression, self-censorship, self-protection and resistance. These are forms of unconscious protection. But more consciously employed silence and secrecy perform a number of functions ranging from smooth maintenance of interaction, to politeness, to the management of shame, to the need to stay safe. Phoenix (2004) says that secrecy can also "signal that there are things too terrible to be said" (pp.162–163). I mention these subtleties as a possible dynamic in any cross-cultural art facilitation in regions that have experienced trauma. Ultimately, individuals can be safer in an art group, as audience members do not have to know who did which part of a joint project such as a mural.

There is also an important tension within feminist literature between the need to include marginalized voices and the imperative to protect and avoid speaking "for" others, which is important for any facilitator to note. Pillow and Mayo (2007) discuss the "politics of representation" and the "research gaze," issues of authority, and who is recording whom, representing and speaking for whom, why and how (p.163). Although Hesse-Biber and Piatelli (2007) state that poly-vocality is central to a feminist understanding of how knowledge is built (p.148), there are "inherent contradictions in the desire to give voice to others" (De Vault and Cross, 2007, p.173). Facilitators who will be helping tell the story of another, in order to give that individual or community a voice, need to bear this tension in mind. Enthusiasm to help and provide voice can sometimes result in misguided actions and inadvertent further trauma, and disempowerment.

This outlines how art heals through storytelling, voicing, catharsis, witnessing, bridging, distanciation and disrupting power inequities. These are the external evidences of a transformative process. But it is important to remember that trauma happens "inside" us. Emotional trauma is held neurologically. Badenock (2017) suggests:

> When we are overwhelmed by pain and fear, the memory is held in the subcortex. Healing involves reawakening the memory of the original experience, and having this experience witnessed by another, so that what was missing at the time of the original experience, can become available for integration.

In short, healing through telling our story is both an internal and external event.

In this chapter we have discussed many ways that art can transform trauma: by revealing the subconscious to the conscious;

through balancing the brain hemispheres; through memory work; by externalizing the interior experience; through bridging the individual into community; through breaking silence and stigmatization; through distanciation of the experience into an objective echo object; by finding a voice and therefore our agency; by storytelling ourselves into more democratic discourses; by adaptation through meaning-making; through strengthening marginalized identities; by envisioning community futures; and through agentic intervention and activism. These are transformations on a trajectory of self-actualizations that are possible within an art practice (Adnams Jones, 2016).

Let us now look at specific examples from the front lines of this work, where facilitators are exploring and refining these principles in the field. What follows are stories by facilitators in their own very unique and diverse voices, recounting their own experiences of working with survivors of poverty, war, genocide, pandemic and tsunami. All believe passionately that creative social acts can help transform people at all levels of their being.

*Chapter 5*

# STORIES FROM PHILADELPHIA, KENYA AND RWANDA,

## with Survivors of Poverty, Inner City Violence and Genocide

*Lily Yeh and the Barefoot Artists organization*

## Early memories

My ancestral home is in Hainan province but I was born in Guizhou, China, and grew up in Taiwan. I had dedicated parents, always supportive and encouraging. I was drawn to visual images from a young age.

When I was in elementary school, girls and boys were assigned different after-school activities. I remember that the girls had to learn cooking and sewing, which I found boring and tiring. How I wished that I could do the boys' assignment of board carving. Five layers of colors in plaster overlaid their wooden boards. With strokes of varied strength from their carving knives, different colors revealed themselves. That seemed such fun.

During my middle school years, the summers felt long. We did not have summer camp or any structured activities. To amuse myself, I would recreate beautiful photographic scenery from a calendar in watercolor on large pieces of white paper, like a sunset on the beach, mountains in the mist. When school started, I rolled away my pictures and forgot about them.

Years later, I stumbled on these watercolors again quite by chance. At first, I didn't even recognize them. They seemed flat and primitive in composition and color. But I was impressed by the sincerity and the patient details displayed in the paintings. Then a faint recollection emerged from the thick fog of memory. The images of the faraway places transported me momentarily back to those long summer days.

Once, I visited an exhibition in Taipei of masterworks from the Old Palace Museum. A tall landscape painting caught my attention. Staring at the weeds along the riverbanks at the lower section of this painting, I actually felt the breeze and the gentle stirrings in the flowing stream. I was mesmerized by the long wavering brush strokes that shaped mountains, forests, clouds, the path and the tiny village into being. What intrigued me was how the artist turned numerous ink marks and shadings into such a serene and luminous landscape.

When I was little, I was fascinated by the story of the "magic sand." Two small children in the story, looking at a picture of a lush rain forest, would throw the magic sand over their heads murmuring "Magic sand, make us small." As in the dream world of Alice in Wonderland, the magic sand would make them so small that they were able to enter into the picture and explore to their hearts' content. When they had had enough, they would come out of the picture and command the magic sand to return them to their full size. What a wonder! Well, Chinese landscape has that magic and I have experienced it many times.

## Studying Chinese landscape painting

My parents loved to travel. In family albums I have seen many of their photos of breathtaking scenery such as the West Lake, Yan Dang Shan, Omei Shan. I often felt the deep yearning of my father to be in the awesome grandeur of nature where he would find comfort and rest.

When my family settled in Taiwan following the Communist takeover of the mainland, they were not able to travel much. My father became passionate about Chinese landscape painting. That was how he was able to experience nature.

In old times, many scholar-officials longed to travel to faraway places but they were bound by their duty to live in the urban environment to serve their government. So they traveled into nature with their mind's eye through painting, where their hearts could be refreshed and strengthened by the nurturing energy from nature.

I was taught to read a Chinese landscape painting usually from the bottom up in a vertical scroll and from left to right in a horizontal one. Often one finds a path in the lower section or on the left portion of the painting. Meandering sometimes along a riverbank, over a bridge or a trail in the forest, through a fishing village, or a remote hermitage, the path often leads to faraway places shrouded in mist or to mountain peaks covered by clouds, or the luminous sky.

When I was 15, Father took me to a teacher and I started learning traditional landscape painting. It became the love of my life. For seven years, from high school through college, I dedicated myself to the study of this tradition. It defined my identity and anchored my development as an artist.

## An unusual encounter

When I was a freshman in college, I had an unusual encounter with a very special painting in my teacher's house. It was an old painting by an unknown artist. As my teacher unfolded the scroll painting, I felt that a magical world opened up in front of my eyes. There were hefty granite rocks standing in the foreground, with thick trees in the background. A narrow path roamed through a luxuriant forest. It felt like summer. The ink washes of different shades suggested dampness in the air, the dots over the surface, moss over the rocks. The footpath stopped at a simple dwelling with a thick thatched roof. On the right side of the house, which faced a fast running stream, a water wheel was turning. It felt cool at this juncture, maybe because of the increased paleness of the painting indicating the reflective surface of the stream. The little walkway continued over a wooden bridge, winding through the thick foliage on the other side of the stream and eventually ending at the bank of open water. Beyond the water and hills, one saw nothing but the rising mist. It was a modest, simple and quiet world and yet I found my heart beating very fast, full of excitement and wonder. I thought to myself, "It's all here!"

I could not understand my response to this painting for a long time. Gradually I came to realize that what I experienced was an unusual place where time stood still and a deep quietude was revealed through the rhythm of an everyday life scenario. Empowered and inspired, I felt as if I stood in the center of an energy field, directly connected to the fountainhead of creativity. I knew I needed to be a part of this space.

## The dustless world

Through painting I came in contact with a special place, which the Chinese describe as the "dustless" world. "Dust" here refers to not the physical but the mental pollution of ignorance, greed and ego that contaminates our mind and world. This dustless place is serene but dynamic, translucent in its rich spectrum of colors, and full in its emptiness. It is a place of trees, rivers, people, mountains and mist, and yet through them, it reveals a place of pristine beauty and mystery. This place has become my spiritual home.

Looking back, my art training as a traditional painter had many perils. I learned the techniques through copying, first my teacher's work, then later that of the ancient masters. I invented, but always within the boundaries of the tradition. In many ways, it restricted my techniques and limited my imagination. But I loved the tradition and was content with its confinement. It took the journey to America to break me from its hold. It was sudden and shattering.

## My trip to America

On graduation from the National Taiwan University in 1963, I received a scholarship from the Graduate School of Fine Arts at the University of Pennsylvania. It made my studying abroad possible.

The transcontinental airplane tickets were too expensive for most families then. Like many students studying abroad, I came on a big cargo ship that made two stops in Japan, went through the Panama Canal, docked at Charleston, in South Carolina, and finally disembarked in Newark, New Jersey. It took the ship a full month to take its cargo and nine students to our destination.

Up to my graduation from college, I had led a sheltered life, nurtured by my loving parents and siblings. Although life was a huge struggle for my parents and people of their generation, due to the suffering of long years of war and the pain of families being torn apart, my immediate family was lucky enough to escape the chaos and had settled down in Taiwan.

When I visited the University of Pennsylvania for the first time, its beauty, the well-groomed campus with lush lawn, tall trees, and splendid modern and historical buildings, filled me with delight. My studio was in the glorious Furness building, the old library, with its orange-red facade that glowed in the setting sun and gargoyles perching on the roof. It was exhilarating to see students of many different nationalities gathered here to study. My teachers were kind and fellow students friendly. A wonderful beginning!

There was a lot to adjust to, such as my living situation, different foods, and the different philosophy of life. In Chinese culture, one addresses a person by their family name first and then the given name. In America, it is just the reverse. In the Chinese way, when one addresses an envelope, one places the name of the country first, followed by that of the province, then the city, then the street, lane, house number, then name of the receiving person. In America, again it is in exactly the reverse order. Of course, this is only a very superficial description of the different approaches in the two cultures. I began to experience the place of individualism in Western culture.

I remember that my first apartment in West Philadelphia was located on a fast and noisy thoroughfare. Sometimes the abrupt transition from my private space in the apartment to the traffic-filled street was a bit jarring. But I quickly made the transition from my home in Taipei, hidden in secluded lanes and shielded behind walls, to my new urban living. I have been impressed by how American homes stand confident and proud without the protection of walls.

Looking back, how I have adapted! In my early days in America, eating salad was strange and not tasty. Now salad is my main daily meal, essential in keeping me healthy and fit. Since I was eager to embrace my new environment I soon found myself relishing the openness, flexibility and freedom. But some things took longer to understand, especially contemporary art and the glorification of profit-making in American culture.

Before coming to America, my creativity drew inspiration from traditional landscape paintings, especially those created in the 10th–14th centuries. I was satisfied to create idyllic landscapes of faraway land in the shadow of the ancient masters. Confronting contemporary art during my first years in the States shook me to the core of my aesthetic, my creativity and my purpose for making art.

There seemed to be no standard—a bicycle handle or a toilet bowl could be called art; huge paintings derived from commercials and cartoon strips populated prestigious galleries and museums. Instead of brush strokes, some canvases contained only knife-puncture marks. I thought to myself, before anything was created, the surface was already ruined. Obviously, I had totally missed the mark. And the happenings! A mostly naked figure splashed in ink crawling on a piece of cloth on the floor accompanied by the music spontaneously created by a cellist represented a new way of making art. It was mind-exploding to me, frightening and disorienting.

As confusing as it was, I am now filled with gratitude for the immense opportunity America has offered me, and most of all, the vast horizon and challenges from this new art environment. Without going through the cauldron of this experience, I don't think I would have the strength personally to break away from the comfort of the tradition that I came from.

## Taoist and Confucian influences

Growing up in Taiwan, the Taoist philosophy guided our way of life and the teachings of Confucius formed the backbone of our education. Taoism expounds the virtue of being humble, inconspicuous, "knowing the Yang but residing in the Yin." Yang refers to the masculine aspect of things (strength, brightness, aggression), and the Yin, the feminine (gentleness, darkness and receptivity). Taoism explicates the power of the weak and the humble, and the virtue of emptiness:

*We join spokes together in a wheel,*
*But it is the center hole*
*That makes the wagon move.*

*We shape clay into a pot,*
*But it is the emptiness inside*
*That holds whatever we want.*

*We hammer wood for a house,*
*But it is the inner space*
*That makes it livable.*

*We work with being,*
*But non-being is what we use.* [Chapter 11]

*The supreme good is like water,*
*Which nourishes all things without trying to.*
*It is content with the low places that people disdain.*
*Thus it is like the Tao.* [Chapter 8]

*Tao Te Ching*, written by Lao-Tze, 6th century BC,
translated by Stephen Mitchell, 1988

The essence of Confucius' teaching is Ren (仁). The character shows two people together, suggesting relationship. The word extends to mean humanity, compassion and kindness. I would translate this as "Do not do to others what you don't want others to do to you." These teachings anchored and guided me in my new life in America.

When I left Taiwan, I also left that special "dustless world" that I could access from time to time through painting. Ever since, I have traveled far and wide looking for it, a place of longing and belonging, a place to feel centered and at ease. It was in the broken land of North Philadelphia, I "found Life—stepping on my feet!" (Langston Hughes's words in his poem, *Aesthete in Harlem*, 1931).

## A calling to step into my life

In the summer of 1986, I was invited by the renowned dancer and choreographer Arthur Hall to convert an abandoned lot next to his building in North Philadelphia into an art park. Arthur founded the Ile-Ife Black Humanitarian Center and the Arthur Hall Afro-American Dance Ensemble. From his immense talent and deep understanding of African American history, he created a unique dance form that fused traditional African music and dance with the experience of black people in America. His visionary and inspiring work enriched 20th-century American culture, and the mastery of his teaching has impacted the lives of several generations in Philadelphia and nationwide.

Before I met Arthur, I was a studio artist and a professor teaching at the University of the Arts in Philadelphia. I wrote a simple proposal to the Pennsylvania Council on the Arts. To my surprise, the Council awarded me a small grant of $2500 to launch the project. That was when I first felt scared. I had no idea how to build a park outdoors. Counsel from experts in the field said: "Kids are going to destroy everything you build." "You are an outsider, don't go in." "The grant money is a drop in the bucket. Do a feasibility study and forget about the project."

While I was struggling with my fear and the desire to escape, the work crew of the city demolished a series of dilapidated houses next to Arthur's lot. I thought to myself, this was a perfect time to withdraw with honor. Then I heard a little voice in my head saying, "If you don't rise to the occasion, the best of you will die. The rest will not amount to anything." The voice was gentle, the message thundering. I decided to give it a try. I had no idea how to build a park, but at least I could try doing something with children.

Since I did not know the neighborhood or how to make art outdoors, I needed help. Arthur suggested Jojo, a talented drummer and jack-of-all-trades. Meeting him changed my life. Looking back at the beginning of my journey, it feels like a story told in a fairy tale. The main character is called to go on a journey to an unknown place. If the person is courageous enough to respond, she meets her guide. Joseph William (Jojo) turned out to be my teacher and my guide.

Jojo was fierce like a lion, always roaring and angry. He wore bandanas on his head and a tool belt with hammers and knives dangling around his waist. I went to his home, a partially renovated house next to the big abandoned lot that I was supposed to work on. He had heard word on the street and didn't want to have anything to do with me, a crazy Chinese woman. Twice I missed him. On the third try, he was tying his shoelaces. I said, "Jojo, please talk to me. I need your help."

I shared with him my dream to create an art park on the lot next to his house. Jojo was a feared person in the neighborhood but this simple request seemed to change him. Later I realized that the world had been trying to put him down. He reacted with anger and ferocity in order to protect his manhood. But here came an Asian woman asking for his help. He could assist me with his building skills and I could provide him with a modest work opportunity. Our weaknesses created a space where we could establish our alliance. Thus we met on equal footing and began to work together.

Abandoned and broken places are powerful because there we can lay bare our vulnerability. Violence tends to happen there too, but also genuine and deep connections between people. Jojo took pride in his new role in helping this art professor to build an art park and to guard this piece of abandoned land. I was filled with gratitude that I could deliver what I promised in my proposal.

Children admired Jojo, especially the boys because he was the strong man in the neighborhood. As we poked around, wondering how to begin, the kids came. I had shovels and spades ready; I knew the kids liked to play with them. I also figured that if they helped us build, they would not tear down the things that they had made themselves.

## About the center

When I first started the project, I did not have a plan. I did not know how to design a park in such a forlorn place. So, I came into the space and tried to feel it. Then I picked up a stick and drew a circle in the center of the lot. We started digging there. Looking back at that moment, I realized that my effort to find my own center and authenticity became manifested in locating the center of this big abandoned lot. I said, "From here, we will build."

Forsaken places are potent with meaning and possibilities, since the established rules have failed them and no one really cares what happens there. They are the safest places for innovation. It was in the vacant land in inner city North Philadelphia that I felt free to explore new ways of working with people and materials and to have fun amidst uncertainty, chaos and failing attempts. Eventually things sorted themselves out and I began to find my voice. Our team, composed of neighborhood children and adults, figured out a nurturing way of working that drew on the energy and ingenuity of participants and provided space for personal growth and the expression of our caring for each other.

Like the Tree of Life, the little art park project on an abandoned lot grew into a multi-leveled and multifaceted non-profit arts organization called The Village of Arts and Humanities. The decade-long, community-building activities and the ongoing art projects became our shared journey to discover our creativity, uniqueness and the meaning of things and life.

## The importance of taking action

I remember asking Jojo on a very hot summer afternoon in 1988 as we worked in the park with children, "Why do the adults just sit at their doorsteps and watch us? Why don't they come and help?" Jojo's answer surprised me. "Help you? They are laughing their teeth off about your project." I asked why. Jojo said people were saying, "A woman and a bunch of kids, they don't know what they are doing." I felt hurt. But after thinking about it, I said, "Man, they are right on target. We really do not know what we are doing." Then I realized that what was important was that we were taking action and doing something. We might not understand what we were doing in our heads, but we knew it in our hearts. The children certainly did. They gave all of themselves in working with us. For me, it was metaphorically a life and death matter. I was desperate to step into my own journey and make my life count.

I felt that we were guided by an intuitive wisdom, the same force that made the salmon swim against tides year after year and the stars rotate in the night sky. Our actions looked random and hectic; our effort appeared fruitless and without direction. But inwardly we were driven by a force like the ocean tide, which is connected to all life and all things on earth. In our playful and seemingly disorganized way of working, a new sense of order and purpose began to emerge. It caught everyone by surprise, including me.

## A natural way to educate children

Although I intended to involve children from the beginning of the project, I was also afraid of doing so. I had little experience with working with a group of children. I was apprehensive of their energy and exuberance. Since no adults except Jojo came to help me, I eventually settled down to work with the children, who so eagerly wanted to participate.

Although fierce towards adults, Jojo was kind and protective of children. Hordes came everyday, attracted to action and fun. It forced us to figure out meaningful and orderly activities for the children to do. In 1988, we worked for two months in heatwave temperatures ranging between 95 and 100 degrees. We were blessed with our first volunteer, Carol Wiseman, who was working on her master's degree at the University of the Arts. Seeing that the children were often hungry or eating chips throughout the day, she began to bring sandwiches and fruit for them. Recycling sewing materials such as colorful fabrics, buttons, threads and shining beads, she conducted outdoor workshops for children under tree shades. Children collected dried peapods, which were plentiful on the ground. Colorful banners, shakers and beaded sculptures emerged. Together Jojo, Carol and I held the art-making station where children from the neighborhood could participate in various activities. We created 12 small cement sculptures and painted an 8 foot by 10 foot mural. Yes, we accomplished something, and we had fun.

I remember a beautiful story about the forming of a school told by the late poet architect Louis Kahn:

> Schools began with a man under a tree, who did not know he was a teacher, discussing his realization with a few others who did not know they were students. The students reflected on the exchanges between them and how good it was to be in the presence of this man. They wished their sons, also, to listen to such a man. Soon, the needed spaces were erected and the first schools came into existence. The establishment of schools was inevitable because they are part of the desires of man. (Wurman, 1986, p.261)

In a way, that was how the Village program for children came into being. It was formed naturally and without much recruitment. The children came eagerly. They have grown into adulthood now. With affection and pride for their contribution to this early park-building effort, many still feel a strong connection to the park and the Village.

I asked myself why the project left such an indelible mark on them. Maybe it is because under the tutelage of adults, children became a part of the workforce that transformed their own neighborhood for better. The project provided them contact with and attention from adults, room for creativity and self-expression, opportunities to learn teamwork skills, and to be seen in public. Thinking back, that was an effective and powerful way to educate children and to build their self-esteem.

## The beginning of the Village of Arts and Humanities

In 1988 Arthur Hall left Philadelphia, and the building that hosted his organization became vacant and abandoned. Seeing the potential of our humble art project, Stephen Sayre, writer, educator, lawyer and builder, joined our community building effort. His knowledge and expertise helped us to become a non-profit organization, which we named the Village of Arts and Humanities. He and I became its co-founders. For the first three years, still teaching full time at the University of the Arts, I was only able to do projects during the summer months. But Sayre became totally engaged and was able to oversee the year-round affairs at the Village. That was how our organization was born.

To save the three-story building from deterioration and vandalism, Sayre recruited the help of Jojo and other neighborhood adults to do the renovation. Sayre's enormous dedication, leadership and construction skills combined with the support from his team and various city agencies made the renovation project a success. From 1990 onward, the newly renovated facility housed a year-round after-school and weekend education program, with dance and drumming workshops, theater rehearsals, weekly Narcotics Anonymous meetings, and community festivities. In addition, Sayre helped the Village to articulate its mission and purpose; he formulated its activities in many proposals, supported our performing arts program, launched our community vegetable garden and the Village publication, *North Philadelphia*, and much else in its beginning years.

Here I must mention two other people whose contributions were critical and essential to the building of the Village. Heidi Warren came to the Village in 1991 as a volunteer when she was a senior majoring in Urban Studies at Haverford College. On graduation, she began working at the Village as an assistant in administration, fundraising, writing proposals, guiding projects and managing finances. Imaginative and efficient, Heidi quickly became Managing Director and created our administrative guidelines and staff policy and set up our financial system. In addition, she assisted the organization to raise most of its funds and in-kind donations. Her talent and deep commitment helped the Village to build a solid infrastructure with dedicated staff, teachers and hundreds of volunteers. Being a fine graphic artist, she designed numerous promotional and educational materials and headed the publication of *Connecting through Walls*, a newsletter created by artists and prison inmates. In short, during her ten-year sojourn, she helped to develop the Village from a fledgling organization into an internationally recognized model for building community through art.

Then there was James Maxton. People nicknamed him Big Man because he was six feet eight inches in height and 300 pounds in weight. People called him that for another, and darker, reason. He was a big figure in the North Philadelphia drugs trade, using and selling drugs for over 20 years. Big Man had become a destructive force to himself and the neighborhood. The drug habit eventually brought him devastation and despair. Looking for a way out of his life, he came to Jojo for refuge. Having lost everything in his life, he thought that he would perish in the gutter somewhere. The only thing he still had was time.

I was creating a very long mosaic wall of seven eight-foot-tall Ethiopian angels and I needed help. He had no art training of any sort, not to mention mosaics. I guided him and he followed my suggestions. He would tell me, "I will always work within your lines." We found a mutually helpful way to work with each other. Quietly and consistently, he worked on the mural day after day in that hot summer of 1988. People commented, "This is beautiful. You did all that for us?" He liked the immediate result of the work and the positive feedback from passers-by. He promised himself, "If Ms. Lily returns next summer, I will leave drugs." I returned and he became drug free. No withdrawal, no drama. In time, he became a well-established mosaic artist in his own right. He commented with humor, "The only trouble is that I left drugs and became addicted to mosaics."

Because of his personal experience, he had deep understanding and compassion for people who were struggling with drug addiction.

For over a decade, he organized weekly meetings for several Narcotics Anonymous groups at the Village. He became the Village's Operations Director; he supervised four crew members and occasional volunteers in the building of the many art parks and gardens in the greater Village area. For example, one of our projects was located at Daniel Boone High School (now Camelot Academy of Philadelphia) 20 blocks away from the Village. His transformation and his love of art and people made him the most beloved figure at the Village.

## The building of the Meditation Park

People say that inner cities lack resources. But if we look at it with the right mindset, there are plenty of assets in the form of abandoned properties and cast-off building materials. Across a narrow street facing the main Village building was another large debris-scattered land consisting of 12 connected lots where rows of homes once stood.

I worked with the city's Redevelopment Authority to use the land. I began to put together a construction crew composed of adults living in the neighborhood. Most of them were not employed and not skilled in construction. I found out later on that they all had drug problems. But that did not deter me at all. I felt grateful to have this opportunity to collaborate with my crew to build something positive on this wasteland.

The funding of this park came from several regional and national foundations, including the National Endowment of the Arts. Suddenly we were on the radar screen and became visible to the public. I became fearful of making mistakes. I thought that we must get the professionals to help us so we could do everything right. I knew that I wanted to have a sculptural wall around the park with a ground decorated with colorful mosaic tiles. I also knew that the loose soil in the ground needed to be well packed down and laid out in such a way that water would naturally flow to the street. This all seemed difficult to grasp and beyond our capability, so I called the professional builders to give me an estimate if I hired them to do the work. As soon as the estimate came in, I knew the price was too high. I figured that we must do it ourselves and learn in action.

I understood that laying a solid foundation for the wall construction would require us to dig into the ground. Excavating the ground anywhere in an inner city poses difficulties because underneath the empty lots the basements are packed with debris of bricks, cement, broken furniture, washing machines, refrigerators and so on. When the city crew came to demolish the dilapidated buildings, they crushed everything into the basements. We tried to hand dig with spades and shovels. The intense vibration of metal hitting on hard objects would send shock waves through our arms. So, we rented a Bobcat.

## Self-empowerment

We got someone to teach us how to operate the machine. All the crew members, including me, learned how to drive the bobcat. We all felt powerful, like the Bobcat. We were fortunate to receive help from a building expert, Richard Withers, a Christian hermit living on N. Alder Street in the Village. He guided us on all aspects of construction such as the grade and mixture of the concrete, the right amount to order, the depth of the foundation, the preparatory structure for pouring concrete, leveling and curing time. We also got help from the city's surveying department. They helped us with the grading of the land. Then Mr. Johnson, a retired construction supervisor who lived in the Village neighborhood, volunteered to oversee the work of our construction crew. He was on site every weekday morning through the whole construction period.

So, from building experts, we learned how to excavate, drive a bobcat, pour concrete, build a foundation and construct walls. But when the walls were built, they looked very mundane—just straight plain walls. Then I remembered the hill-like shapes on some of the sacred shrines in Mali. I figured that those cone-shaped mounds would look good on our walls. Recycling the broken bricks and stones, we built the gently undulating shapes on the walls. We felt music come into the space and the walls began to sing; the space became harmonious and our hearts felt happy and soothed.

I figured out with Jojo and Big Man how to set mosaic tiles and colored stones into freshly poured wet cement on the park floor. It required tight teamwork. Our construction members and volunteers decorated the entire floor of the park with colorful mosaic tiles and stones. So many pairs of hands working in a well-coordinated way was fun and exciting. The focal point of the park is now a colorful 14 foot by 10 foot mosaic mural, "The Tree of Life," featuring golden star-shaped flowers against deep turquoise and green foliage. In our highly industrialized world, it is difficult to create a public space that requires such intense labor and personal attention due to limited time and high cost. But in our poorer neighborhood, this could still be done. When every inch of the surface in the park was touched by hand with care, it makes the place nurturing and magical. It brings warmth and joy to people who visit the place.

Chinese gardens, African architecture and Islamic courtyards have been my sources of inspiration. In the process of designing the park, I was able to introduce the beauty and design concept from these various cultures to our neighborhood. Life in an inner city is intense and stressful. I wanted to build a space where people could come to relax, reconnect, reflect and re-center. I named the place Meditation Park. If the park looks wonderful, the process of making it was more wonderful and significant. It left me with some of the most memorable moments during my sojourn at the Village.

When thinking how art transforms those who participate, Vic comes to mind. He was on drugs, which had caused an estrangement between him and his father. Wanting to follow in the footsteps of Big Man, he showed a real promise in becoming a skilled worker and a leader. Not only did he master the skill of driving a Bobcat, he took initiatives in helping other workers and in ensuring the quality of the work produced by the team. Vic's father would often stand under a tree and watch his son work. He was so proud of him, and they reconciled and reconnected. Vic told me once that coming to work at the Village from the drug-infested areas felt like stepping from darkness into the light. A couple of mothers came to us smiling, "My son can come home now. He's working now and no longer stealing people's TVs and things for drugs."

One afternoon, as I was working with the crew laying stones and tiles into the wet cement, I suddenly heard a loud and guttural sound released into words that seemed to come from somewhere deep, "*Wooooow! We are awesome!*" It came from a member of the construction crew nicknamed Weasel. He felt so happy about what he was doing and he talked about getting married to his lovely fiancée. It all seemed so hopeful. Unfortunately, we ran out of money and winter was setting in, so we had to stop the construction work.

The project, transforming community through creating beauty, and working together in a meaningful way, did provide the crew members a valuable means to leave drugs for a better way of life. But ultimately each person has to make the shift inside themselves to follow the light within. Some did do that and the project became a way for them to move on with their life towards a future. I ran into Leon Saunders on Warnock Street on a summer day in 2005. Jojo recruited him in the summer of 1990 when the Village crew set up the three-story-high scaffold for the painting of the Ile-Ife Park Mural. Suffering from a drug addiction, he was trying to find a way out. He was not afraid of heights and enjoyed painting up on the scaffold. On a late afternoon, after crew members had completed their work, Leon lingered on with excitement. He heard that I was going to paint a huge rainbow with some rainbow-colored rain; he wanted to stay around to see how it was done.

Leon loved painting and loved being up high on the scaffold. He smiled a lot and had a good sense of humor. But sometimes the sunny expression on his face would suddenly change as if darkened by heavy clouds. I asked him why. Leon said he would be happy working on the job at Ile-Ife Park. But he would be burdened by the thought of what he would do and where he would go after the job. Thirteen years later I bumped into Leon on Warnock Street. His face was smooth and untroubled. Well dressed in suit and tie, he had a nice haircut, albeit with quite a bit of grey. We were both surprised and broke into big smiles. After greeting and embracing, he told me that he now worked as a manager at a local company. Things were going very well for him. He was grateful to have been able to take shelter at the Village during his addiction years. Receiving care and encouragement from the community, he had found strength to move on with his life. He came to the Village from time to time to check things out and to reconnect.

The most remarkable encounter was with Ice, a member of the crew. Few people knew his real name. Everyone called him Ice. He was small, quiet and almost unnoticeable. He saw himself as a laborer in the lower strata of the workforce and always stood at the back behind other crew members. One day I felt very distressed about how chaotic things were in our storage shack. Wheelbarrows and cement bags were piling on top of each other and tools were thrown randomly into the storage space. We could not find the utensils we needed, nor could we remember what we had. I felt overwhelmed and upset. Ice began talking to me, "You know, I been with you for three years and I was a laborer. I have worked myself up now and I would like to help you with the inventory. I have a suggestion. You should put all these on a list." He made the statement with a great deal of concentration, effort and energy. I felt that his words came from an interior depth that really made me listen.

However, some of the participants in the Village did not change their way of life. I heard that Weasel was killed in a robbery attempt. Vic did not manage to follow in Big Man's footsteps. For two decades, he remained heavily addicted to drugs. Eventually he managed to free himself from what he described as the slavery of the drug choke-hold; he began to see the light of freedom. He came back to the Village for reconnection and support. Now he runs the weekly Narcotics Anonymous meetings at the Village and works as a small-scale building contractor.

I never felt unsafe working in the inner city. Once in a great while, we would hear gunshots coming from some abandoned houses. We had lost children in our neighborhood to stray bullets in the cross-fire of gang violence. Somehow, I felt protected by the positive energy of our work and the presence of Jojo, Big Man, other participants from the community and the children. Also in the face of violence, it was all the more important to continue our work to create new possibilities and hope. Somehow one day Ice got wind that "Ms. Lily felt danger." Feeling anxious for me, he said, "If I learn you got hurt or sick, it wouldn't matter where I was in the city, I would drop everything and come here. I will come here and protect you." And he just kept on saying this and that. He did not deliver his message in a linear fashion. He would say it in an archaic and multi-dimensional manner, repeating words or phrases here and there. I tried hard to listen to what he was saying. When I finally understood his words, the most amazing thing happened. I felt that I held his heart in my hands. He gave it to me while expressing his feeling and concerns. This was a mystical experience revealed to me through a quite mundane conversation in this badland of North Philadelphia.

## Finding opportunity on the flip side

At the start of this project in 1986 I was not well equipped with knowledge or resources. But I was well equipped with two essential things—the desire to take action and the understanding of the power of art. The experience of growing up in China and years of studying Taoism and Buddhism made me understand that the world is made up of two conflicting and yet complementary forces that the Chinese named Yin and Yang. The Yin and the Yang is, for example, the shady and the sunny side of a mountain. The two must appear simultaneously and always in the company of each other. With this philosophy, nothing is ever still. These two forces are constantly in motion, in order to become each other. Each element contains the seed of its opposite, and will eventually become its opposite. This understanding makes me see things differently. When I see the brokenness, poverty and crime in our inner cities, I also see the enormous potential and readiness for transformation and rebirth. When I see deficits, I see resources on the other side of the coin.

As I stepped into the project, I was lacking in every way. This weakness became my most powerful tool in realizing the project. Because I was lacking, I needed help. It provided opportunities for people to meaningfully join the project, helping me to realize my goal. It helped people realize their own strength and provided people opportunities to reconnect with each other through work. Through this process, our separate and individual selves were made whole. Empowerment and the healing of people began to take place. This was the first step towards community rebuilding.

## Becoming a leader and embracing action

I did not know how to lead. It was the children who taught me how, the children who came into my project 30 years ago. The children, through their innocence, curiosity, joy and willingness to take part showed me the power and source of their creative energy. Their participation forced me to figure out a different way of doing things. It was a way that was not taught in my school, nor in my family life, nor in society. That was when I learned how to be a leader. A real leader understands the art of following. To lead, one must follow the feeling that comes from the heart and the energy that surges forth directly from life itself.

Since this beginning in 1986, I have chosen to create art with people in poor communities. For me, it has been a special gift to work with people in dire circumstances, to make a real contribution, to make a difference in people's lives. These difficult and compelling situations make life more real for me. They help me to better understand who I am and why we live, and to see the complexity of human nature in its light and dark manifestations. By looking at challenges face to face and acting with compassion and creativity, we can find hope and new solutions.

For me, being an artist is not just about making art: it is a way of life. It is about delivering the vision you are given, sharing your gifts freely, and doing the right thing without sparing yourself. If you do all this, you will feel fulfilled, without fear, and thus can become truly free.

## Three steps forward

After attending many conferences on art, urban planning and community building, I realized that the work I had been doing was not only about an individual artist working with disenfranchised people in an isolated situation. It was also a part of a global movement to make the world a better place through grassroots efforts. Governments, professionals and the private sector can build powerful systems such as transportation, utilities, communication and other infrastructures. They can construct big buildings, highways and technology complexes. But they cannot solve all the problems caused by the enormous growth of urban centers all over the world, particularly problems caused by poverty and population displacement. While good systems can bring physical, social and economic improvement to people's lives, they can rarely address their emotional, mental and spiritual needs. Although intangible, these needs are critical to people's well-being.

Art and culture can function as powerful tools to build compassionate communities, connect people, strengthen family ties and preserve cultural heritage.

When we create art that comes from the heart, it heals and transforms. The art we create with community residents flows out of their experiences and deep concerns. It reveals the pain and sorrow and celebrates the hope and joy of the people in the community. Its process is open and inclusive. This creative power and imagination is the light within each one of us. Through doing projects together, we pass on this light within us to illuminate that within others. Together we unite and shine. This light cuts through the darkness of our ignorance, greed, politics and social blight. Here, I believe, lies the hope for the future.

Community building is challenging and often without glory. It is three steps forward then two steps backward. It is trench-work filled with sloppy and mundane details. Then why do I do it? I do it because it fulfills my deepest longing to be connected with others and to become whole. Despite the endless failings, in that one step, the world begins to change. As the poet Rumi said, "Let the beauty we love be what we do. There are hundreds of ways to kneel and kiss the ground."

## Barefoot artists: creating beauty in broken places in the world

Prior to my departure from the Village, I established a second non-profit arts organization named Barefoot Artists, Inc. This organization focuses mostly on international projects. I was inspired by the work of China's barefoot doctors in the 1970s, who visited the poor, usually peasants in faraway areas. They went without much pomp, practiced their art of healing and then moved on. This felt like a good model for me. The mission of Barefoot Artists is simple: to witness, embrace and act. I designed our logo as a huge flower hovering in a vibrant sunrise-colored background. An image of the globe occupies the heart of the flower. It reveals our desire to bring beauty to broken places in the world, and with it, inspiration, hope and action. This beauty is not just decorative or something that makes people feel good momentarily. It is what our soul yearns for. It arises from our effort to honor people's cultural heritage, our search for authenticity and our deliverance through sincerity and deep caring. This beauty nurtures and heals.

Barefoot Artists is a volunteer-based organization that requires minimum overheads and maintenance and yet has the capacity to carry out large-scale projects with precision and effectiveness. It aims to bring the transformative power of art to the impoverished communities in the world through participatory and multifaceted activities that foster community empowerment, improve the physical environment, initiate economic development and preserve and promote indigenous art and culture. For me, beauty and creativity are not luxuries for a few. They are essential for our well-being. Like sunlight and air, they feed our souls.

Under the auspices of the Village of Arts and Humanities and later Barefoot Artists, I have since traveled to many countries, including Ecuador, Colombia, Ghana, Ivory Coast, Kenya, Italy, Republic of Georgia, Syria, Rwanda, China and Palestine, offering my methodology of healing and community building through the arts. I have come to realize that broken places are our canvases, people's stories the pigments, people's imagination and talents the tools. At the beginning, when I start a project, my intention is to do something for the people. Then I invite people from the community to participate. When people learn the process and skills, they take charge and continue. At the end, the project belongs to the people.

In many places in the world, such as North Philadelphia in the USA, Jamestown in Ghana, Korogocho in Kenya and Rugerero in Rwanda, our projects continue to evolve and grow. I call them "living social sculpture." When the projects are carried out in the right manner and spirit, they build confidence and pride and at the same time bring hope, joy and possibilities to the community. How does this happen?

## My approach

There are steps and structures to this process. It is the essence of my methodology. When I think of my various projects and how they function, I think of the following metaphors (Moskin and Jackson, 2004, pp.25–27):

## 1. The planting of a seed.

A seed, though small, is potent. It knows when and how to make things grow. It contains all the growth patterns and qualities of a plant, be it a small bush or a huge tree. I see that a seed is like an inspired idea. It has authenticity because it contains life in its small but potent form. Inspiration comes not from our head; it is given from the source of life. If one is connected to one's heart, one is connected to the primal energy source. Inspiration is from that energy source that makes our heart beat fast. It is like our inner light. It guides us. Ideas that come from that place have immense power for growth and impact. An artist's work is to realize those ideas so that they blossom, come to fruition and are not wasted.

## 2. The growth of a tree.

I see that community evolves in the way that a tree grows. As the seed of a tree breaks ground (reaching downwards), its stem reaches upwards towards the sun, the source of light and energy. As the seedling grows stronger, it begins to sprout leaves and branches. The deeper the roots grow, the taller and stronger the tree grows. As the tree grows downwards and upwards, its branches reach simultaneously in all directions. With the rain and dew in the night, the tree puts out flowers. It begins to attract insects, birds, animals and people because of the resources it offers: the shelter, shade, cool breezes, nourishment and beauty. This is the way I see that the Village has become a community.

It grew organically and naturally. It emerged and is still in the process of creating itself through many people's hard work and dedication. The deeper the roots grow, the more the tree can open up, reach out, survive stormy weather and realize its full power and potential.

## 3. Deep ocean kelp.

Deep ocean kelp is securely rooted in a fixed place with a small attachment. Although the plant is pliant, it is tremendously strong. Riding and responding to the ocean current, it can reach far and wide to gather food and look for new opportunities. The Village works this way. It takes root in a particular community, as in the inner city of North Philadelphia. Yet it has regional, national and global impact due to the clarity of its mission, its values and artistic sensitivity, the simplicity of its primary structure, the flexibility of its methods and its openness to people's participation.

### 4. A school of fish.

Schools of fish are interconnected, in tune with each other, sensitive and responsive to the environment and quick to reorganize. They move in unison and are dynamic.

### 5. Shedding and frogging.

In lean times, plants shed leaves and even branches. A certain kind of frog burrows underground in the dry season. When rain comes, the leaves and the frogs surface and take action. At the Village, we burst into full bloom when resources are plentiful. In lean times, we "frog" some of our programs. Whatever we have learned and begun is not lost. We simply "frog" the activities until the resources (rain) arrive.

### 6. The drifting of a coconut fruit.

Imagine a coconut in a river or on the ocean shore. The coconut drops into the water and gets carried away according to the force of the current and the formation of the land. If the new environment is supportive, the coconut will take root and begin to propagate. Although the original coconut tree grows only in one fixed place, its impact can have infinite possibilities. This is how the Village can have a local and regional influence and, at the same time, a national and global impact.

### 7. Throwing a pebble into a pond.

This is another image to show the impact of the Village. The pebble is thrown and touches the water at a particular place. From this place, the center ripples push outwards towards the edge of the pond. This reflects the impact of the Village on a local level, then regional, national and international. The physical center is the Village and, particularly, the circle in the center of Ile-Ife, the first park. When I started, I drew a circle in the middle of the vacant land with a stick that I picked up from the ground. I announced that from here, we would build. Looking back, I see that the circle was the physical manifestation of my own center, through which I came in contact with the primary energy source that makes the earth go round and the stars rotate. What connected me with that energy source is that I listened and took action in order to realize the inspired idea I received as a vision.

## Following the light inside

How was it possible for a woman with very few skills in park building, and even fewer skills in community building, to become a catalyst for such creative energy, rebuilding a whole community? The answer is simple. I followed my passion and was guided by the light inside me. That light does not belong to me alone. It is innate in all of us. Everyone has it (Moskin and Jackson, 2004, p.6). I have often been given credit for helping people transform their lives. However, it was I who felt isolated and separated. It was I who longed to make contact with that which is essential and real in myself and in others. In short, I longed to belong to something bigger, more powerful, sacred and profound. I did not know where to find it. So I became quiet. I listened, waited, observed and tried to get ready. Finally, when life called, I became involved. I traveled far and wide to look for it and I found it first in the inner city of North Philadelphia. Later, I found it in the hearts of many other people who also longed to belong and to connect. This prepared me for the extraordinary place called Korogocho.

## Local to international—Korogocho, Kenya

Fascinated by the people and the land of Africa, I had longed to visit that vast continent for years. The opportunity came in 1993 when I received a Lila Wallace Arts International Award to travel and work in East Africa for three months. I spent one month traveling in Kenya and Tanzania, visiting many renowned parks such as the Masai Mara, Serengeti, Nakuru, Lake Turkana and Ngorongoro. The experience of going back in time in a place so far away from my routine existence, so close to wildlife and nature, and the experience of silence, uninterrupted by telephone, radio, television or traffic was profound. There was a sense of peace and deep rest that I have not known before. I felt the alluring magic of this continent and its beautiful people despite the great difficulties of traveling in Africa.

Even more profound was my experience in Korogocho, one of the largest slum neighborhoods outside Nairobi. This shantytown of 150,000 people, living in only 1.5 square kilometers (0.6 square miles), is built around a huge garbage dump and is inhabited by rural migrants trying to make a living near the capital city.

The first time I visited Korogocho, I was terror stricken by the density of life in the labyrinth-like streets, with people and animals crowded together, and numerous children in tattered clothes. There were ramshackle houses constructed with pieces of wood and recycled metal and plastic sheets. The stench from the massive trash piles mingled with the smell from cooking and traffic, and open sewers made breathing a challenge. In the dump, dark red flames belched up thick black smoke from the burning trash that encircled a large, dead, dark green pool, and I thought this to be hell on earth.

The scene became all the more startling and unreal when viewed under the bright blue Nairobi sky filled with clusters of brilliant white clouds. There were hundreds of marabou storks, nearly five feet tall, hovering over the trash piles. Such beauty and such ugliness in one view! Here thousands of children and adults work daily in the vast trash field to eke out a living. They are called mukuru (garbage) people. They experience violence on so many levels—intense pollution, the lack of clean water and air, lack of security and the ravages of hunger. It is the violence of poverty and the deprivation of opportunity and human dignity.

What is one to do in the face of such devastation? My immediate response was to bring colors. No one, including me, could have imagined that beauty could exist in such a place. I come to find out that creating art in forlorn and forsaken places is like making fire in the frozen darkness of a winter's night. It brings light, warmth and hope, and it beckons people to join in.

## Father Alex Zanotelli

During my residency in Nairobi, I stayed at the simple and lovely compound of Paa Ya Paa Art Center, the oldest and highly respected cultural organization in East Africa. It was my hosts Elimo and Phillida Njau who introduced me to Father Alex Zanotelli, who lived in a wooden shack a short distance from his church, St. John's Catholic Church, in the heart of Korogocho. I soon discovered that this man, dressed in an old blue jersey jacket, a worn pair of pants and sandals made of cut-up tires, is a living saint who was baptized by the poor living in the hell of Korogocho.

Father Alex established St. John's Catholic Church to provide the Catholic faithful with a place of worship. To help the people living in Korogocho, Father Alex worked with the destitute and the abandoned to set up various cottage industries, such as a recycling trash collaborative for garbage collectors (Mukuru), a batik studio (Batik), a furniture-making workshop for young men (Kindugu), a bead workshop for young mothers (Udada), basket weaving for older women (Bega Kwa Bega), and a performing dance group (Kairos). Under his leadership, the Catholic informal school took care of 800 children who could not afford to go to regular schools. The drama of life and death unfolded daily.

The church compound contains the church and several smaller classroom structures on the periphery. A barren and dusty courtyard occupies the center of the compound where many church activities take place and where 800 children play. The church is separated by a shaggy wooden fence from the vast dumpsite. In the middle of the dump is a small lake filled with stagnant water and green algae.

## The art project in Korogocho

I said to myself that maybe I could do something to bring some color and joy to this place. Yet at the same time, I felt that there was no way I could work here amid all this devastation and filth. What followed was an intense struggle within myself, to go forward or to back out. I was guided again through the voice of my son Daniel who was traveling with me in Kenya. Sensing my intense conflict, he simply commented, "Mom, this is your project. Be brave." Thus, with fear and trembling, I stepped forward to face my challenge, a challenge that impacted me profoundly and helped to chart my life onward.

The first question was what kind of art would make sense here? How could I engage the community in art-making and how could we create images that came from the community? Since I could not work simultaneously with hundreds of people, I decided to focus on working with a smaller group of people who could go through the process of creating art with me. With assistance from Father Alex, I started with 200 participants from St. John's Catholic Church.

## So close to death

One morning as I was working in the churchyard of the church, I heard chaotic and excited voices coming from across the green stagnant water. Someone jumped into the lake to commit suicide. Some people went into the lake trying to save the person. Many people, children and adults, dotted the landscape in a restless motion, hither and thither. A big city truck arrived to help.

I continued looking for some walls to paint on. There were no images anywhere on the walls, just dirt and dust. I figured if I could put colors on these walls, the environment would begin to change.

What to paint in a place filled with grave danger and devastation and with so few resources… I decided to call on the presence of the angels to protect this sanctuary, its people and community. So I started designing angels. The inspiration came from the Ethiopian angels we had made in Angel Alley at the inner city Village, and the masks and statues exhibited at Paa Ya Paa Art Center nearby.

As I painted an angel wearing a long gown in peacock green and blue, bedecked with orange and red flowers, a person suddenly came from behind my back, and walked towards the side of the wall on which I was painting. Bending down, he picked up my water bottle for the day, and gulped it down in one breath. He then threw away the bottle and threw himself down at the corner of the wall and went into a deep sleep. He had huge eyes and a dark complexion. He was so thin that his limbs looked like twigs and his lower face shrank to a pointed chin. He was wet and wore only a thin bathing suit. I stood only a few feet away from him, yet he was totally oblivious to my presence. I felt that it was best to let him sleep while no one was in the courtyard to disturb him. So I just continued painting. I placed a white dove in the hands of the angel and a jeweled crown over her head. It was quiet and peaceful.

Moments later some people came and brought him clothes, and he staggered up and put them on. The clothes looked wretched. Did they come from the dump? He was struggling with multiple illnesses and so Father Alex had the man taken to the hospital. We did not know whether he recovered or where he went. And so life went on.

## Painting is like performing magic

How appropriate, I thought, to bring the images of angels to this Catholic church that provided comfort and hope for the poorest and the most destitute among the Kenyans. Yes, angels. I painted MaMa Angel, Warrior Angel and Peace Angel, to guide, protect and comfort this community. People were very curious about what I was doing. No one had created murals here before. I got on a tall ladder made of raw branches and wooden planks and started sketching on the wall. From time to time, the fragile ladder shook a bit. I had to concentrate both on the act of painting and balancing.

After sketching the figures on the wall with chalk, I then outlined them in black. The bright colors I used—orange, red, cadmium yellow, bright green and sky blue—breathed life into the images. After quite some time, I turned around and saw a throng of people watching, holding their breath, wide-eyed and in total amazement. I realized that the act of painting in that situation had become a public art performance.

Colors here are more than just pigments used to capture the images we see with our eyes. Representing different aspects of nature— red and orange, the sunset colors; yellow, the sunlight; green; the forest; and blue, the sea and sky—these colors energize and bring joy. I stepped down from my ladder for a short break. When I returned, I saw a little boy standing on the ladder imitating me painting. Another little child, standing near the wall with his little finger stretched out, stooped down and picked up some yellow drops on the ground. He looked at the color carefully and then pressed his finger against the wall. He was utterly delighted by the little yellow fingerprint he had created.

## A Ninja painter

When I first visited Korogocho, I avoided direct contact with people. I was frightened of the dangers in this profusely polluted environment. My travel book told of many exotic and terrifying diseases in this land. But my policy of no contact did not work very well. Every time we walked down one of the roads in Korogocho, children—running towards us from far and near—screamed with joy, "Mzungu, how are you? How are you?" Mzungu in Swahili means white man or outsider. I found out that when Father Alex walked down the street, he would greet the children sweetly, "How are you?" He would hold their hands fondly and walk together with them. Father Alex's faith in God and his deep love of humanity transformed any danger into a celebration of life and the occasion of being together.

I would work all day without eating and I did not drink much so that I did not have to use the pit toilet. When the wind blew, it brought the smell and dust from where trash was dumped, so I covered myself totally, wearing a long-sleeved shirt, long trousers, a hat over my head, a scarf over my face and a pair of big goggle-like glasses over my eyes. Feeling embarrassed by my fear, I secretly hoped that no one took any notice. If they did, I hoped for their understanding. In my moment of great unease, it was a child who came to my rescue. After taking a good look at me, he said, "You must be a Ninja painter!" From then on, I called myself a Ninja painter. What a gift from this child!

## Paint-shaking dance

I tried to involve as many people as I could in the mural painting process—adults and especially children. Before we opened up cans of paints, I asked children to give them a good shaking to help mix the paints properly inside. It became a paint-shaking dance with a lot of fun and laughter. I outlined the figures; I asked adults to paint different sections with ready-prepared, flat colors. For children, I created simple geometric designs on the walls outside their classrooms. Taking turns to paint the patterns on the wall, children participated and felt proud of their contribution.

## Transformation of the environment

As the walls in the church and classrooms were being transformed from mud-splashed surfaces into brightly colored murals of angels and flowers, the people in the community also began to change. People were curious and excited. I noticed there was more laughter and joy in the courtyard. Slowly, more people wanted to help and be a part of the action. My hours of working in the church extended from six or eight hours to eleven hours during the last days. I wanted to finish the murals on time for the dedication ceremony before my departure back to the States. After five weeks of working, with the increasing intensity of work, I felt the energy in the church community building up. The singing practices became more frequent, the choral voices more attentive and focused. The hauntingly pure, gentle and high-scaled voices of children permeated every corner of the church complex. They too were rehearsing for the dedication ceremony. That was a happy and deeply fulfilling time.

## Sculptures in the church courtyard

Elimo Njau, Director of Paa Ya Paa Art Center and my host, introduced me to a fine Kenyan sculptor, Lawi Moshi, who carved powerful animal figures and statues of complicated intertwining humans. I asked Lawi to carve some figures for me on the tree branches we found lying around in Paa Ya Paa's forest-like garden. Coming from the tall, straight and majestic eucalyptus trees growing plentifully in Elimo's garden, they were ideal for carving with their smooth, soapstone-like texture. Our collaboration resulted in seven angelic figures, including a winged being, two mother-and-child figures and other protective beings, vigilant and silently watching. Then Lawi carved the statue of a child on his own, with a raised hand, so then we had eight figures.

We looked for a home for the eight wooden figurines, and found it at the end of the church courtyard, a ten-foot-high abandoned concrete block with metal spikes protruding from its top platform. A rough, fragile wooden fence separated the concrete block from the vast dump below. To the right stood the latrines, and to the left lay an oven-like structure with a flat concrete slab protruding from the wall for burning trash. I felt that this lowly place would be the right home for our angels, who needed to reside in a place where people dreaded to go. This situation reminded me of the virtue of water expounded in *Tao Te Ching*:

> *The supreme good is like water.*
> *Which nourishes all things without trying to.*
> *It is content with the low places that people disdain.*
> *Thus it is like the Tao.*

> *Tao Te Ching*, written by Lao-Tze, 6th century BC, translated by Stephen Mitchell, 1988, p.8

The figures stood guard in silent vigil, overlooking the community and the huge body of stagnant water beyond the fence. When people burned trash on the concrete slab, the smoke of the garbage became an offering, like incense for the angels. Thus, through creative actions and good will, we were able to transform the barren and bleak courtyard into a place of beauty, joy and hope. We named this process "urban alchemy."

## Into the dump

Some of the children in my art workshop also worked at the dump. In 2005, our team decided to go into the dump to better understand their environment. With heavy boots on, I gingerly took steps so not to step on "undesirable materials." Many people working in the dump were addicted to alcohol and drugs. This helped to dull people's senses and made it possible for them to work in such impossible situations. Korogocho was an eerie landscape of industrial and organic waste—hill-sized piles of bones buzzing with flies, hospital toxic materials, plastic scraps that screeched under our feet as we walked over the springing artificial ground.

I turned my head and found little Paul by my side. He had no shoes on. I was greatly alarmed by the danger of him walking barefoot on this poisoned ground. I said to Otieno, the man who accompanied me to the dump, "We must get shoes for little Paul." He did not respond. I turned around and found 20 other children. None of them had any shoes. It was a shocking reality. In this nightmarish landscape, some 3000 people slept in the garbage land, having no place to go to at the end of the day. This way, they started working early before other people descended into the Mukuru land.

One morning, we were in a section of the dump covered with plastic bags, paper bags, debris and broken bottles. We saw a group of boys, nine or ten years old, with no shoes but every one had a bag strapped over his shoulder. Facing each other in a circle, they were examining their finds of the morning. One little boy did well. He retrieved a handful of metal spoons from the ground. Discussing how much the spoons were worth, they were joking and pushing each other in affection and humor. Then I noticed the unusual hairstyle on one of the boys. It was cropped tightly over his whole head except the front center portion where a circular patch of hair was rather long and pressed forward. Looking around, I discovered that they all had the same hairstyle. Some of them were grooming the frontal patches of hair with plastic forks; some were grooming each other. I was stunned. Even a place like this could not deter people's desire for beauty. What a revelation! The boys pushed, hugged, ran around and laughed. Despite the daily struggle to survive, in a place where over 60 percent of the residents are HIV positive, they celebrated life. No one could take this precious gift away from them, the gift of their joy.

## The realities of life

Many children here sniff glue due to boredom, hopelessness, peer pressure and its affordability. Korogocho community has not escaped this cruel reality either. Strolling through the streets, one would often run into people sitting idly or lying about on the ground or at street corners, drinking or dazed by drugs, which included bhang, chewing miraa, drinking changaa, sniffing glue or taking psychotropic drugs.

One day, while we were on the road near the dump, we saw a lot of commotion and excitement. People were running in a certain direction. Our guards told us that an airplane was coming to drop off garbage, which contained unconsumed food.

Nairobi is a dangerous city and Korogocho much more so. With the expensive video equipment, we needed protection. We hired some guards who were friendly and helpful but towards the end of our trip, we got wind that our guards were planning to hijack our rented equipment. Fortunately, we took steps to avoid the disaster. Poverty and desperation can easily drive one astray.

Our guards showed us where to cross a narrow bridge shabbily put together with wooden and metal pieces. Underfoot flowed the Nairobi River, brown and foamy with pungent-smelling deposits and refuse. Someone found some packaged food. He crossed the bridge and walked down to the riverbank. Stooping down, he washed his hands and the small package in the river, oblivious to the filth and smell in the water. Then he opened up the package and ate the stuff inside.

## The dedication ceremony

As the project progressed, the joy and hope in the community increased. Their delight was contagious and palpable. Five weeks of intensive work brought the project to its completion. When we installed the eight carved wooden angels, the beauty of the figures, in addition to the several large and colorful murals, visibly moved the community. I was wondering how to say goodbye to a community that had helped me to understand the deeper meaning of life. How to tell the world of the suffering of people here, and their tremendous strength, joy and creativity?

As we were preparing for the dedication of the art works, Father Alex and Paa Ya Paa invited prominent guests from outside the community to join us. The guest list included local politicians, community leaders and people in diplomatic circles, such as representatives from German, Italian, Swiss and American embassies. Words spread and people were curious about the works we had accomplished, an international artist working with the dumpsite community.

The morning of the celebration, we heard that the American ambassador, Aurelia Brazeal, had decided to join us. People were beside themselves with happiness. By 10 o'clock in the morning, the church compound was completely filled with over a thousand people. Dressed in his elaborate beaded robe decorated in deep blue and red colors, Father Alex led the procession that moved through the whole courtyard, blessing each and every one of the newly created art works. To commemorate the occasion, several community groups performed songs and dances. Artists from the community presented their works to the public. On this day, we celebrated our talent, energy, collaboration and success. No one had imagined that Korogocho could be a place of such beauty and exuberance. It was a day of tremendous blessings and possibilities. During the ceremony, Father John, a Comboni priest from Italy, remarked, "If you want to see a miracle, today is a miracle."

At the closing of the ceremony, Father Alex thanked everyone for being there. The children sang the song they had rehearsed for the occasion. "Welcome, welcome, our dear friends from faraway lands. We welcome your visit with smiles and open arms. But, please do not forget us when you leave. Please come back to visit us again." One scene in the children's performance has stayed with me to this day. Ashen-faced with white powder, amid children in ragged clothing, a thin, lanky boy threw open his arms towards the sky asking forcibly, "God, why do you make us so poor? Why are we suffering so much?" It was a howling from the depth of his being about his condition and that of all the children and people living in Korogocho.

That day, I again realized the power of art and the impact of people working together. Pushing open the heavy hell-gate of Korogocho, our innovative action brought in sunlight and fresh air through the presence of the people from the outside world, who would have never set foot in this deprived and traumatized community. Witnessing the creativity and resilience of the people, some of our guests were deeply moved to take action to help. To me personally, what the Korogocho community has taught me about humanity and courage has been so profound that I returned repeatedly to do summer workshops over the following decade.

Every Wednesday evening, Monica and her colleague Claudine would visit the street children in a small rented room on a very narrow lane. They felt that although the youth in their programs looked tough and defiant, they were quite tender inside. When we met with them in the evenings, these youth behaved rather differently from their daytime demeanor. They sounded softer. Many still quite young, they welcomed the attention from adults.

Monica introduced me to Mama Katherine, her assistant in working with the youth group. On the way to her house, we passed her tiny store, where she sold household goods from a window-sized storefront. Such small businesses are everywhere in Korogocho, selling bananas, fruit, yields from people's gardens, corns freshly roasted on tiny stoves by the roadside, clothes, fried fish, cooked food, shoes, kitchen wares, utensils. Much of the hardware was found in the dump.

The further we walked, the narrower the street became until it was just an unpaved alleyway sloping slightly downward forming a continuous shallow ditch where water drained. Tiny mud houses stood on both sides. Astride the ditch stood three or four tiny square shacks roughly covered with metal and wooden planks for roofs and walls. These were the toilets for the residents. When people washed clothes or vegetables here, the discarded water also washed away human waste.

Mama Katherine's home was spotless and tastefully decorated. The interior of the house was covered with smooth, polished wallpaper, including the floor. There was no debris or dust on the floor on which her baby grandchild crawled freely. What imagination, strength and dignity within the heavily polluted environment.

Mama Katherine led us all towards the end of the narrow alleyway. A little mud hut on the right was our meeting place. The room was filled with tightly placed, slim, wooden benches facing a wooden table. A blackboard hung on a sidewall. Mama Katherine, Monica and I took our seats on the bench behind the table. Approximately a dozen children and teens followed us inside and many faces looked in through the window. More people squeezed in. Eventually, there were about 30 people in the room and we could hear people's breathing. Soon the night came and the room became pitch black. Someone brought in a kerosene light. We placed it on the table in front of us and the yellow light lit up the people sitting in the front.

Drug addiction cannot be cured by a single act. It requires a highly organized program with dedicated staff to help youth with addiction problems. Monica talked briefly to the group, and James, a 19-year-old young man, responded first. He was very thin and his voice was very soft. He talked about the difficulties of fighting against addiction. He expressed that he would like to be free of drugs. He had tried several times but failed. A little boy, nine years old, shared his story. Both parents were on drugs, and he had been thrown out of the house. No relative would take him in. He had to fend for himself and he started to hang out with the glue-sniffing youth. Different people talked about how they had asked for help from the local government. They had visited local council offices, and had tried to find jobs. But no one would listen, or cared whether they lived or died. To me, the situation sounded desperate and hopeless.

Monica then introduced me. I figured that if I could provide an opportunity for the youth to do things that would benefit the community, it would be a win-win situation. How about starting by children cleaning the street once a week? Mama Katherine said she would organize the children and teens to clean up the commercial area in the main streets where selling, buying and polluting took place. In return, the children would receive a good meal in a local restaurant— meat, potatoes, ugali, vegetables and soft drinks. They would also get clean shirts, shorts and shoes. This offer was quite exciting to them. They agreed that we should start the following Friday.

It was getting quite late when we finished the meeting. The streets were quiet. Mama Katherine, Monica, Nyash and I strolled through the empty streets enjoying the cool evening breeze. Nyash was a very thin man, about 5 feet tall, with a crop of matted hair. He liked to wear a pair of oval shaped, gold-rimmed glasses, which he found in the dump. Although his pair of glasses had only a frame with no glass, he wore them fondly. Wearing them made him feel wiser and more learned. He was among the first group of young men with whom I worked during my first visit to Korogocho in 1993, and he has helped every time I have returned. Seeing him is like seeing an old friend.

Suddenly we heard footsteps running towards us from the back. Maybe some boys playing ball, I thought to myself. Before I could turn around, someone held my collar and tried to pull my jacket off. Trying to protect me, Monica kept on saying, "Attack me. Leave her alone." I felt a hand in my pocket trying to take my camera. I told the teen who was robbing me, "Don't tear my jacket off. I will give you everything." He said, "Are you afraid of us? Don't be afraid of us. We have to do this to live. Very sorry." I said, "No problem. I understand." I gave him my two cameras, money, pens and a flashlight. His voice was soft and kind, a beginner robber, not yet hardened by his acts of violating people. It is too bad we met under those circumstances. I would have loved to work with him in one of my workshops.

## Weaving incessantly

One of the groups Father Alex helped to organize in Korogocho is Bega Kwa Bega, which contained elderly women who worked together to weave baskets of different sizes and designs. They dyed the materials and boiled them to fasten the colors. They wove constantly as this was their livelihood, putting food on the table and putting their children through school. They received lots of orders for their baskets from Italy and Japan. I sponsored a photo-taking portrait workshop for the Korogocho community at the beautiful Paa Ya Paa, since few people have photos of themselves or their children in Korogocho. I hoped that people would relax, enjoy the fresh air and lush trees and have their photos taken in some scenic spots. The Bega Kwa Bega women's hands never stopped weaving while fully enjoying themselves in the beautiful surroundings of Oaa Ya Oaam.

Leah, one of the teachers in the youth program, also conducted a class for girls on social behavior and health. Her dedication and concern for their well-being earned her trust from the girls. They shared their stories with her. Some girls told her that boys would force them to have sex behind the toilet space at the back of the school. Some of the boys would offer them packaged food they had found in the dump as bait. But several days later, after the girls had eaten the food, the boys would ask to have the food back. When the girls could not return the food, the boys would ask them to repay them by having sex with them again. One young girl told of the betrayal by her mother, who would send her to get grain from a certain man down the street. When she went, she realized that he was to have sex with her before she could bring the grain home. After listening to these young girls exchanging stories, Leah guided them to think of methods to protect themselves and ways to escape from dangerous situations. This kind of preventative thinking and strategy is essential to many girls' survival in a community where over 60 percent of peoople are HIV/AIDS positive.

## Map of life

Although the survival of girls here is particularly tenuous, the whole community is under siege with the onslaught of drug and sex-related diseases. The most threatening is the HIV/AIDS epidemic and its devastating aftermath. During my visit in 2004, I was invited to work with George, a community leader, educator and director of a dance troupe, on HIV/AIDS prevention for children and youth. While working with the children in the Boma Rescue Center, I would also spend time working with teachers and students in Korogocho, teaching AIDS prevention through the arts. I asked George what he had in mind about prevention methods. He suggested "abstinence." I thought to myself, "How does one present abstinence in visual images?"

After thinking about this for a couple of days, George suggested something else—creating a map of life. All neighborhoods in Korogocho are full of hidden dangers and pitfalls, such as thieving and robbery on the street, brewing alcohol, selling drugs and hosting prostitution. The map of life would alert youth to stay away from perilous areas and behaviors, so they could continue to travel on the road of hope to a healthy future.

We usually had around 50 people in our workshops. I organized them—teens and young adults—into five groups and each explored and charted a map of life for a different neighborhood. In my mind, the various neighborhoods looked pretty much the same, bleak and dilapidated. But the maps that emerged from the workshop were not places of monotony and destitution. Instead, they demonstrated places of great problems but also of energy, activities and hope.

Some of the drawings indicated the kind of needles used in shooting drugs, while some showed people pulling guns on each other. One of the drawings showed a thief lying on the floor with a tire around his neck in flames. I had read in my guide book about thief-burning with gasoline-filled tires. People are desperately poor in Korogocho and when they catch a thief, they take justice into their own hands. So here it was, in one of the drawings. If one can avoid the pitfalls in dangerous places on the map, one has the chance to reach the prosperous downtown with its multi-story buildings, lovely homes and jobs—a symbol of navigating success.

After the groups had completed their large drawings, I asked them what they would aspire to become. Words like doctor, nurse, teacher, policeman, footballer, beautician and politician emerged. I asked them to write the words on the upper portion of the large drawings. This gave the young people a moment to focus on their future, rather than being constantly bombarded by the needs of the present. One boy said his mind was blank. He had no idea what he wanted to be when he grew up. He had never thought about it. I said, "Now maybe you can think about it." To energize the children, Nyash began singing, "Chura, chura, draw and draw. Chura, chura, draw and draw." He was so happy with his invention that he started dancing, twisting around and clapping. Echoing his rhythm, George joined in, smiling and laughing. Their joy filled the space and was felt by everyone in the room.

When this group finished their work, I refined the images a bit, sharpening the edges in some areas, and pulling some fragments together. When they saw the result, they felt proud of what they had created together. George was beside himself with happiness. He said, "Now we know how to create banners. I have always wanted banners that show images of ourselves rather than those created by Mzungus from the outside. Now we know how to do it."

To celebrate our accomplishments, George and Monica worked with youth group leaders and community representatives to organize a parade through the Korogocho streets and a teach-in at St. John's Catholic Church. Featuring the newly created paintings and banners with their written messages, the parade functioned as an "alert tool" to let people know the danger of HIV/AIDS and the importance of abstinence and restraint. It also effectively announced the location of the HIV/AIDS prevention teach-in. Although it was an impromptu event, it was impressive in its scale and energy. People were singing, clapping, laughing and drumming. Hundreds of people, mostly children, followed the parade, running, pushing and having fun. It was a motley crowd, surging forward and kicking up dust and excitement. The parade stopped at St. John's Catholic Church where the teaching took place. How wonderful that a preventative action against HIV/AIDS could be so imaginative and fun!

## Devotion

Korogocho is a place of deep religious devotion. I took a stroll on a Sunday morning around the rim of the dumpsite. It was a place filled with energy and life. I saw people bowing down in front of a white cross, praying with great passion. I saw more people kneeling with crosses in hand in a different courtyard, praying. A chorus of harmony and joy rang out from a church building, sounds of preaching coming out from cinderblock rooms and tiny shack-like structures with corrugated metal roofing. And then there were the Pentecostal Church members, dressed in white robes with sky blue sashes around their waists or draped down from their shoulders, marching. Energized by the deep and sonorous beats from the drum at the head of the procession, people sang, clapped and prayed with great focus and conviction. Sometimes some people in the procession had to run a bit to catch up with the brisk movement of the group. Then there were preachers whose loud sermons attracted big crowds in open-air roadside churches. Worship went on everywhere, accompanied by noisy traffic and pedestrians selling and buying recycled materials from the dump.

The Sunday service in St. John's Catholic Church lasted for hours. Children, adults and elders, often dressed in their Sunday best, made up the colorful crowd. Even though I did not understand Swahili, I felt strengthened by the solidarity of the people, the warmth of their welcome and the moving, heavenly sound of the chorus. Gill Horsefield, a medical missionary sister, said:

> To pray seems to me to be a matter of survival. There are so many situations one cannot bear on one's own; there are so many situations one can do nothing about except pray. The people so often ask you to pray, and rely so much on your prayers; it becomes an imperative. (Horsefield, 2002)

## The Talking Walls

Imagine my surprise when in September 2014, 21 years after my first project in Korogocho, I received this message from Daniel Onyango via Facebook:

> A very good morning and much greetings my Name is Daniel a community young leader from Korogocho I remember meeting you some years back when. I was very young and was inspired by your art mural in St. Johns which inspired me and some of my friends to start an art project Talking walls in Korogocho where we do arts installation on walls with color and positive message. We have so far done 1.5km wall in the street of Korogocho and we want to continue more to bring life and color to korogocho but most to inspire art development in the slum. Please visit our pages Talkingwalls to see some of activities and also Kochfest page for updates on what has been happening.

This illustrates how awakening creativity in people is a powerful way to keep the spirit of a project alive.

## The Rwanda Healing Project

In 2004, I was at an international conference where I heard my guide, Jean Bosco Musana, describe the suffering of Rwandan people. It touched me so much. Because my heart was moved, I responded. I told Jean Bosco to wait for me at the airport, as I was coming.

So, Jean Bosco took me to the genocide villages. When I first went there, my heart sank. It was a very grave and sullen place, with no smiles and no colors. There was no beauty. A hundred families had two faucets, and sometimes the faucets were broken. The people walked two or three miles for a drink of water from a polluted river. There were mass graves.

A terrible genocide had occurred here. Such a thing can happen anywhere, if we do not look inward and take care to balance the light with the darkness. We need to make friends with the darkness inside us, and we need to embrace that, integrate it and be gentle. Then we can fall into the light. But if we cut off the darkness and exclude it, it turns poisonous and becomes deadly. That is what I became so aware of: my own imperfection and my own darkness when I was in Rwanda. We are all human. We are all fallible. That's what genocide teaches us. If we don't check that, it creates a climate that allows tyrants to speak everyone's unconscious desires. I can only check my own shortcomings. When I learn to forgive myself more, then I'm able to forgive other people. When we're aware of our own darkness, we are more able to forgive the other and understand the other. That's the beginning of peace.

I was constantly scared at the beginning of this project. I asked myself, "Why did I put myself here?" I do this to myself. These broken places, they imply risks and there is real physical danger that I encounter, but nothing compares to the depth of what I feel—the profound sense of fulfillment in my life by doing this work. Once you experience this, then you always want to go to that depth, and maybe even deeper. I am willing to take the risk for this depth of connection, impact and meaning in my own life. I feel that if I do this, then I can die well.

When I came to Rwanda, I didn't have much money. I had $5000. They asked, can you bury our dead properly by burying their bones underground? I was so frightened because this meant technology, ventilation and aeration. Otherwise, bones get soft, and this was to be a national place of mourning for Rwanda. We started by digging into the grave, and everything I feared happened. The cement was porous and absorbed water and then the bones started to soften. I became frantic and then, lo and behold, I found China Bridge and Road Construction Company, which happened to be working in the Gisenyi area near us. How lucky could I be? They said, "Go and raise your money. We're going to help you build it."

Before the art project, the people there did not know each other. They mourned in their own silence and solitude. They were not a community. But the art project brought everybody together. Together, we made the Rugerero Genocide Memorial Monument. I said, "Let's put our minds together. Together we will create our future. Yes, let's make art, then will come beauty and then joy." So I taught the village how to make mosaics. I suggested we use broken tiles because we are all broken in one way or another, especially in Rwanda. We made a mosaic to seal the surface.

In dedication, they gathered all the bones. They put them in caskets and brought them into the bone chamber. Everywhere you saw the color purple, which is the color of mourning. The monument was completed in 2007. We had a wonderful celebration, to give the monument to the people, and to the government for safe-keeping.

Looking back, this grave actually looked like the Mother Goddess from Neolithic times. Each year they now commemorate the 1994 genocide. Thousands of people come out and they open up the bone chamber. They walk in. They open up the caskets. They look at the bones. Fifteen years later, when I returned, the grief was so deep that many people collapsed. It was too much to bear. This is when we must look at the difficult, the destruction, the death, the human greed and the violence: look at the genocide. We must embrace the dark and the difficult and the fear and the ignorance. It's an eternal conflict between the complementary duality that is the essence of life.

How do you work when there is no common language or history? I engaged volunteers, and we got children to paint with bright colors. You show the children the beauty. Inspire them. I put the best of their work on the wall. In this way, art is not imposed, but rooted in the community with honor and respect. Before, this was just a place where they temporarily stayed. Now it has character. They identify this painted village as their home.

The community continued to paint their dreams—images of computers, cars, motorcycles and goats—and sometimes dreams come true. Every family now has a goat. My friends in Philadelphia asked at Christmas time, "What can we give?" They gave goats, and now those goats have given birth to little goats and created resources. This is how culture creates assets. In the beginning, the survivors' village had nothing. Now the people have milk.

Rwanda has resources. There are two rainy seasons, so Barefoot Artists was able to get funding and then help them to also get a rain harvest tank. Every family now has access to running water and then, with added solution, they have safe water.

Then, universities came to us and asked how they could help. Making art in destitute places is like making fire in the dead-cold night of winter. It gives out warmth, gives out light, gives direction and rekindles hope. The University of Florida and Jefferson University

Hospital sent about 70 young people to work and learn from the community. And then Engineers Without Borders came to build wonderful sanitation facilities. Every family now has clean sanitation. Volunteer Alan Jacobson was inspired to create a sunflower-seed oil production business. People are taking out loans to start little businesses, and now they have jobs.

The women of 45 years and older said they needed help. They wanted to learn traditional basket weaving, and how to harvest yucca, beat it, scrape it and wash it in soap. When you build a project, creativity is never linear. You need to respond to whatever people need, to make it sustainable. But as some of them could not even see, how could they weave? We invited the eye doctor to come, and now everybody has nice glasses and they can see. When they weave together, they bond in sisterhood. They support each other and have hope for the future.

A group of young orphans, whose parents were killed when they were between seven and ten years old, were destitute with no way to make a living. They decided they wanted to learn to sew, and now they sew beautiful things. Barefoot Artists was able to help them start a business. Each one now has a sewing machine so they can make a living, and provide for their family. Most recently, we managed to sponsor an engineer. He came and taught solar energy and production. By the third training session, he had produced 37 solar engineers. Often the homes have no tables, chairs, mats or beds, but now they have solar energy and so they can start something. There is solar energy for the sewing group, so they can sew day and night to make money to send their children to school. In the community parade this year, they marched with the solar panels, not imported from America, not imported from Europe, but produced and made right in the survivors' village in Rwanda.

As artists, we always celebrate. We celebrate life, beauty and our talent, and we celebrate who we are.

## Conclusions

After many years of working at a grassroots level with communities around the world, who are uplifting themselves through art, I have developed some core beliefs (Moskin and Jackson, 2004):

- To build hope and a sense of future, you must first have self-esteem.

- Doing justice is to honor, respect and cherish self and others.

- Forsaken individuals and forlorn situations contain boundless possibilities.

- Through hard work, creative imagination and a nurturing environment, people have the power to realize their dreams.

- Deficits can be turned into resources, and despair into hope and renewal, through an alchemy-like process of actions and transformations.

- Conflicting forces can be harnessed into a powerful, cohesive energy that serves to build rather than destroy.

- Every action should have multiple benefits.

- You can realize your dreams, if you live the life you believe in.

- Everyone has the capacity for creativity, joy and compassion—an internal flame that can be rekindled through the creative process.

- In serving and in order to serve others, you must find authentic meaning in your own life.

- Art that comes from the heart does all the above, as it heals and transforms.

I have learned these things from my own experience. And I would offer the following advice to anyone else considering a similar journey to my own:

- Learn all the skills you can, and work hard. They will prepare you for your journey.

- Follow your passion, for there burns the fire of life.

- Be mindful of your inner voice, for that is the light that will guide you to your own path.

- Cherish your weakness, for there lies your strength.

- Embrace your fear, for that is where magic happens.

- Broken and neglected places are our new frontiers. They provide open and free space for imagination and innovative action.

- When we step into our own life, it unfolds like the stories told in fairy tales.

- Have the courage and authenticity to continue your journey all the way.

- This journey is about discovering and fulfilling the purpose of your life.

- I create murals and sculptures to shape space where genuine meeting can take place. When that happens, one often experiences love.

Because I have seen abandoned trash-strewn lots transform into parks and gardens. Because I have seen spirits that were once crushed by drugs and abuse inflate with hope. Because I have seen the uprooted and displaced glow with confidence and strength. Because I have seen the forgotten and despised rise to reclaim their heritage. Because I have seen the light of hope and possibilities pour into the hellhole of garbage dump communities. Because I have seen joy and aspirations return to the broken and the despairing. Because I have experienced all these things, I know that it is possible. It is possible to turn brokenness and pain into beauty and joy. It is possible to transform the violent energy of our time into a culture of kindness. All things are possible through the openness of our mind, the gentleness of our spirit and the determination to take action.

## Chapter 6

# STORIES FROM SOUTH AFRICA,

## with Survivors of Poverty, Patriarchy and the HIV/AIDS Pandemic

*Dr. Carol Hofmeyr and the Keiskamma Trust Art Project*

The village community of Hamburg in the Eastern Cape of South Africa, and indeed many other such rural communities in South Africa, have suffered long-standing loss, poverty, degradation and breakdown of its social structures. The history of colonization and apartheid in South Africa made an ideal breeding ground for the spread of HIV (the Human Immunodeficiency Virus). In addition, the disease was harder to manage because of this history and social setting. It is against this background that the spread of HIV in these communities must be viewed. It was against this background of trauma that we made art.

I work in the art project of the Keiskamma Trust, a non-profit organization founded in 2001 in the village of Hamburg. My story and the story of the art project and the works we have made together are told in this chapter.

In 2000, my husband and I moved from Johannesburg, where we were born and educated and had worked, to the Eastern Cape, one of the poorest of South Africa's 11 provinces. For two centuries, this area was the frontier between the Xhosa and the Dutch, and later, the British. The colonists' first encounter with the Xhosa, who are part of the larger Nguni people (which includes the Swazi and the Zulu), took place here.

In this area, people's lives center around their cattle. Cattle represent wealth and are used in ceremonies such as appeasing or thanking ancestors, or to buy brides.

Before the Xhosa met the European colonists, they lived in communities with chiefs and moved seasonally from their permanent homes near the forests and mountains to the coastal plains to find grazing for their cattle. Once the European traders arrived, conflict over land and cattle began and led to the hundred years of frontier wars of dispossession. In 1856, after constant battles and skirmishes with the European settlers, a young woman called Nongqawuse had a vision. She saw her ancestors in a pond, and they told her that her people must kill all their precious cattle, plant no crops and wait for a rescue from ancestral kings who would emerge from the sea. This was a desperate last attempt to salvage a nation on the edge of defeat. But no one came out of the sea, and the defeat of the Xhosa people was complete. Thousands of Xhosa people died and remnants of a once proud, strong nation limped into towns and begged for food and work from the European settlers.

The village of Hamburg, at the mouth of the beautiful Keiskamma River, was founded in 1856, the same year as the terrible event that came to be termed the "Cattle Killing." It was initially a settlement of German mercenaries in the employ of the British army who were offered land in the colony when the Crimean War ended. They did not realize they were to be settled on inhospitable land across the river from the Xhosa people to act as a buffer for the British settler farmers further west.

After the final defeat of the Xhosa people, the Eastern Cape became a British colony, then part of the Union of South Africa and then part of the Republic of South Africa, under an Afrikaans apartheid government. During this time, parts of the Eastern Cape became so-called independent "countries," or puppet states of apartheid South Africa, with undemocratically elected presidents. This was apartheid's "grand plan" to keep the best areas for those South Africans of European descent. By this time, the German settlers had left for nearby towns, leaving their farm workers on the smallholdings. The village of Hamburg therefore was mainly a holiday and fishing destination. Although holiday makers in those years were exclusively white, they provided income for the sparse black population who struggled to farm on poor soil and in the face of the strong winds and frequent dry spells.

The creation of the independent "homeland" of Ciskei between the 1950s and 1980s ended the visits of holiday makers to the seaside village of Hamburg, which had become a thriving holiday resort. White people felt afraid to be in "black" areas. Trust of each other was purposefully and systematically broken down. Separation intensified the distrust and fear.

These homeland areas, too heavily populated for subsistence farming, were partially bolstered by border industries set up to make the areas appear economically independent. Migrant labor, already part of the social fabric of South African life, increased, and people often traveled 1000 kms to work in the mines, only returning to their homelands once a year. This whole system resulted in poverty, breakdown of family units, loss of connection to land and loss of a sense of identity. This was the ideal ground for the growth of the HIV virus, and Hamburg was sadly no different.

In 1994, all these puppet states fell away. South Africa was again one country. Nelson Mandela, a Xhosa chief, indeed rose out of the sea—from imprisonment on a tiny island off the coast—to save his people. South Africa was an example of hope and peaceful change for the world. But by 2000 this was not so obvious in Hamburg on the edge of the Keiskamma River. Rural villages struggled to find work for all the people who had been resettled there during apartheid times. They were cut off from the mainstream of South African life by bad roads and lack of infrastructure. Only the most determined, or those few with parents who were employed in cities, managed to get tertiary qualifications and employment in nearby towns.

When I arrived in Hamburg in 2000, health and education services were in disarray, as three separate countries had to be integrated into one province, the Eastern Cape. Identity was again an issue because borders had changed once more. Hamburg had not benefited from the effects of political change. Indeed, in spite of the exceptional natural beauty, it seemed to me the people living there had little reason to hope.

My personal journey in all this was one similar to many white South Africans of British descent. My forebears, three and sometimes four generations back, had come to the colony looking for opportunity and a new life. They were often the poor and dispossessed in their own countries. I grew up in an advantaged situation but was unaware of this privilege except for small, occasional insights into the lives of some of my fellow South Africans. Virtually my only contact with black South Africans was as domestic workers and gardeners. I had no opportunity to meet any other black people in normal social circumstances until I went to university. During my childhood and early adulthood, I had no idea of the huge injustice and inequality that were the norm. Separation and inequality were bolstered by fear of the "other," which was conveyed in subtle and not-so-subtle propaganda. I remained ignorant of the extent of the harm done by colonialism and apartheid until relatively late in my life.

After our first democratic election in 1994, the Truth and Reconciliation Commission heard stories of gross injustice, forced removals and torture. As I read these narratives of the hearings of the commission, I knew that somehow deep down, I had known this was happening at the time but had chosen to believe the propaganda and denials of the apartheid government. My dilemma in the 1990s was whether any white South African had the right to be in the country.

My own art work at this time sought to find an answer. Throughout the 1990s I traveled extensively and made art work about the first Europeans to arrive in southern Africa, and those who followed them. For example, the early Portuguese explorers had planted crosses along the coastline, claiming southern Africa for their God and their king. To the Portuguese, these crosses were a symbol of their power and the power of their Christian king, which sadly and ironically became the herald of suffering for the peoples of this land, and lasted over five centuries. In making this the topic of my art work and by looking deeply at the advent of Europeans in Africa, I resolved that I had nowhere else to go, that I belonged, and needed to be part of what South Africa was becoming.

My belief in the Christian meaning of death and resurrection underpinned my work then and now. The crosses planted so proudly in the 15th century seemed to herald real suffering and crucifixion for the land and its people. But my faith made me believe that resurrection must follow. By 2000, when we moved to the Eastern Cape, I had decided I had a duty to stay on and make things better and rebuild some of the trust and hope that apartheid and colonisation had destroyed. My conviction was that by demonstrating total trust, and by working together with the local population, I could rebuild something I felt I had been complicit in destroying.

At that time, I read a searing novel by J.M. Coetzee, called *Disgrace* (1999) about relationships between black and white South Africans set in the Eastern Cape after 1994. In the novel, set on a flower farm in an area close to Hamburg, a father is disgraced by a scandal in Cape Town and visits his daughter on her farm. While he is visiting, his daughter is raped by a relative of her trusted black farm manager, on whom she is totally dependent to run the farm. The manager protects his relative and while the father finds this unbearable and unjust, the daughter decides to carry on and give birth to the child resulting from the rape. J.M. Coetzee chose to leave South Africa, but, like the protagonist's daughter, I chose to stay, and was prepared to accept what it meant to be unfairly advantaged and carry the responsibility that brings for past wrongs. In the 16 years since then, I have had times when I have found it hard to accept this, but I am always brought back to what it means to be here, and the responsibility I feel.

So when we moved to the Eastern Cape in 2000, my husband and I bought what we thought would be a weekend cottage in the village of Hamburg. Because of being part of a "fake country" or homeland, Ciskei remained relatively unspoilt. The Keiskamma River widens into a fertile and beautiful estuary and sandy beaches stretch for kilometers in both directions. Like all South African towns and villages during the apartheid years, there was a white area, with substantial houses, mostly holiday homes, and an area for black people to live, and also a place where new arrivals or growing families set up shacks for themselves, just to have a home.

Before over-population and over-grazing of the land, the Xhosa people built their homes from mud, bricks and thatch. Today, most homes are brick with corrugated iron roofs. In addition, many people live in shacks they erect themselves out of wood and corrugated iron. If they are lucky, these houses have an outside tap, and since 1994 may have electricity. Every established homestead has a wooden cattle "kraal"—an enclosure where the cows are kept at night and family ceremonies take place. Apart from traditional beliefs, nearly all the Xhosa people living in Hamburg are church-goers of many denominations.

The gravel road to Hamburg curves along the river and the first houses on the hill beside the river are shacks that appear insubstantial. However, they are colorful and full of life, with children playing and old people chatting. Further down the road, the original German settlement begins and then overlooking the sea are the much more substantial holiday houses of mostly white people. One good outcome of Hamburg having been in a "homeland" is that black and white areas became much more intermingled than in most other small towns in South Africa.

The village center on first sight seems quaint and lovely. There is a liquor store, a small general dealer and not much else except the inevitable bars or "shebeens." The center of the village also houses the art, music, health and education programs of the Keiskamma Trust. The superficial picturesqueness of the village belies the suffering endured there. What my husband and I found when we started to look around the small village of Hamburg was a community devastated by political change, poverty, illness, poor health services, poor schools and people losing hope in their ability to change this. The euphoria of the first democratic election in 1994 had worn off. Most people did not have any work at all. All lived close to hunger, with inadequate shelter.

I felt obligated to do something to help bring back trust and hope. Instinctively, or by an act of blind faith, I decided I must teach print-making as that was what I knew. I was a medical doctor who had given up medicine in 1990 to study art, and had decided never to practice medicine again. I had specialized instead in print-making. I had done this because I saw that medicine can often fix the body but cannot offer any cure for hopelessness, cynicism and despair. Before stumbling on art-making through working with clay, I had been totally cerebral in my way of living and being. I was disconnected from tactile, physical, bodily knowledge and experience. I think this was partly the cause of my own depression. Later I came to see that this wound we all carried would also be the very ground for the spread of the Acquired Immune Deficiency Syndrome (AIDS) virus.

I began to deal with my own sense of despair about suffering, my own sense of worthlessness and helplessness and depression, by making things. My idea was that I could teach others to do the same. I could show trust and faith in people and hope to restore this between us. At this time, it was the wounds of dispossession, loss of trust, poverty and loss of esteem that I saw were in need of healing. Although we knew the pandemic of AIDS was coming, it was not this that at first engaged me. In fact, I had not done any medical work for ten years. There was too much else to occupy me. I took one step at a time, all the while coming to know and gradually love the people in the village. I came to see more clearly the almost unbearable hardship of their lives, the despair of having no money to feed their children, the pain of poor medical treatment at local clinics. Yet they had humor and an ability to keep on trying to find ways just to feed and cloth their children.

I failed with the first initiatives I tried. I thought I could teach print-making and people would flock to learn. But no one knew what print-making was and even when they did, no one wanted to learn. The first people who came to lessons thought that when I said I had a big "machine" to make art, they would learn computer skills and be able to get work. They soon gave up.

Then to provide work for hands to create, and to make things to sell, and to clean up the beautiful environment that was covered in plastic bags, I brought two Basotho women from another project far away that I had read about, to teach us to crochet handbags, mats and hats, with strips cut from recycled old plastic bags. This had limited success as we could not use the many old torn bags we had collected and had to get brand new ones. I also was completely duped by some unscrupulous and creative people in the community. I offered payment for bags filled with plastic rubbish collected in the area. Some people simply went to the dump and fetched back the bags of rubbish I had off-loaded there, and I paid for them again, several times over, until I caught on to this ploy.

Then, I decided to teach embroidery and make embroidered items to sell. I had been reluctant to do this because I could not embroider myself. I asked the founders of other South African embroidery projects to come and help me, but they were too busy. They told me to get a book and learn. So I did.

While struggling to learn embroidery on a road trip with friends from the UK, one friend, Jan Chalmers, turned out to be an expert embroiderer and agreed to bring her friend, Jacky Jesewski, to teach us all. This first act of generosity and sharing of Jan and Jacky led to ten years of their committed teaching once or twice a year, and also set the stage for other skilled people to come and share their knowledge. From then on, we did not look back.

The story of the Keiskamma Art Project in Hamburg is one of countless acts of kindness by people anxious to give what they have. By 2004, we had over a hundred trained embroiderers. We decided to embroider our story, and in this way to use the story to see who we were, why we were here and ask questions about our heritage and our history. We asked, "What does it mean to be part of South Africa's frontier, a place where division and prejudice in South Africa were born?" I was descended from conquerers and they from the defeated, yet we could rebuild trust and understanding.

With the Nguni people, a man's worth is measured by his cattle, and cattle are the men's responsibility. All-important ceremonies involve cattle and often the sacrifice of a cow. Few women own their own cattle, and women of childbearing age are not allowed near the "kraal," which is a sacred space. In a subversive way, our women's project of embroidering cattle and earning money from it gave them independence from their patriarchal menfolk.

Initially, all the women had to draw their own cows and then embroider them. Many had not drawn anything since childhood and most felt very shy. But they all did draw and embroider their own cows and those images remain very precious to me, awkward and naive as they are. Later they divided themselves into designers and embroiderers. Some discovered they were skilled artists.

Then I had another idea. Cattle theft by the British, Dutch and the Xhosa underlies the frontier wars. We had so many embroiderers, we would be able to make a monumental work. With the help of historians, we began to make a tapestry modeled on the Bayeux Tapestry, which was made in the 1070s and told the story of the Norman conquest of England. It is 70 meters long. We aimed to make one just as big, by telling our own history. It was my hope to tell again the story of colonization, wars, dispossession and apartheid and show we are made, and live within, the layers of our own history, and that all people everywhere are the same. All people have experienced conflict and conquest. It is part of our history as a species to be both conquered and conquerer. In realizing this, we take our place in all human history and are connected to all people everywhere.

This work was our first national success. We stopped sewing when it was 120 meters long, much longer than the Bayeux Tapestry. It was bought by a large South African bank, and now wraps around the legislature in the South African parliament in Cape Town. I have photos of women triumphant when they saw what they had been able to achieve by working together. They saw how strong they actually were, where they belonged, that they have a community. They made and told their story and people in South Africa took notice.

We did not realize then that this art work was the first of many telling our story and thereby connecting us to the wider world and at the same time offering context, hope and income. In the photo of these women triumphant, in front of the Keiskamma Tapestry at the National Arts Festival, you can see Noseti Makhubalo. She is dressed in traditional Xhosa dress, which she made herself with apron and headdress, and she has her arms spread out above her head in triumph. To me she embodies the soul of the Keiskamma Art Project.

I first met her when I was trying to find a way to clear the litter of plastic bags in the village and make useful things from them. Noseti was the translator as she could speak Sotho and the two women teaching us could speak only Sotho. Then, later, when she heard we were starting to sew, she arrived with a sewing machine balanced on her head in the traditional African manner of carrying heavy objects. I visited her at home one evening and saw she had no food for supper for her four little girls. To feed her children, she normally poached abalone and would dive dangerously at night into the sea to illegally find the protected shellfish, risking drowning or arrest. But the evening I visited, she had nothing. It was the first time I had had to imagine what it would have been like to have no food for my own children. This changed me.

Then Noseti was pregnant for the fifth time with a second set of twins. Late one night she went into labor. Her husband called an ambulance. It did not come for several hours. This was usual at the time. The ambulance finally came and took her to the local hospital 60 kms away. Again, she waited several hours before being transferred to a bigger district hospital. The first twin, a boy, was born dead in the ambulance, the cord around his neck; the second one, a girl, survived.

I wrote a story about this to try and deal with the deeply shocking things I was experiencing, inspired by this quote from Vaclav Havel: "Hope is not the conviction that something will turn out well, but the certainty that something makes sense, regardless of how it turns out" (Havel, 1993).

## STILLBORN

Yesterday could be seen as an early Renaissance painting. The main picture shows the burial ceremony. The priest is there. There is meaning to this death. There is ceremony. There is symbolism. The second live twin is placed in the grave and then removed to be freed from the forces of sickness and death that took her brother. The children play, oblivious of the drama in the family, happy to see their cousins. They are sent to find the donkey down the road. Life must go on. More symbols, an apple tree grows near the cattle kraal. The fall and the birth and the death of Jesus are here in this painting.

Below the main image in the same glowing rich colors, the full story of the day is told in miniature pictures. The story is told in linear time. Each event has its place in the sequence. Susan and her pig are a backdrop to all the events of the day. It starts with the butchering of the pig inside her hut as people wait to buy pieces of it. She uses some of the money to buy a new piglet.

Myself, setting out, leaving Susan with her dogs, Careful and Life, promising to take her to buy the new piglet from Nora as soon as I get back. Noseti getting into the car with the exquisite second twin, mother and child dressed beautifully, on an outing. The four little sisters wave goodbye and we promise to bring chips to them when we return.

Then, synchronistically, we find "Nora-pig" hitch-hiking with her bags. She rides most of the way with us. Then signing for the body of the second twin at the hospital mortuary with Justus and Terrence, Noseti's brother, while Noseti and the old aunty wait in the car.

Then riding home and finding Nora-pig again on the side of the road with her full bags. Then the funeral ceremony at sunset. Then nightfall and me racing back to fetch Susan to get her new pig. She is furious because we are late to get the new pig, and life is more important than death.

But yesterday was not like that. Yesterday was more like a modern painting or play. For me, the scene in the mortuary overshadows all the rest. It is in black and white. The characters are absurd. There is a loss of meaning and only dark despairing irony.

Our cars pull in to the subway under the ugly cement roof between oppressive brick walls. It is dirty. Other vehicles pull in with anonymous relatives wrapped up in blankets. It is cold and a draught blows through the subway. There are empty stainless steel trolleys left randomly. We approach the office. A cheerful mortician greets me and Terrence and then Justus with a "Long time no see." I carry the coffin in the black plastic bag. Noseti holds the living twin in the front of the car and stares forward. We show the file to the mortician. Then we go into the room filled with stainless steel trolleys, one with a cover. The walls are painted a dirty cream enamel. There is no attempt at comfort or tidiness or gentleness in this finality. The mortician opens the cold-room door and comes out with a baby swaddled in bloodstained cloths with its tiny head lolling to one side, blood in its mouth. Why all the blood? It, he, must have conducted a post-mortem. The mortician still has gloves on. He holds the baby like a butcher showing a cut of meat to a customer, up in one hand. He asks if Terrence works for me, presuming a black man with a white woman is a domestic worker. I take the baby and lay it in the coffin. Terrence passes me the plastic red rose and I put it in with the baby. The mortician sings cheerfully about a red, red rose. He tells me to go and wash. I take the coffin back to the car trying to be tender, just as Noseti would be.

Noseti sits still, facing forward, but feels the bump as the little box is laid in the car. She begins to cry. I hurry to drive off and leave quickly to get home and away from all this that I cannot bear. There is no hope here.

On the way, we find Nora-pig.

If yesterday is a post-modern work of art, it is an installation or a mixed media work with all the elements present but unrelated. Each would use its own style and medium to present itself optimally and making sense of the whole would be unnecessary. Shock value, humor, play and reference would be the major content of the work. The viewer would not be expected to find cohesion, meaning or even good craftsmanship.

At art school, we were encouraged to put arbitrary absurd images into the ordinary. Once, a teacher suggested a wrapped foetus flying through the air above a relatively ordinary landscape.

So in the art work there would be Susan's dead pig. It lies decapitated, slit from neck to anus, disemboweled on the table in the middle of her hut. A Francis Bacon fragment. Two men using a saw and a gum pole cut up the carcass piece by piece. For this they receive the bowels and liver and kidneys and spleen. Around the room in the half-light, like parts of Goya's last works, sit men and women, waiting to buy their pieces. Each face is a caricature. Each face has more than its share of life's experiences etched on to it.

In another corner of the picture, Susan goes about her business. Her always comical face changes expression but she is solid, whole, continually arresting, interesting. First, she can be seen sitting in the room with the carcass and the people holding bank notes, payment for meat. She eventually made R1200 ($120).

Then she is nagging for a lift to Ntilini to buy a new piglet from Nora-pig. Finally, she is furious in the dark, striding, stomping down the road back to her house at 7pm. "Where have you been? How can you leave me? They say my madam doesn't care for me. She leaves me in the dark." My answer that I went to the burial of the stillborn child carries no weight with her. The child is dead. What could you possibly do there?

Then Nora-pig appears on the scene. This stoic little grandmother, with her bags and her sweets. She is a businesswomen. Her business is to hitch-hike up and down the road to East London buying maas (thick sour milk), vegetables, sweets. She returns to Ntilini and sells her goods there. Sometimes she has to sleep on the side of the road if she does not get a lift. But yesterday she was lucky. We picked her up in the morning on the way in, Noseti and I. She had a striped plastic bag full of umfino (edible green spinach-like plants) and an empty 50-liter container. We had the empty coffin in a black plastic bag.

On the way home, we found her on the side of the road near Igoda and we loaded the now full plastic container and sweets and guavas, which had been exchanged for the umfino, into the back of the truck with the tiny, now-occupied, coffin.

Life does not make sense, so we can just play with the balls it throws us. There was a pattern not of my making. And in the end, the feeling it has left with me is not a renaissance, optimistic worldview, life just opening up, or a modern despair, or a post-modern absurdity. It is rather a calm, following a struggle. A peace, when the worst has been looked at and left behind for now. A persistent, indestructible hope for the future.

Somewhere in that horrible cream room of the mortuary I came face to face with my own nightmares. My own persistent dreams—of buckets of cold, bloody, dead foetuses from my medical years—ended there. This little wrapped one put an end to them. He had a name. He is Sipho, child of my friend Noseti, only brother of six sisters. He has a grave next to the woodpile beside the cattle kraal and we will plant a fig tree and some flowers there. His sisters will grow up knowing about him and accepting him as part of their life. And I thank Noseti and her family for closure in one of my own nightmares.

Until the death of Noseti's baby, I had not disclosed my medical background. If I had been known as a doctor, I could have made phone calls and saved Noseti's son by getting him to the right hospital in time. After this I began to work in the clinics, although I had not worked as a doctor for ten years. Noseti has been beside me now for 16 years as an example of courage and optimism with so little to base this on. She became the artist who designed our iconic cows and continues to create art works, now mostly at home, as she can't walk easily due to severe rheumatoid arthritis.

But we were yet to learn that the success of our first monumental work, like our euphoria in 1994 with the first election, was the edge of an abyss. Nothing can be fixed quickly or easily. There are always two steps back, after three steps forward. First, distrust surfaced when the tapestry was sold. I should have expected this but did not. Many years of hurt, shame and distrust are not healed so quickly. I thought it was obvious that my motives were pure, but someone in the community suspected me and spread the story I had taken the money for the long tapestry for myself. In fact, the money from the sale was slow in reaching us due to normal bureaucratic processes, but the women were desperate and did not understand, and so marched down the village street, chanting and dancing in the angry *toyi-toyi* manner of stomping feet, and clenched fists holding imaginary weapons, typical during South African political protests. I spent days lying on my couch, not going out, feeling sorry for myself and very angry. But many of the women supported me, showing huge courage in that small community, and eventually I went out, broke the door of the project studio that had been locked by the dissenters, and started over with those who trusted and believed in me. I remain indebted to J.M. Coetzee for his book, which shows that white South Africans cannot expect to have anything easy.

Luckily, we re-opened because much worse suffering was to come to that community, but at least when it did, people had learned to trust, and we had a strong group of women to support each other. Once I began to work in the clinics in the area, I immediately gained trust, which would have been much harder had I not been a doctor. I was privileged to know and try to help people with their most intimate concerns and they needed me for this, more than anything else.

I had thought medicine was not important to true healing. But all needs are relative. In fact, when you need simple pain medication, for example, no amount of art can help. Both go hand in hand, and bodily needs scream for help long before spiritual ones can be heard. What allowed me to think that one aspect—spiritual healing—was more important than physical healing was in part due to my being privileged. I was face to face with the hierarchy of needs, which I had previously been able to disregard.

It was the monster of AIDS that lurked at the edges of our fragile success with the Keiskamma Tapestry. When the pandemic then started to sweep the country, Hamburg was badly hit. Fear was everywhere and we had no treatment. Once a person was infected, death was certain. I had worked with AIDS education projects before, through a project run by Artist Proof Studio in Johannesburg, where we had used art to teach people about HIV/AIDS. The idea was to give people a positive experience through making an art work, and expressing themselves, so that they were open and not fearful when taught about HIV. Fate would have it that I was uniquely prepared when the previously unknown virus struck. I had nursed a friend of mine who had contracted HIV through a blood transfusion and was one of the first people to die of AIDS in South Africa. This was as close as I had come to seeing the disease's unremitting course when untreated.

I went to World AIDS Day services held at the Johannesburg hospital in the 1990s and saw the grieving mothers of gay men, and the grief and fear of their partners. Although I could imagine their pain, I somehow still felt removed from it, little realizing how I was being prepared for my own intense decade of approaching work.

HIV has been called the most successfully adapted human virus to date. I have seen virologists wonder at the design and functioning of this virus. As far as we know it can only survive within a human host and it arose somewhere in Africa where a very similar virus mutated from primate hosts to use human beings as hosts. The virus itself initially does not cause any symptoms at all. Once it enters the human body, usually through sexual intercourse, it invades blood cells, specifically those that protect the body from infection, and slowly destroys them. Thus, the infected person's immunity drops and they become susceptible to many different illnesses. In Africa, particularly in South Africa, HIV and tuberculosis bacillus form an alliance where each illness increases the progression and severity of the other.

A person infected with HIV will at first seem totally healthy. This is the reason the virus is so successful. People infected are not aware of it and spread the virus long before they get ill. Pregnant women can be totally healthy and their babies can be infected, usually at birth, as they pass it through vaginal fluids. Once the virus has begun to deplete the infected person's immunity they become ill with many different diseases, and later, without treatment, the infected person develops full-blown AIDS. At this stage, the patient is very ill and will die unless treated.

In 2004, our government still denied the existence of HIV and refused to sanction the use of anti-retroviral medication. Treatment was not an option for people in Hamburg. Tragically, it was the young adults, the best and brightest in the village, those who managed to study and find work in cities, who were the first to be affected. They crept home in disgrace to die secretly behind closed doors because families were too ashamed to acknowledge their illness.

South Africa, as with all countries where HIV first showed itself, experienced severe discrimination against anyone known to be HIV positive. This further encouraged the spread of the disease as people were afraid to be tested and know their status. I am not sure why people living with AIDS are still so violently discriminated against. Perhaps it was due to homophobia as the disease was first recognized in homosexual men. But in Africa it is a disease of heterosexual adults and children. People infected are often shunned and turned out of homes through fear and prejudice.

In addition, the government in South Africa in the 1990s was tragically unwilling to face the disease and protect our newly democratic nation. This was to my mind an inexcusable omission. By the time the epidemic spread from the north across the Limpopo River, we had robust scientific information on the biology of the virus, its methods of transmission and how it might be prevented. We had a well-developed health system and instituted sound surveillance procedures. In spite of this, we watched helplessly as the prevalence in pregnant women increased each year (blood samples in pregnant women were tested anonymously, peaking at 30 percent in the Eastern Cape). All our efforts to encourage abstinence, monogamy and use of condoms seemed futile. Effective treatment eventually became available, but remained unaffordable in the public health services.

Of all the missed opportunities, the most regrettable was related to the prevention of mother-to-child transmission of HIV. By 1998, it was proven that a relatively affordable short course of anti-retroviral drugs could reduce the risk of infection at birth by 50 percent. By failing to implement this evidence, we missed the opportunity to prevent tens of thousands of avoidable infections of babies, most of whom died. Some doctors who defied the ban on prescribing drugs for the prevention of mother-to-child transmission of HIV in state services were fired. It took a constitutional court action brought by the Treatment Action Campaign to compel the health services to implement a program for prevention of mother-to-child transmission in 2002. The proportion of children infected with HIV fell dramatically, but the survivors faced inevitable orphanhood. Keeping the mothers alive was more difficult, because the cost of long-term treatment was considerable.

In 2004, as the pandemic peaked, we continued making art work, and the Keiskamma Trust decided to become involved in this national disaster. It was one of many non-governmental organizations that stepped into the breach to provide the life-saving treatment for adults and children infected with HIV. Most were critically ill at the time. Of the first 174 people initiated on treatment by the Keiskamma program between July 2004 and February 2006, 42 percent were bedridden, 89 percent had CD4 counts (a measure of white blood cells fighting infection) below 100 (37 percent below 50), 61 percent had a good response to treatment, 21 percent died and 3 percent were lost to follow-up (Hofmeyr, Georgiou and Baker, 2009).

In this same year, we made the Keiskamma Altarpiece as a memorial to those who had died, and those who survived and had taken on the care of the many orphans.

Fortunately, but tragically for all those who died and all those broken families, in 2008, the South African Department of Health instituted the largest anti-retroviral program in the world. Survivors in the Keiskamma Trust treatment program were transferred for further care to the government services. By 2017, the prevalence of HIV infection among pregnant women in the Eastern Cape had stopped rising, and in time it will fall as more and more people access treatment and become non-infective.

This is the political and medical background in which we were making art in Hamburg. Statistics don't always reveal to the reader the effect faraway decisions have on individuals trying to live quiet lives with dignity and meaning. One of my most disturbing and shocking encounters exemplifying the harm the disease causes happened in early 2004. An old lady who worked in my home, Susan Paliso, then 82, took me to see a young woman, the daughter of a friend of hers. Susan and I trusted and understood each other. She was in our house when we moved in that first day in July 2000. She was on her knees scrubbing a very stained carpet as if she had been doing it all day, but as I got to know her, I realized it was both part of her instinct for survival, and her sense of humor. She insisted to us she had to work there, that it was her house. She had the right to be there. We employed her reluctantly, but through all 17 years of my time in Hamburg she has been my guide and friend, made me laugh and shown me what resilience, courage and humor look like in the face of what I see as unendurable suffering. She still works for me and refuses to retire at 94 years of age. The story of the death of her favorite and last-born son is told in the Keiskamma Altarpiece. But this is getting ahead of the story.

When Susan took me to the home of her friend, it was the first time I had been invited into a home hiding a person dying of AIDS. She lay in the corrugated iron shack terminally ill, convulsing. I could do nothing but call an ambulance to take the dying woman to hospital. At the time, I noticed a small boy who looked about six years old, but was actually 11, peeping around the corner inside the shack. He was small and very thin, and his scalp was a mess of sores. I was to see many sick children later but he was the first child I recognized to be infected with HIV.

Susan told me the dying woman was his mother. Later that week, his mother died in hospital and her own mother, the small boy's grandmother, was admitted with a stroke and also died a few days later. The boy, Nkululeko, born in 1993 and whose name means "Freedom," lost the two people closest to him in one week. He went to live with his aunt but he grew sicker and it looked as if he would also die. It was then I decided I had to get hold of anti-retroviral treatment myself, whatever the cost. I could not let him die while somewhere there existed treatment that could save him.

By mid 2004, I could no longer deny that the village I had grown to love would be devastatingly affected by this disease. I had seen how it divided families and communities. I had seen that the worst of it was the shame it created in all associated with it and I remembered something I had heard at one of the World AIDS Day memorial services during my other life in Johannesburg. An AIDS doctor and Jewish theologian had talked about the AIDS virus spiritually. He had said, then, in the context of gay men, that the AIDS virus grows best where there are fault lines of prejudice and shame. It aims to divide even further and thus facilitate its spread. It thrives where there is blame and breakdown of relationships in families and communities. He said then that we have no treatment but we can fight it by not allowing it to reach its ultimately divisive goal.

I remembered this and thought that we had a real community in Hamburg. We had worked together on the art tapestries for four years. We could make a big art work to tell our story with HIV/AIDS, to comfort and honor those infected and affected, to offer spiritual hope to those dying, to offer comfort to those grieving, to mend the fault lines in our society. Although I said earlier that bodily needs are more basic than spiritual needs, one spiritual need seems to me to be more basic than even food. This is the need to be accepted and loved. I saw people would rather die without treatment than be shamed and rejected by their community. At least the spiritual epidemiology of the HIV virus could be broken by not allowing it to divide us.

I had personally found comfort in the 16th-century altarpiece painted by Grünewald and carved by Niclaus of Haguenau for a hospice in Isenheim that cared for people dying of St. Anthony's fire, an incurable and painful condition caused by a fungus that grows on rye bread. This altarpiece, made between 1512 and 1516, shows the crucifixion on the front panels. It opens twice, in panels, to show scenes of hope and of glory. The crucified Christ in this painting is diseased and unappealing, in fact causing revulsion in the observer, just like some onlookers feel when watching dying AIDS patients. But the message was that Christ carries all diseases to the grave and rises beyond them. This concept had comforted me personally as a doctor, always on the edge of despair, watching people in pain.

The villagers of Hamburg and the surrounding areas were nearly all church-going people of many Christian denominations. We could make work with our hands to convince ourselves that there was life beyond the awful deaths we were witnessing. So we set to work on a new art work—the Keiskamma Altarpiece. As with the historical Keiskamma Tapestry, when I started it I had no idea what it would involve—two sets of doors that open like a book to reveal further layers of tapestried story within. When it came to the mechanics of putting the opening doors together, nothing would have been displayed if it were not for my husband's skill in figuring out this kind of problem. Once again, we just jumped in blindly to make a monumental art work the same size as the original renaissance work—4.5 meters wide when open, by nearly 3 meters tall.

Again, the premise was that if we told our story, alongside another story about other suffering people, we would feel we belonged; that we were part of a larger community of people suffering; that we had relevance; and that we could also be comforted by the hope of life beyond the suffering. To achieve this, we had to feature ourselves in the work. However, this presented some problems for me. How could we show the diseased Christ figure without seeming blasphemous to more conservative Christians?

One day, I was pondering this and driving though a nearby village when I saw the dignified figure of a young Xhosa widow. Her traditional dress of blue told a story of loss of her young husband, probably away in the mines, and many children left for her to care for, until she inevitably became ill herself and left her children to the care of her mother. We used her image, standing in front of the crucifixion, with children on both sides, and her elderly mother sitting, waiting.

On either side of this crucifixion in the place of St. Anthony and St. Sebastian stand Susan Paliso, my closest friend in Hamburg and a grandmother who had by now lost her last-born child Dumile to AIDS, and Legina Mapuma, in her eighties, matriarch of a large family in Hamburg. Both had become friends of mine and my admiration of their strength increased the more I got to know them.

The Grünewald altarpiece opens to show choirs of angels heralding the annunciation and nativity and then the resurrection. Christ has laid aside all disease and Grünewald depicts what has been described as the greatest painting of the resurrection in Western art history. With our tapestry, we decided to show our village free from suffering and disease, whole and happy.

The last opening on the Grünewald piece reveals Niclaus of Haguenau's carvings of St. Anthony, St. Jerome and St. Sebastian enthroned, and the painted panels on either side show Anthony and Sebastian tempted and suffering in purgatory.

With the Keiskamma Altarpiece, we decided to depict the grand-mothers of the community and their grandchildren as the strength and hope of our society in this time of suffering. They stand as saints of our time in the place of the saints of old. We worked in the tradition of art history, using the work of Grünewald as a starting point, because he had also lived in the hospice when he made the work and had therefore had intimate experience of the suffering of the victims of an incurable disease, because, just like the great medieval epidemics, AIDS is an epidemic, killing many in its wake. In this tradition, the making of our tapestry story, and the final viewing of it by our community in the cathedral in Grahamstown, allowed the fearful and those suffering to see that they are not alone. They could now tell their own stories and people would take notice. They felt acknowledged, even if we had no treatment at the time, even if they lost loved ones, even if they died.

One of the best moments of my life was seeing the women, and a few men, of the Hamburg community, rise to sing and dance as their work was unveiled for the first time in the Grahamstown cathedral. With this art practice, I had had no plan to facilitate "art therapy," but rather to let the artists and embroiderers recover hope and awe even in the face of extreme suffering, by connection to others in the same situation, and by creating with our hands our belief in life. It is a tribute to the women of Hamburg that they were able to do this, not me.

Alongside the making of art, and always woven in and out, were the patients I was seeing as a doctor. I wrote something describing what I was experiencing at the time.

## AIDS AS I KNOW IT. 2006

I can't remember when I was first aware of it. Perhaps in the Florida Keys in the 1980s when I was afraid to try on earrings at a market. But then the virus was not in my lived world or experience.

Then Barbara, and greater fear. Fear of being contaminated. Fear watching its heartless, painful progression.

Then Hamburg and a child. A baby with new clothes, baby blanket, but wizened, marasmic loose skin on its legs and tummy. Wide black and white eyes.

Then a shack dark with fear, a small boy watching covered in sores, smelling bad, his mother "stroked," unconscious, writhing, ugly.

Then the same child, clever, self-conscious and the beginning of anti-retroviral therapy. Curled up with pneumonia for the third time. Feverish, no mother to wipe his brow. His young aunt caught up in an abusive relationship ending in yet another death, her husband. Still the child watches, waits.

Nomonde. She said she had been gang raped. Another child clinging to a beautiful model-thin mother. Not letting her out of her sight. I still see the child running out of her grandmother's home as my car passes. For two years after her mother's death I brought her gifts as I passed.

With what can we patch the holes? Holes in each house. Some so threadbare one feels patching has no place. All must disintegrate and disappear and with it the pain of loss and helplessness and shame.

Mrs. Mbiko. I have watched, desperate, three times as we tried to save her children and grandchildren. There have been several other deaths in her house. I only watched two closely and one peripherally. Where are they all, in that deserted homestead, which used to buzz with life?

Then Noroyi, struggling back from the outside toilet shack, unable to walk, dehydrated, outcast from her own home. We took her in. That is, Eunice did. Into her home, even her own bed, nursed her. Again, we bought anti-retroviral drugs.

But I remember we saw anti-retroviral therapy as a desperate measure. We hadn't been told we could believe in them. We believed the dangers the government said they brought but wanted to try because we had no other hope.

Of these first six people I have mentioned, four are now dead. Nkululeko and Noroyi live.

Nomonde, the baby and her mother and Barbara all died. Their deaths are caused by multiple factors: timing, lies, pride, discrimination and laziness. A problem emerging too big, too costly to treat, too painful and too ugly to face, to try and stare down, tell it to back off, go away.

The relief of death. This too I remember. The name no longer on my list. The face no longer worrying me awake at night. The pain gone, obliterated with the wasted body, the sores, the diarrhea, a third of the village.

Lists obsess me, those sick, those on anti-retroviral therapy, those dead, an ever-longer list. Still some relief as I move the name to another column. Not my worry anymore.

This we have done for six years now.

I am grateful to the staff of Umtha Welanga AIDS Treatment Center in Hamburg with their endless work and caring, the patients with their resilience, courage, sense of humor, life, my family and friends who have supported me and lastly myself who has done my inadequate best.

We continued making art and people recovered slowly in many small ways. Using one's hands to create makes the creator feel they have accomplished something, and this was my initial premise. It had worked for me and allowed me to access and communicate thoughts and feelings for which I had no words. The process of creativity gave me some sense of being a unique person in the midst of many other people also unique like me. But this idea of how art heals grew larger, to include the telling of stories about ourselves and who we were, using well-known Western art works that had personal meaning for me. We used Western art works only, because they were what I knew and understood and were meaningful to me. I could use them to communicate without words on a very deep level.

By using these famous images as a base of inspiration for our own work, we were able to get in touch with universal human experience and express our own story in this context. I used them because they were part of my culture and my belief. I used them because they affected me deeply and I wanted to communicate on this level. I did not consider any further academic reasons and at the time, I had no idea that this might be viewed later as politically incorrect by some. I was simply sharing what I believed and discovered and this resonated with people who had a different culture from my own. This use of iconic Western art works was deliberate and important to me as it allowed me to express my own belief and communicate it to the community I lived in and ask them to use it to express their own story. It gave us a framework within which we could truly collaborate.

The figures in our own iteration of the altarpiece were of people we knew who were larger than life, and this use of scale elevated the people of a remote village to positions they had not thought they could claim. In doing this, I hoped to draw us closer in understanding to each other, to show common humanity rather than difference. I had come late to art-making and had no in-depth education in the arts except for literature. I was 40 years old before I discovered the breadth and depth of expression available in visual art, music and dance. But I could share my experience of visual art and thereby make it evident we are all one and that human experience is universal. At the time we made these images, this motivation was mostly unconscious and instinctive. Great art touches us whoever we are and shows us how important and unique and yet how common and universal our experiences are. We are allowed to take our place with all people everywhere.

During the making of the Keiskamma Altarpiece, while we were concentrating on giving hope where there seemed to be none, a physical miracle took place. Another charity sought us out and offered us anti-retroviral drugs from America as part of the President's Emergency Plan for AIDS Relief in Africa (PEPFAR). This was amazing. As we made the art work, depicting spiritual hope, we witnessed people get physically better where we had never believed they could. People who saw this phenomenon have called it the "Lazarus effect."

Because of the young boy, Nkululeko, for whom I personally accessed anti-retroviral drugs, and for a few others that I was unable to watch die, we were seen, at the time, as one of the few organizations with experience in using AIDS medication. Nkululeko got better and so did many others when we could access the medication.

Part of the joy at the unveiling of the Keiskamma Altarpiece in Grahamstown Cathedral in 2005 was the knowledge that people need no longer die. Another unexpected and indirect outcome was the formation of a supportive group of people who met each day and grew to know and care about each other, while making art and craft. All who worked there belonged, and were accepted and cared for. In this situation, stigma fell away. We had rebuilt connection without deliberately planning to do so.

I realized that making things, decorating them, dancing and telling stories and painting what we see and experience is something intrinsic to being fully human and fully alive. Because I had not had this as part of my conscious experience until I was in my late thirties, it was a revelation to me and I felt the need to communicate this to others.

I am fascinated with San art and the cave art of stone-age Europe, I think because it proves to me how basic and essential art is to our humanity. Long before white settlers arrived and before the Bantu-speaking people moved into Southern Africa, Africa's first people, the San, followed by their later, close relatives the Khoi Khoi, were painting their lives and meanings on cave and cliff walls. Archaeologists believe they have excavated the oldest evidence of human beings ever making art, found at Blombos Cave in Stilbaai, on the Indian Ocean in South Africa. In caves and on rocks all over Southern Africa, visual narratives and depictions of the lives and beliefs of these ancient people can be seen. Some San people mixed with the Xhosa people when they arrived in Southern Africa, so they are closely linked, and some of the clicks in the Xhosa language show this relationship. This ancient culture that is almost lost can still be found in facial structure, the names of rivers and mountains and, most of all, in the art they left us to ponder, which gives us a sense of their spirituality and mystery.

Keiskamma artists have a close association with a last surviving remnant of these ancient people, a group of Naro San painters and print-makers on the edge of the Kalahari in Botswana. Our links with them helped us to understand a little of the ancient people who have covered our land in paintings. We have learned their connection to the land, to plants, to magic and to the importance of narrative, dance and painting.

After the sadness of the realization of what the AIDS epidemic was doing in our midst, we looked around us and made another large work praising our own environment and all the different people living in it. As with our other works, this was based on a very famous art work from the early Renaissance, the Ghent Altarpiece by Jan van Eyck. This European work with its detail of plants, animals and people, with its sense of one particular place, described with care and detail, allowed us to look at ourselves within our own environment, in Hamburg, on the Keiskamma River, near the Indian Ocean.

The Creation Altarpiece is a tribute to the place where we live, the wildlife and plants and the people living there. It helped us to look up from the devastation of lives and families around us to see where we are now, and our relation to this place, and to celebrate and offer praise. Since then we have made several works related to the environment and especially our own place in it. We have also visited and looked at the environment of the Naro San people, and seen how they live in a very different place. We observed their deep connection to their landscape and all it holds. This act of making art, of praising the beauty around us, in the midst of loss, has helped us feel tied to the place, and that we belong.

Since making these three pivotal works, Keiskamma artists have been engaged in many other works, some to do with the environment and others describing life around us and what is happening to us as a community. Always the key ingredients are communicating a story and making something lovely at the same time. Initially, we make the works for ourselves, to teach us something, or to understand better. Through the making of it, a mysterious learning takes place, which is not cerebral but grounded in our being. Behind these two overt aims lies the slower unfolding of a deeply connected group who care for each other. Visitors are drawn into this community and feel the sense of welcome and friendship and of being part of something larger than ourselves. My own way of explaining this is to say this is a work of God. We only have to take up pencils, needles and wool and start to make things and we get drawn along by something much bigger than ourselves. I am almost daily astounded by this.

By 2010 the community of Hamburg and its surrounding areas was again frustrated. While anti-retroviral drugs were available, many people could not access them due to extreme poverty. They were only available in the hospitals. Our own Keiskamma hospice had had to close due to lack of funds. So we had attempted to start a step-down unit at the local hospital to fulfill its function, with our own community health workers. This was not successful. There seemed to be nowhere in our region where people with AIDS could find love and care. Our patients seemed worse off because the drugs were available but their circumstances made it impossible to get hold of them. Because the South African government was now providing the drugs for AIDS, we could no longer access the drugs ourselves. In addition, nursing in many South African hospitals was of a low standard with nurses who still treated HIV-positive people carelessly and with disrespect. Poor people were discriminated against. We knew many people who died unnecessarily in government hospitals. Our patients feared to go to hospital. They said people only died there.

At this time, I wrote another essay:

## TEN YEARS LATER…THREE *PIETAS* (REPRESENTATIONS OF THE VIRGIN MARY MOURNING OVER THE DEAD BODY OF CHRIST)

Elie Wiesel tells an old Jewish story of the prophet in Sodom standing on a street corner shouting to people to repent or be destroyed. Many years later he was still there in the same place, still shouting, but nothing had changed. A visitor asked him how he could keep shouting when obviously it made no difference to anyone and no retribution had occurred. He answered that when he had begun prophesying it was to save others but he kept doing it to save himself.

This morning I read the stories I wrote when I first came to live in Hamburg. I was struck by the raw feeling, the shock of what I saw, the horror of it all, the constant struggle to make meaning. But somehow the person who felt that is gone. I had not saved myself. Instead, I had lost myself to numbness. I just keep going, work and rest and make no comment, seemingly remaining unaffected. So tonight I have written about the day, recording impassively. It is no worse than any other day and I almost forgot it all as soon as work was over.

## First pieta

The first mother and child were the Bengu family. Baby Bengu was HIV positive, a twin, one year old. She had retinoblastoma. The baby presented some months ago with a new squint. The mother's story was that when she got to the eye clinic they found nothing wrong and sent her home. The eye-clinic doctors said they told her the diagnosis and wanted to remove the eye and she refused.

A month later the eye was protruding 5 cms in the baby's face. She went back and they removed much of the now inoperable tumor and sent the mother and the baby home with morphine syrup. The baby initially did well and the eye socket healed. They live in a very remote village 40 kms from the local hospital and an hour's walk from a local clinic. The mother came back and forth to the clinic for dressings, often carrying both twins herself, one in front and one on her back as she walked.

Now this morning she was in the hospice. We had heard the swelling in the eye socket was again enormous. We wanted to help. I talked to her through Mrs. Zita, our nurse. "Did she know the baby would die, that the tumour would grow and grow?" Yes, they had told her. Mrs. Zita interjected, "She is talking you know…the baby that is."

All the while the mother held the baby with a huge bulging swelling of the eye socket. The baby looked constantly at her mother's face. The mother cried silently.

"How can we help? Can we care for the child until she dies?" No. She wanted to care for her at home.

"What does she need us to do?" Just make sure they have food for the whole family. See if the oncologists will just remove the massive swelling for cosmetic purposes.

I promised and rushed out and forgot the mother and baby for some hours.

## Second pieta

This mother was older. Fat with a small beard. Her son lay in the side ward of the clinic. He looked 60 at least, but he was only 41—emaciated, breathless, coughing, with thrush on his lips, and clubbing of his dirty, long fingernails. He told me the story. The mother kept interjecting in Xhosa, which the nurse translated. She remembered more than he did, in spite of the fact that he was away in Port Elizabeth when fell ill.

He was a policeman and had been on anti-retroviral drugs for three years from 2001 to 2003. Then he stopped the medication. He was so well. Then recently he got tuberculosis for the third time and was admitted to hospital. To clarify the medical history, I asked, "When did he last work?" He answered that he stopped working when he killed his wife. He had been discharged from hospital in 2009. "Why had he allowed himself to become so ill?" He said that collecting tuberculosis treatment had been difficult at first because he was in jail, then on bail, then had numerous court cases in the high court in Port Elizabeth. So he did not get better.

Later, he was bedridden, and the health visitor did not bring treatment regularly. Then his mother brought him home from Port Elizabeth to Hamburg. They lived 200 meters from the isolated rural clinic. She kept coming to the clinic to beg them to visit him, and then begging him to come to the clinic. For a few weeks, he had refused. Today he had agreed.

She suddenly became agitated. She held up her hand with four fingers. "I have lost four sons," she said in Xhosa that even I could understand. This is the last. She cried. I said to the man, "Look at your mother. How can you continue to refuse admission and proper treatment?" "She is always like this," he said to dismiss her. I persisted, "Of course she is, she fears losing her last son." He agreed to be admitted. I called the ambulance. He had a slim chance of survival.

Later, his mother and I looked at his medical card. He had three children. She had never heard of the third one. Finally, my professional demeanor broke down. We asked, the nurses and I, of the mother, "His wife…why did he kill her?"

"She was stealing his money. She tried to poison him twice and he landed in hospital in the intensive care unit. She abused him. Finally, he came home and shot her point blank in the head with his police gun."

My last view of mother and son was her wiping his mouth tenderly and then stroking his hair.

### Third pieta

Again it was a young mother. She was pretty. HIV positive with a nine-month HIV-positive baby. Both looked well. We talked about the baby's treatment and hers. The nurse interrupted my history taking. She was para 1 gravida 3, she told me (three pregnancies with only one full-term, live birth). The inaccurate medical classification told another inadequate story. One child had drowned, one died of meningitis at three years, and now this last one was HIV positive.

These communities, families and individuals keep on with work and daily life. We all become mechanical. We work and talk and slowly our soul and love of life and joy die. We hardly notice until we remember who we were before this slow plague.

## My personal *Guernica*

As I worked in rural clinics, I became more and more angry and frustrated. I wanted to make an art work to express my outrage but hesitated because I felt in danger of cracking the fragile shell that allowed people to cope with indescribable losses. I thought they coped by believing it was God's will and that they must accept this. None of my family members was affected. I was not sure I had the right to express my own anger through artists, designers and embroiderers who lived this loss day by day and had to cope by whatever means they could, just to continue living.

I thought if I allowed anger and grief to express themselves, I might destroy their only coping mechanism. After some discussion with the artists and embroiderers, they agreed they would like to work on this angry piece and express their own feelings as well as my own. Here, in this work, consciously, we decided to try and help people to cope by expressing their own pain and grief. We held workshops for adults and children to come and talk about loss and then make a clay pot in memory of their loved one. We facilitated classes with children to draw the crying, grieving figures in the way Picasso had done prior to making his large work. We started to depict pain and anger as Picasso had done.

And so, in 2010, the work that I feel was the most important of all we have made so far was made. It is important due to its fulfillment of a direct need to express both anger and grief and thereby bring some measure of peace and control. The Keiskamma Guernica was based on the *Guernica* painted by Picasso in 1937 after the small Basque town of Guernica had been bombed by fascist forces on market day. It was one of the first instances of the bombing of civilians and was purposely done to have greatest effect. Many innocent people, including children, were killed. Picasso had heard about this while working in France, and had decided to express his outrage in a monumental work for the 1937 Paris Exhibition. He had created a painting now known as *Guernica,* which has become a symbol of suffering caused by war.

We exhibited our iteration of *Guernica* in July 2010, at the National Arts Festival, and we put all the names of those who had died on small metal grave plates, and hung pillow cases on a long wall, each one containing the hospital notes of one of our patients who had died. The idea was to bring these lost people back into our midst, to show the extent of the loss and honor them.

At the exhibition many, many people thanked us for the opportunity to express their grief and anger in this way. Some people asked why we had abandoned hope and allowed our work to be so negative and dark. But it surprised me that the actual people who had suffered and lost family members found some comfort in this harsh expression. I had initially been hesitant, thinking people who had suffered such loses might not be strong enough to cope. I was proven wrong.

As I have grown older in the company of people where early death is all too common, and food and a clean, dry home are never certain, I have learned many things about myself and become much less idealistic, or certain, in my ideology and beliefs.

I know nothing heals the pain of being human permanently, but many things make it bearable and sometimes meaningful. For me, making art gives dignity and meaning to life, which so often strips these precious things away.

I also know that moments of success and triumph are followed by long periods of hard work and difficult relationships. I often have times of wanting to give up and run back to my privileged security, to not have to know about things I have had to confront and see in this community where I live, to pretend all is well. But I have come too far on this road to do this. I know too much. I have seen too much, but I have also seen the courage and strength of women with no security for themselves or their families and I have been altered permanently.

It would be negligent to talk of working in a community and about healing in this community without acknowledging that all who visit here and share skills gain more than they give and are also relieved of the "embarrassment of riches" as they are accepted and befriended as they work alongside people who have so few material possessions. There is a deep guilt and wound in many people because they are so lucky, so privileged, and have so much. They feel they have no way of meaningfully sharing what they have and even if they did, it would make so little difference to the world's vast suffering.

The Keiskamma Art Project unintentionally offered many people, who came and visited and wanted to share and live alongside the women for a while, a chance to understand and give what they could. They have never been judged for being advantaged. They have always received much more than they have given, in friendship, gratitude, insights and understanding. As with everything, it is relationships that count.

In addition to those who came from more privileged environments to help, it is the people I work with in the rural communities of Hamburg and the surrounding area who are the essential elements without which nothing could have been accomplished. They gave what they had and that is how the program succeeded. In this work, I am the person most seen, often the face of our organization. This gives an inaccurate picture. I am a part of a community of people who have worked together for 17 years to fight poverty and illness in their community. The miracle was that everyone involved gave what they had, and like the loaves and fishes, it has multiplied to feed thousands.

In assisting a suffering community to create art that tells their own story, I have learned a few things. I believe the Keiskamma Art Project has done far more than simply make art and craft works, and provide income for many women. It has allowed women to work together and support each other, to develop self-esteem, to understand other different cultures, and to look closely at the fragile environment. In making art as a community, and learning from other more skilled people, it has also allowed sharing and understanding to develop between people of very different backgrounds. I have seen that medicine saves lives, but art actually gives lives meaning.

*Chapter 7*

# STORIES FROM PALESTINE, ISRAEL, TURKEY, SYRIA, JORDAN, INDIA, FRANCE AND GREECE,

with Survivors of Poverty and Ideological
Violence, and those Living in Refugee Camps

*Max Levi Frieder and the Artolution Project*

I have been hooked on creating community-based public art with children for the last eight years of my life. Recently, I facilitated a mural in the Azraq Syrian refugee camp on the border of Syria and Jordan, and as I looked at the beautiful children painting in the most bleak and difficult desert landscape, having fled the ravages of the Syrian civil war, I was transported to being a seven-year-old again, when I saw a film called *The Devil's Arithmetic*. In this film, families and children were killed in gas chambers in the Holocaust, and since I was a child, these images have given me re-occurring nightmares. The film made me feel that I was lucky to be alive, that I needed to appreciate every day and that I had a responsibility to do something meaningful in the world with my life.

When I was 20, I was hired to innovate the fine arts program at an arts camp in the Adirondacks in upstate New York. I had an unlimited budget, every art supply you could imagine and talented children and teenagers who were creative, inspired and passionate. It was the ultimate educational laboratory with the freedom to experiment with all the ideas I had ever dreamed of trying. After three months of doing 25 wildly collaborative murals and sculptures and seeing the corresponding reactions, a voice in my brain started to whisper, "Maybe this could be the start of something big."

As this seedling of an idea planted itself in the depths of my mind, follow-up questions began to germinate. "What if this powerful art form was used with the most disenfranchised and traumatized children in the world? What would happen?" It was as if the two ideas went hand in hand. And the more I imagined the pairing of these concepts in different contexts, the larger this idea grew. Every day, it became my goal to figure out ways of using the language of collaborative public art in the greater world.

While working on my Bachelor of Fine Arts degree, I fervently pursued a community-based public arts focus within my painting major. Through field experience, I facilitated the creation of collaborative murals in New Zealand and Costa Rica and at the Rhode Island School of Design. I graduated as an energized artist, motivated to go out into the world and use my curiosity and excitement to explore the power of creative expression. I undertook this endeavor knowing that failure would be an inevitable part of the process, and that I would be lucky if I could get one out of every four projects actually off the ground. Over a number of years, I was able to partner with organizations in the Middle East (Israel, Palestine, Jordan and Turkey) and Latin America (Colombia, Mexico, Cuba, Brazil and Peru) and develop programs working with children and teenagers who were survivors of violence, poverty, war and ideological trauma, physical and sexual abuse, mental and physical illness, and also with people in refugee crisis. As the projects began to grow, I gained insight into how people interact with art when made publicly, and together. The emotional nature of this profound work impacted me at a visceral level.

I was captivated by the intense sensations that came from this work: the paint-infused adrenalin, the meaningful conversations and interactions, the mutual appreciation, the reason to talk to everyone in a community, the expressions on the faces of the children, and each dense day feeling like a lifetime. From refugee camps to children's hospitals, I started to see that there were similarities in the reactions and interactions of the children, teenagers and families. I observed the communities and children's love for painting together, their fulfillment in seeing a finished public work that they had created, and the shared feeling of being part of something larger, something important. The more I submerged myself in these creative ecosystems, the more questions arose from this practice. These questions ranged from, "What might the ultimate potential of this work be?" to "What might the long-term influences of these projects be?" and "What could they become?"

Although I had a hypothesis as to the influences of the programs, I was not satisfied. I had images in my mind of Sebastian from Peru, Muhammad from Palestine, Punkaj from India, and Rooba from Syria waking up at sunrise, in their various corners of the world. I imagined them getting out of their beds, gathering their books and backpacks together and walking to their schools in the morning. Each child would be greeted with the colorful mural about their own life, stories and hopes for their own future that they had painted with their communities. From this bird's eye perspective, I was inspired to ask, what do they think? What are the stories they tell? Does the art and memory matter to them, and how does it affect their lives? What about their parents, teachers and neighborhoods?

Through digital communication, I have been able to stay in contact with many of the children, artists and teachers with whom I have worked, and the same questions keep arising, from people in very different parts of the world and in different cultures. They often ask, "When are you coming back? How can we do more projects like this? What comes next?" I started to see that it wasn't just an appreciation for the original experience, but a thirst for more programs, a desire for a "next step," a need for water to cultivate the seeds that we planted together. The art-making process was bigger than any one of those children or teachers. But there was a larger problem in the field, of resources, and a practice that triggered some very deep and difficult internal questions. These questions lead to my co-founding and development of Artolution.

Artolution began as a community-based public arts initiative in 2009. In 2015, I joined forces with like-minded community-based mural artist Joel Bergner, whose work had followed a parallel trajectory for years. As co-directors, we decided to launch Artolution as an international organization that partners with community-based public artists, educators and institutions around the world. Artolution is a public arts organization that seeks to ignite positive social change through creative, participatory and collaborative art-making. We facilitate projects around the world that connect diverse peoples in order to address common social objectives. Our projects bring together children, youth, families, artists, educators and community groups. Our founding objective is to address critical issues related to conflict, trauma, and social marginalization by cultivating sustainable global initiatives that promote reconciliation, healing and creative dialogue.

In my work through Artolution, I have facilitated the creation of over 300 collaborative canvases and wall murals and public percussive sculptures in 15 nations throughout Latin America, South Asia, North America, Australasia, Europe and the Middle East. I have collaborated with over 75 global organizations to make these projects a reality. These groups have included museums, schools, hospitals, the United States Department of State, the United Nations and a variety of non-profit and humanitarian-aid organizations. The foundation of these initiatives is based on facilitating opportunities for communities to empower themselves by becoming agents of social change through creative and cooperative public art-making.

Over the past eight years, my practice has been with a wide variety of radically different cultures and demographics with their own requirements and interpretation of the arts. Real-world situations mean I have had to maintain a great deal of flexibility due to a variety of intense environmental variations.

Our projects engage youth and communities who have faced social exclusion and trauma, including refugees, street youth, the incarcerated, people with physical and mental disabilities and young people living in areas of violent conflict or extreme poverty. We utilize visual public art mediums such as mural art and community sculpture, as well as street performance genres including dance, theater, puppetry and music. In our workshops, participants explore important community issues and collectively decide on the subject and content of the artistic productions. This culminates in the collaborative creation of works of public art.

Through this process, we emphasize the building of positive relationships among participants, skill-building, the sharing of knowledge and the encouragement of community activism. These projects have been organized and facilitated in partnerships with local artists and educators, grassroots community groups, schools, religious centers and international institutions in over 30 countries internationally. Our process educates and provides skills and resources to local artists, educators, youth and communities to be actors of positive social change, explore critical societal issues and create opportunities for constructive ongoing public communication.

My work seeks to understand why the phenomenon of community-based public arts is important in the world today and how it can be cultivated for artists, educators, organizers, therapists and activists as a field for the future. I ask what role community-based public arts can have in facilitating dialogue, healing and learning for the future of our world. I ask how participation-based public arts can influence the lives of traumatized, stratified, under-represented and multi-generational communities, and I share here some experiences with current projects— their influence, assessment and future scalability. I am seeking to investigate and question the implications of projects I have coordinated globally. These inquiries will strive to crystalize the importance of cultivating a sustainable approach to developing community-based public arts. This exploration uses the data I have collected over the past five years, facilitating and addressing community-based public arts projects through fieldwork, and documented through written observations, field notes, auto-ethnographic narratives, photography, videography and analysis.

In this series of international pilot studies, I am intentionally trying to bridge the conversation between different sub-fields of the arts, and put them into a format where they fuse into a hybrid, pulling the greatest strengths from each discipline. These sub-fields include mural painting, recycled sculpture, music and performance implemented through art education, alternative education, public arts, community arts and cooperative learning (Borwick, 2012, p.21). Hallmark (2012) makes this point clear when examining the relationships between participation, facilitation and representation (p.94). Both of these sources emphasize the relationship between the practice of creating art with a community, and how important the process and product are perceived by the participants.

Community-based public arts are rooted in the choice to utilize the arts through interaction in the public sphere. When an act of community-based public action takes place, it is a cyclical act where the audience, viewers, artist and participants all become contributors to the long-term impacts of the initiative. Blurring these pre-established societal lines becomes a catalyst for investigating alternative pedagogies, trauma-relief, artistic communication and the building of social capacity. The skills needed to do this work were acquired on the job during my projects with traumatized children, adolescents and adults. Many of the participants had suffered physical and sexual abuse, war or ideological trauma. Others were victims or perpetrators of violence, had suffered mental or physical illness, or were in refugee crisis. Each of these situations and participating populations has informed the curriculum.

Each site and project required fluidity, flexibility and support according to the capabilities and experiences of the participants. As the facilitating artist and educator, I put high priority on integrating the arts in an encouraging, healing and culturally sensitive way, supported by the *Inter-Agency Network for Education in Emergencies'* Minimum Standards (Anderson and Roberts, 2005, pp.8–10). These opportunities have shown me the incredible power the arts can have in the lives of traumatized, stratified, underserved communities of all kinds. This work is informed by the field, as well as the essential work of a variety of multi-disciplinary artists and scholars, including Suzi Gablik (1993), Suzanne Lacy (1994) and Claire Bishop (2005). All of these sources discuss the evolution of the arts as based in a practice of initiating dialogue.

Community-based public arts can provide a creative space where traumatized, conflicted and dislocated children, adolescents and adults can create art as a source of dialogue and healing. Each of these situations require a unique approach, with a structure that is applicable across international contexts. I am searching to understand the underlying thread of this process, so that it can one day exist on an ongoing and sustainable basis. Through this research, I seek to find the commonalities across different examples of this work that can help develop an evolving application-based model. There is a need for articulated research surrounding socially engaged public art education as a vehicle for addressing larger social trauma, disparities and local issues (Cameron *et al.*, 2013). The potential benefits and challenges that lie in facilitating civic conversation and growth through community-based public arts initiatives will be shared throughout the stories. Community artist John Latham describes co-experience as a way to make shared experiences; the application and description of the values of the field come in the form of the *co* of *cooperative*, especially when applied to shared art-making (Richardson, 2011, p.237). The selected sites and participants range in culture, geography and experiences and in community and socio-historical contexts. However, there are common ethnographic trends that span across the different examples of international environments.

The participants in these projects have faced traumas that cannot be described at length here. They entail children, teenagers, women and men who have faced displacement (Syria/Palestine/Greece/France), war (Syria/Palestine/Israel/Greece/France), severe poverty (Syria/Palestine/India) and different levels of post-traumatic stress and depression. There is a limitation on how many of these problems can be addressed, but it is acknowledged that underneath the narratives, the pre-existing trauma and experiences is a factor in the background of the participants.

Throughout the research I conducted for my Master of Education degree in Community Art at Teachers College, Columbia University, I was influenced by several seminal educators. John Dewey, Paolo Friere and Maxine Greene all envision arts practice in which socio-cultural factors act as shaping aesthetic dynamics. John Dewey (2005), in *Art as Experience*, explores how art-making catalyzes meaning and experience-making. Maxine Greene (1995), in *Art and Imagination*, delves into the importance of arts as a window into imagination as a way of knowing ourselves as makers, and the corresponding meaning to the affected environments. Paolo Freire, in *Pedagogy of the Oppressed*, investigates critical pedagogy as a paradigm of how teaching can shift interaction towards a more autonomous perspective for all parts of society. Freire (2006) proposes that the teacher becomes a co-producer of knowledge, facilitating a tangible empowerment through collective and non-hierarchical collaboration. Context is always importance. For example, we can assume that during the Gaza war in 2014, the emotions of the participants in Palestine and Israel were tense, and post-traumatic stress was part of the expressive decisions being made in the art projects of this specific time.

Given the displaced, traumatized and under-represented communities in the following narratives, including refugees in Palestine, Israel, Jordan, Turkey, India, France and Greece, these projects take the difficult background situations of each and work with them. Health improvements associated with community arts can be due to the relief of different stress factors. According to the Center for Arts and Cultural Policy Studies, "The arts improve individual health. Either engaging in creative activity or simply attending some kind of artistic event appears to improve physical health" (Guetzkow, 2002, p.10).

In the projects described below, adults and children work together, the intention being to enhance and maintain social bonds. We can assume that at its best, socially engaged art can help us to open our eyes to others and ourselves. Greene (1995a) explains that by having such experiences we are lurched out of the familiar and the taken-for-granted, and we may also discover new paths for action. We may experience a sudden sense of new possibilities and thus new beginnings.

Community-based public arts are rooted in cultural storytelling. The cross-cultural visual sharing of communal stories is the priority. Murals and all public art forms originally stemmed from the ancient world, and told the stories of myths, religions and cultural traditions. Murals and public arts have historically required collaboration between different kinds of people (tradesmen, funders, artisans, etc.) in the act of creating something that takes on a new life. In this way, we can see that murals and public sculptures are living entities embodying social communication.

There are many challenges to facilitating community arts projects in contexts of trauma. Much of the time, this work is facilitated through the use of a second or third language, or through working with a translator. There is planning, physical preparation, group orchestration and interactions with the participants. Facilitation comes in varying forms including being an artist, educator, activist, manager or organizer. It is crucial that this conversation involves local and international individuals who are concerned with the future of this field. The culmination of a project becomes reality only through the documentation, videography, photography, writing of the stories, analysis, editing and web publishing of all content. In many ways, this performance relies on a fusion of theoretical knowledge, experiential instinct, culturally specific engagement and facilitation. There is the long-term goal of one day developing an international forum of facilitators, as well as the dialogic potential to expand the audience of this work.

There are five themes that run through the various projects described here: storytelling of issues, public sharing, imagination as health, creative facilitation, and co-creatorship; and these themes will be evident in each narrative. The ultimate goal of this work is relational, interactive and catalyzing. Bolin (1999) discusses the importance of using art-making to create an environment where meaningful art-learning and world understanding takes shape (p.5). The dynamic of "caring" is rooted in sharing—a holistic approach where the arts act as a catalyst for conversational play, as narrative inquiry, as material craftsmanship (Hallmark, 2012), and a recognition of their role in creating personal and collective change (Gargarella, 2007). In the different environments, each participant needs to become a problem-solver for their part of the larger experience. Dewey (2005) explains that the participant must have the "opportunity and occasion to test his ideas by application…and to discover for himself their validity" (p.193). The palpable encounter of making something public and permanent becomes the way to validate the learning in a group environment.

Collaboration in an artistic form is a series of dynamic, changing processes. Without a structure, chaos would reign; however, without malleability in that structure, it is very difficult to develop an event without a pre-defined framework. For the transformative nature of a project to exist, there must be a dynamic and constant creative exchange. Krensky (2009) comments on this by explaining the importance of the contribution of community arts to the formation of identity and efficacy for the individuals involved (p.54). This formation of identity transcends the arts and goes into a deeper realm of how we interact as mutually respectful *co-creators*, a "complex mix of attitudes, intentions, constraints, and behaviors" (McCarthy and Kimberly, 2001, p.23).

Researcher Stephens (2006) makes the assessment that: "Community-based learning has the power to encourage and sustain the intellectual curiosity of learners" (p.46). Curiosity can be harnessed to discuss important issues, relieve trauma and build bridges across boundaries. Three different United Nations Educational, Scientific and Cultural Organization (UNESCO) studies concluded that non-formal education, such as an art project in a refugee camp, is critical to stimulate community-based learning that takes place outside formal primary, secondary and tertiary education. This is increasingly recognized as a crucial means of addressing 21st-century social, economic and environmental challenges (UNESCO, 2011, 2012, 2016). The arts can act as a catalyzing force or framework for discussing problems, including marginalization, discrimination, racism and conflict. Freire (2006) theorized the pedagogical act of *conscientization*. This occurs by means of dialogue and sharing information on injustices with the goal of changing perspectives and actions in their everyday lives (Denzin and Lincoln, 2008, p.153). The role of the art facilitator is not to create that public *conscience*, but rather to be a conduit for what is already within the participants. The role of the facilitator is to be a catalyst for the participants—to make their experience as impactful as possible, through encouragement, process explanation and material facilitation.

The projects described here ranged from three days to three weeks in length, determined by the partner organizations, as were the number of participants and the location for each workshop. The process follows a plan adapted to each environment. The mural painting begins with the showing of photographic images of other community murals from around the world, and the description of each location so that the project is understood to be part of a larger, worldwide connection. Participants are then asked to individually draw ideas about their own futures, dreams and ways to represent their communities. They are then asked to hang the drawings on a wall and reflect on each other's work. The facilitator holds a communal discussion on how to create a unified composition of a visual story comprising of the ideas of all the participants. All the drawing ideas are considered in how the final story takes shape. The participants then paint the color background, covering the ground of the wall or canvas. They then transfer their drawings onto the colored ground using chalk in the agreed composition. The final phase has the participants filling in their drawings with paint, shading, outlining and filling in the details. The entire process is holistically inclusive and shifts according to the needs of the local group. Although children are the focus, adolescents, adults, local teachers and community members are also involved from the original ideation to the painting and final public presentation. This includes instruction for local artists and educators.

The second artistic element introduced into a project is known as the *Foundstrument Soundstrument,* a project in which participants collect durable trash and recycled materials, and then use the objects to construct a large-scale sculpture that is designed and built as a long-term public percussion instrument. Each piece of the foundstrument is painted synaesthetically, meaning that the participants are asked to decide what color they think best represents the sound made by each object when it is hit with a drumstick. They then participate in the construction of the larger sculpture, which is assembled using wire, screws and zip-ties, with multiple sets of drumsticks attached with cables. This project is accompanied throughout by educational percussion and performance workshops, and local musicians are invited to be involved in the process. The materials used are based on what is locally available, which also includes natural materials, collected trash and local materials. The location for the display is agreed on by the local community to be an appropriate place for musical expression. The final sculpture is installed and continues to live in the community as a permanent work of interactive public art.

Following the painted mural and the creation of the foundstrument comes the third aspect of each project—the photography and video-graphy documenting the process and product from each site, and the subsequent distribution (with appropriate approvals) through the internet. Written narratives arise from the experiences of facilitating, observing and reflecting on the projects. These three categories of outcomes do not take into account the importance of the non-objective outcomes, including the relationships and connections developed, the educational experiences of the learners, teachers and community, as well as the continuation of future initiatives at each site.

At its core, the experience of being part of a larger public process also turns participants into a collective audience. After creating a communal art work, the engagement process shifts participants into the role of public viewers. This shifted position transforms artists into the intended audience for this greater body of inquiry (Denzin and Lincoln, 2008, p.152). Each of the varied audiences in the creative ecosystem of interactions surrounding the creation, observation, dissemination and analysis of each of the stories can be simplified and divided into three primary categories: communities, facilitators and organizations. Their daily viewing and interaction stimulated by the public arts pieces needs to be taken into account. They are linked together through the process of making art.

My underlying goal is to ensure that more facilitators will be able to continue this kind of programming on an ongoing, knowledgeable basis. Community-based public arts have a deep connection to the institutions that make this work a logistical reality: civil society organizations, education in emergencies, public health and alternative education development (Andemicael, 2013, p.22; Garavan, 1997, p.43). Although these disciplines vary, these public arts projects create a junction where the arts can act as a series of bridges for creative approaches to serious local and global issues. Talbot (2013) points out that the academic research concerning options for education during emergencies has an urgent need to strengthen the literature in the field (p.4). This is especially true with art education, where the arts have been under-represented, and many times are not a priority for local education systems, international organizations or governing agencies. I am seeking to affect this by sharing the following stories, so that community-based public arts can be prioritized in the future.

## Palestine/West Bank

*Shoafat Refugee Camp Elementary School Mural: Shoafat Sector C, East Jerusalem, Education Department, Artolution.*

The Shoafat Refugee Camp is composed of multiple generations of Palestinian refugees dating from the 1967 war and continuing until today. Located in the contested region of East Jerusalem, the camp has neither Palestinian authority nor Israeli military forces patrolling the region, with exceptions only during times of conflict. I entered and worked in the camp in collaboration with the Educational Department of the Municipality of Jerusalem.

Through working with the Municipality of East Jerusalem Educational Director, Ranan Nali'en, we were granted access to the elementary school where boys aged five to twelve attend classes. This school is located inside an abandoned metal fabrication factory. The school has existed for five years and during its first two years it operated while part of the factory continued to manufacture sewer manhole lids. Due to the constant noise and metal shards many of the children got very sick. The school eventually took over the entire building. This space was in need of beautification.

As the young boys gathered to discuss their ideas for the piece, the outcome was unexpectedly playful. Although a translator had been provided, I was surprised at how strong our communication was without a common language. The boys came up with a simple concept; to have a dragon whose fiery breath turned into the students' dreams for their community. The future "fire" would end up in the stomach of a giant bear. As we started drawing on the wall, a group of the school's teachers, in beautifully patterned and pristine hijabs, started drawing along with the children, completely unprompted. As this continued, I noticed that one of the teachers began drawing on a wall across the front entrance. This was unexpected, as we had not received permission to paint there.

Before I could interject, swarms of children followed this teacher and spread the scrawling drawings across the wall within minutes. I figured that since it was the teacher's initiation, it must be acceptable. The principal watched from afar and was surprisingly supportive of this unfounded growth of the project. As the paint came out, the color took on a mosaic-like evolution, which became a patchwork of abstraction. Slowly but surely, the walls became covered in bright images, a world of colorful chaos and imagination.

Ranan voiced to me her immense satisfaction that, in this otherwise extremely politically charged location, the statement here was of the children's imagination for a better world. At the completion, the teachers, the principal and the students all were yelling, singing and dancing excitedly at the unexpected success of the painting. This abandoned factory-turned-children's-school now has the shimmering world of the children's imagination welcoming them each morning.

# Israel/Palestine

*ALYN Hospital Mural: Pediatric and Adolescent Multi-Cultural Rehabilitation Center, the Inter-Religious Communication Council of Israel (ICCI), Face to Face: Faith to Faith, the Auburn Seminary, Har Herzl, West Jerusalem and Artolution.*

The ALYN Hospital is an unprecedented anomaly in the Middle East. It is a hospital in West Jerusalem with specialized and intensive care for children and adolescents with brain and spinal cord injuries. This hospital invites patients from both sides of the Israeli-Palestinian conflict, and their families, to receive treatment and support. At that time, it was the only hospital in Israel that accepted people from Gaza. Each child must have a family member stay with them in the hospital at all times, with the primary focus being on rehabilitation and healing. During my time at ALYN, I met children who suffered from various diseases as well as physical and war trauma.

Painting with both Palestinian and Israeli children together at ALYN was a haunting illumination of their resiliency, in spite of their pain and suffering. Most of the children were paraplegic and quadriplegic, and being able to make a simple mark across a canvas meant the world to them and their parents. We gathered the children and their families together to create drawings and come up with the idea for the mural. One stood out. It had been created by a mother whose infant son had severe brain damage. The design was composed of a violent scribble, tearing at the center of the paper. The scribble inside the drawing of a child's head was a single bold word, "FIX." As we stared at the drawings, the silence refused to be broken, despite my encouragement and the coaxing of our two translators. Finally, after ten minutes, a tiny woman at the back of the room tentatively raised her hand and simply said, "Trees." With this basic and universal word, a forest of color came from these healing families, Palestinian and Israeli alike.

I was told that one of the Palestinian boys working on the mural had been brought to ALYN from Gaza after his family had been killed by an Israeli missile that had landed on his house. As he joyously caked paint onto the canvas from his wheelchair, I noticed that he was painting directly next to a Cheredi Orthodox Jewish rabbi and his daughter. As the two children painted from their wheelchairs in unison, the lines

Kujenga Pamoja ["Together we build" in Swahili] Park at the
Village of Arts and Humanities in Philadelphia.
*Photo by Lily Yeh*

The Rugerero Genocide Memorial near Gisenyi, Rwanda.
*Photo by Lily Yeh*

Lily celebrating with children in a colorful parade at the
Rugerero survivors village in Rwanda in 2006.
*Photo by Jean Bosco Musana Rukirande*

Keiskamma Altarpiece (closed) at the National Arts Festival in South Africa.
*Photo by Justus Hofmeyr*

Noseti Makhubalo in her home with the Democracy tapestry.
*Photo by Miki Redelinghuys*

Women of the Keiskamma Art Project celebrating the success of the
Keiskamma Tapestry at the National Arts Festival, South Africa.
*Photo by Justus Hofmeyr*

Foundstrument Soundstrument and Tra the Paint Creature (Max Frieder) and the children of Samos Refugee Camp, with Artolution, We Are One Collective, Calais Action, Prism the Gift, Big Nazo (risd) in the Samos Greek Refugee Camp, Vathy, Samos Island, Turkish border of Greece.
*Photo by Max Frieder / Pru Waldorf / Majida Ali, 2015*

Noor the paint-handed girl in Azraq Syrian Refugee Camp, with Artolution, International Rescue Committee (IRC), Global Citizen, Refugee Nation, Mawada Initiative in the Azraq Syrian Refugee Camp, Northern Syrian border of Jordan.
*Photo by Joel Bergner / Max Frieder / Hamzeh Al Khasawneh, 2017*

Children sitting around the "fire of education" mural with Artolution, Give a Hand Foundation, Vidya Center. Indira Camp Slum, Okhla Phase I, South Delhi, India.
*Photo by Joel Bergner / Karla Thomas / Max Frieder, 2015*

"The Strength of the Jungle Gorilla," with Rashid (who walked from Sudan to France) in Calais "Jungle" Refugee Camp with Artolution, Pikey Wrong-Stockings, PArt of Us, Calais Action, Doctors Without Borders (MSF)—Calais Refugee Camp, Northern French/British border, France.
*Photo by Max Frieder / Angela Prusa / Kenybell Umda, 2016*

Performing the "Duplicity Dance"—Children of the Butterfly
Peace Garden of Batticaloa, Sri Lanka.
*Photo by Paul Hogan*

Children performing the "Interrogation Dance"—Butterfly Peace Garden of Batticaloa, Sri Lanka.
*Photo by Paul Hogan*

Painted mural of "Blessing Way of the Painted Dove" in the
Butterfly Peace Garden of Batticaloa, Sri Lanka.
*Photo by Paul Hogan*

Sally Adnams Jones carving the finer details of a red cedar totem
using a knife in the traditional Hul'qumi'num manner.
*Photo by Jane Marston*

Members of the cultural art program offered by the Simon Charlie
Society, practicing traditional totem carving skills.
*Photo by Sally Adnams Jones*

Red cedar, "Yin-Yang" mask, carved by Sally Adnams Jones.
*Photo by Sally Adnams Jones*

of institutionalized separation melted away. With tears in his eyes, the rabbi in traditional black and white came up to me and confided a story, which has been impossible for me to forget. He said, "My daughter has moved her arms more in the last hour painting than in the last six months combined. This is what the blessing of art can create." The mural now greets every child who enters the hospital, and is a testament to the curative nature of color beyond the pain of division.

## Israel

*US Consulate General, America House, Jerusalem and YMCA Reconciliation Mural: painted by Palestinian and Israeli Children at the YMCA, West Jerusalem and Artolution.*

During the recent conflict between the Israel Defense Forces and Hamas—also known as Miv'tza Tzuk Eitan or Operation Protective Edge—a small ray of light came in the form of color and co-creation in front of the YMCA in the center of West Jerusalem. In this rare location, there is a summer camp that brings Palestinian and Israeli children together with Palestinian and Israeli guides. The US Consulate General organized a collaborative project that would create a mural with both populations to be permanently displayed in America House in East Jerusalem.

As the children arrived, one could not tell the difference between Israeli and Palestinian. With the foundation of "humanity before culture" we began to paint. All the participants became the same: artists. However, as the day progressed, the language separation became more apparent, and groups became more noticeable. After we finished the ground, we began brainstorming the theme of the mural. At this point, we began siphoning our conversation through the two translators. Although the children were hesitant at first, the idea finally emerged of people of all cultures coming together to eat under the same roof. With food and home as a foundation, the drawings came to life.

Ideas grew from this and one of the Palestinian guides painted a red key with a foetus inside. The "key" referenced how to solve issues of hate and violence, which lay in the next generation—how children were raised. The guide spoke of how the war had affected his life.

As a Palestinian teenager, he had been afraid to leave his house and go into West Jerusalem. He spoke of the incredible fear that lay between the sides, and that much of it came from the biased education of both sides and the underlying mistrust taught from birth.

As the foetus grew, the umbilical cord split and attached to Palestinian and Israeli flags on opposite sides of the canvas, politicizing the message. However, throughout the rest of the piece, there were images of animals, people and tree houses. A new story began to form. The director of the program looked at the image and spoke of the fear on the left of the painting merging into the key, and coming out as a gathering of both sides sharing a meal. She spoke about this current time as a summer of crying, yet these children were laughing as they painted; both cultures, one image. This mural was in an exhibition at the US Consulate, and is permanently displayed at the US Consulate's America House in East Jerusalem.

## Israel/Palestine

*Parents Circle Families Forum Mural: painted by bereaved Palestinian parents in Beit Jallah, Palestine, completed by bereaved Jewish parents at the Tel Aviv Cinematheque, Parents Circle Families Forum, United Nations and Artolution.*

The Parents Circle Families Forum brings together Palestinian and Israeli parents who have lost family members, and it had a recent campaign called: "It won't stop until we talk." This mural project began with 20 Palestinian mothers in Beit Jallah, Palestine. When entering Beit Jallah, I was guided by Robi Damelin, a bereaved Israeli mother and spokesperson for this group. As we arrived at the Palestinian Parents Circle Center, Robi said something that will stick with me for the rest of my life: "Healing and reconciliation can only happen with a good sense of humor."

The group of Palestinian women came to the center from across the region to talk and participate in a knitting circle. As they arrived, Robi, the only Israeli in the room, began the morning by sitting down with the women for a conversation about the conflict. As I worked on setting up the canvas in another room, I could hear the ensuing discussion. Many women voiced an extreme sadness and anger with their situation and the life in Gaza. The conversation evolved into tears and screams. Robi maintained the grace to continue the dialogue. The sorrow in these women's lives was powerful, and the mood was one of a people who needed to speak their pain. As the women's conversation came to a close, I was invited to join the group and present the mural project to them. I began by describing the Artolution Network and the various murals I had facilitated in other communities. I was surprised at the excitement and enthusiasm in the faces of these grieving women and felt privileged to have the opportunity to work with them.

The women entered the projects with a tentative engagement. With little instruction, the painting began, and the expression grew exponentially. Although political messages of "Free, Free Palestine" and the calligraphic name of a killed Palestinian martyr came into the picture, so did something else. Something beyond words. A woman quietly grabbed a brush and let it dance across the canvas in small marks. These small marks grew into huge slashes, full of energy. This caught on, and many of these women let the paint become a medium for translating their pain and frustrations into colorful actions of the hand. From behind, it looked as if these women, all clad in colorful hijabs, were part of the painting themselves.

One woman began to tell her story. She chose to paint a tree divided into two branches: one branch Israeli, one Palestinian, coming from the same base. Both had leaves falling, symbolizing that both groups had lost lives, yet came from the same roots. The truth of the image was too powerful to forget. As we began to finish the painting, all of the women came into the room to pose for a photo. There were looks of simple joy, as though the weight of the world was lifted off each of their shoulders, even if just for a moment.

As I said "*shukran*"—thank you—to the women, I knew that this moment was frozen in time. One of the women had been imprisoned in Israel for five years after participating in the last Intifada, another had lost her husband in a violent riot, and yet another had lost a child in the recent conflict. Still, this moment was beyond the pain. As we began to pack up, one of the women grabbed my arm and pulled me to the painting. Her face was mere inches from mine showing me every stroke, while she painted her final marks of exuberant oblivion. After everything was packed away, the director of the Center, Mazen Faraj, made a final statement of essential importance. He said, "Thank you for thinking of us, many don't. You have helped these women find themselves." As the women left to return to their lives, we rolled up the canvas to be brought to the "land of the other"—Israel. This canvas was to become a painting made by "enemies" turned into fellow artists, painting on the same creation.

Half the painting was covered with ideas, emotions and color; the other half of the canvas was completely white. Every day, since the beginning of the Gaza War, the Parents Circle Families Forum has set up a tent in the center of the Tel Aviv Cinematheque Peace Square, with chairs in a circle, to have a communal and public conversation. Although the core of this group is made up of bereaved parents, the forum invites anyone from the street to come and participate. As we drove directly into the heart of Tel Aviv from the hills of the West Bank, we brought the canvas to hang around the exterior of the central tent. The tent was already set up and was adorned with a large sign saying in Hebrew and Arabic, "It won't stop until we talk." And so the conversation began.

Two well-known Israeli artists were asked to put the first marks on the mural. Both had lost their sons to the conflict years before. The painting gained momentum, and people from the street began to join. A large number of children were eager to paint. With no instruction, this organic community of Israelis created in harmony, with the conversation of war intensely humming in the background. Everyone knew to leave the side painted by the Palestinian women alone, and the division was indicative of the conflict itself: a conversation framed by separation.

Although the topic of conflict was in everyone's hearts and minds, most of the content of the mural was of hopeful images: birds, trees, and a life aiming towards the future. Throughout the creation of the piece, the media, along with a crowd of spectators, gathered and asked about the painting. As the evening came to a close, Miri Aloni sang *Shir Lashalom*, a song for peace. She also sang this song minutes before the assassination of Yitzhak Rabin on November 5, 1995, a reminder of the trail of continued violence from many years ago.

As the piece finished, two faces arose from this side of the canvas, mirroring the same two faces on the Palestinian side. Both were of peaceful sleeping faces. No matter the side, humanity was the core statement here. As we packed up the canvas, I felt that it was a tragedy that the Palestinian mothers who had poured their souls onto their side of the mural might never meet the small Israeli children who had also put their hearts on the canvas. Still, they had a conversation that will live on in that painting. Many times, dialogue is impossible when trauma breeds blind hate. But when trauma can be directed into creativity, the result may answer the foreboding statement, "It won't stop until we talk."

To continue this painting dialogue, the Parents Circle Families Forum decided to create another mural as a follow-up to the bi-cultural mural painted a week earlier. The organization received special governmental permission to transport over one hundred Palestinians from across the West Bank into the heart of Tel Aviv for a series of dialogue circles in the Tel Aviv Cinematheque. To accompany the verbal dialogue, we painted a second canvas mural, which allowed the conversation to take tangible form. The painting started with children of both the local and visiting communities. On the pristine white canvas, two children started the painting, one Palestinian, one Israeli, neither aware of the other. As people began to rotate in and out of the mural, there became a fluid transition between people of all kinds.

Strong political images and writing appeared. There were Palestinian messages of freedom and Israeli words of co-existence. The layering of conversations in Arabic and Hebrew became a background coming from different hands, and different personal experiences. Flags also appeared, one painted by a small Palestinian girl and one by an older Israeli man. The finished painting resulted in people of all minds and expressions facing in different directions, looking apart and at one another. The process of this creation was completely open to free dialogue, with no obstruction. A year later, the final peace square mural was brought to New York and displayed in the United Nations headquarters. Bereaved families from both sides, the Deputy Secretary General of the United Nations and I all spoke about the importance of communication across cultures, in spite of conflict. The result was a physical conversation between people of different worlds living together in the same story.

# Turkish/Syrian border, Turkey

*Syrian Refugee Mural Project: Zeitouna, Karam Foundation, AptART (Awareness and Prevention Through Art), Al Salam School; Artolution, Rehanli.*

The sky was orange as the blisteringly cold wind blew in from the mountains of north-west Syria across the border into Turkey. I stood atop a rickety set of wooden scaffolding, above a crowd of hundreds of Syrian children, painting a wall on the front of Al Salam School. Four dedicated and inspired Syrian girls stood at my side, giggling with nervous enthusiasm. I knew these girls had never experienced anything like this. As they painted their dreams for the future, the calls to prayer subtly erupted from the mosques in the distance. The notes were a tranquil, meditative calm amid the stressed environment.

I was working with the Karam Foundation alongside other artists, writers, soccer coaches, dentists, photographers and story-tellers. We were in Rehanli, Turkey, for ten days, providing trauma-relief programming for 1500 Syrian refugee children. As the mural project came to an end, I was surprised to discover a connection I had not anticipated. The pink-hijab-clad girl sitting to my left on the scaffolding brought her brush to a corresponding line in unison with mine. She looked at me, and gave a slight smile. As she turned back to the mural, she began humming a tune. I listened, thinking she was echoing the call to prayer. But, as I paid more attention, the girl broke into English lyrics, "Near, far, wherever you are…" She was singing the theme song to *Titanic* by Celine Dion! I stared in disbelief. She looked back, smiled and continued to sing the familiar tune, without understanding any of the English words. Without hesitation, I joined in, brought back to the world of my distant childhood.

A wave of surreal nostalgia took hold of me as I started yelling the lyrics at the top of my lungs. We were accompanied by the orchestral notes of Celine Dion and the continuing Muslim call to prayer—a chant of irony and beauty. As all the girls joined the singing, we completed the painting of a boy on a striped elephant, an image from her dream. I looked to the snowcapped Syrian mountains of neighboring war-torn Aleppo, and the wintry fields and wandering roads of Rehanli, and realized, with a burst of wind in my face, that life comes full circle.

# Palestine

*United States Consulate General, America House Ramallah Mural: al-Am'ari Palestinian Refugee Camp, United Nations Girls' School, United Nations Relief and Works Agency (UNWRA), Artolution, Ramallah.*

The al-Am'ari Palestinian Refugee Camp was established by the Red Cross and the United Nations in 1949, in the center of the Palestinian capital of Ramallah. Directly outside this camp is a UN Girls' School, which serves over 700 local girls who come from the camp every day. Unlike many other kinds of refugee camps, this camp is composed of huge concrete apartment blocks that have housed upwards of three generations of Palestinians for over half a century. The American Consulate General has an America House outpost in Ramallah, and wanted to create a wall mural in the local refugee school, and a canvas mural for permanent display in the Ramallah America House. However, on the day before the project, a local Palestinian teenager was killed in a riotous conflict with the Israeli military. This postponed the project for a week, and illuminates the instability of everyday life in the region.

As the Consulate vehicle passed through the government checkpoint in the Central Israeli city of Modi'in, with its Los Angeles-style pristine landscaping, I felt as though I had entered a different world of wandering people and fires on the side of the road. After driving through the hectic and congested streets of downtown Ramallah, we arrived outside the barbed-wire-enshrouded al-Am'ari Refugee Camp. The school was flooded with girls and the excitement was palpable. The awaiting principal greeted us with stern encouragement. The theme of this mural was to be about female empowerment, violence against women and female abuse within the local community—prominent issues in the camp. After we presented this topic to the teenage girls, their drawings displayed serious signs of violent abuse as a commonality among the girls. Images ranged from women being beaten, faces with bruises and blood, subservience, and women kneeling in prayer among the cacti. However, along with this darkness, a butterfly emerged, pulling a chained house out of the camp with the chain snapped in two.

During the dialogue, the final idea was to have a "balance scale" in the middle of the wall. One side had a cactus to represent the waiting of the women and the Palestinian people, encircling a sad girl's face. All of the images of abuse and violence were on this side of the scale. On the other side was the butterfly, flying with the broken chain. As the image came to fruition, the response was of immense surprise that the girls could complete such a positive monument to their difficult life situation so quickly.

The strongest impact of the project was the response of the art teacher and the principal. Both stressed a desire to make this model of collaboration sustainable, and to continue painting the whole school. This is the most powerful response adults can have to this kind of initiative. As the painting neared completion, four girls refused to stop, embracing every last second of the experience. Before finally departing, one of them started speaking quickly and radiantly in Arabic, translated by her friend. She said, "I feel like I have found myself through the paint!" With the nods of the other three, the girls walked back to the refugee camp, giggling.

## Syrian/Jordanian border, Jordan

*Azraq Syrian Refugee Camp Mural Series: AptART (Awareness and Prevention Through Art), UNICEF, Mercy Corps and Artolution, Trauma Workshop, Azraq.*

The Azraq Syrian Refugee Camp is one of the most bizarre places on earth. It is a refugee camp that looks like a perfectly gridded, sprawling, white, suburban housing development in the middle of the most desolate and inhospitable desert landscape imaginable. This otherworldly suburbia is composed of white, sheet metal house-shacks that span as far as the eye can see. In the middle is a Western-style supermarket, stocked with food from floor to ceiling where residents can purchase with a ration system. Azraq Camp is designed for over 130,000 refugees, and currently has approximately 7000–12,000 people, with refugees fleeing illegally into Jordan daily. Designed and built by a coalition of international donors and organizations, the camp cost over $64 million to build. However, the Jordanian government only allowed it to be built in the most desolate region of the country, isolated and away from the rest of Jordanian society. Unlike many other refugee camps, this camp did not evolve organically to fit the needs of the inhabitants, but rather, was constructed in a machine-like manner with a Western conception of pragmatism at the forefront. Some people have even chosen to go back to Syria rather than stay in the camp. The dusty endlessness surrounding the refugee camp is broken only by abandoned Bedouin encampments, and bulldozers gouging rock from the earth.

As we entered the lunar-pseudo-suburbia, two heavily armed Jordanian guards checked our car and ultimately allowed us to pass. There was no public transportation within the camp, and people and families wandered in a sea of dust, moving from one corrugated, monopoly house to another. Lone silhouettes of fully covered Muslim Syrians inhabited the landscape in a bizarre inconceivability.

We arrived at the Mercy Corps Adolescent Friendly Space located in Village 3, one of only two sectors inhabited out of an existing six. A glimmering, green, artificial turf football field had been constructed inside a space surrounded with razor-wire, chain-metal fencing. We were greeted warmly and set up a ten-meter canvas along the fence. We prepared containers of paint and began the workshop with 20 of the Syrian boys, who discussed their ideas about the future, and what they wanted to say to the world. We told them that this piece would eventually be cut up and displayed in an international exhibition in Amman and Brussels, where people from around the world would get to see their paintings. This was an opportunity for them to speak to the world.

As the boys began to draw, the images were full of violence and the ravages of war. There were planes dropping bombs, tanks shooting rockets, people with bloody limbs missing, people dying, people being killed, and images revealing a longing to return to Syria, in spite of the war. While looking at the drawings, we discussed how to turn these ideas into something productive. The answer was, "How can we rebuild Syria?" Together, we decided on a simple hammer, a school and a forest of planted trees—basic human desires for the rebuilding of a lost home and a lost life.

The Syrian refugees pray to rebuild Syria, as destruction turns their homeland into an apocalypse. Still, these children have hope. They grabbed onto each morsel of positive attention as we painted together, enjoying a simple and earnest smile, or a pat on the back. It was as if the world was somehow being reborn, if only for a second. But that second turned into hours as the canvas came to life and became an artifact made by the hands of a homeless generation.

One of the boys had burns across his entire neck, torso and arms. Another had a scar the size of my index finger from his ear to his nose. Still, they danced to the beat of Bob Marley and the Beatles' joyful tambour, in the middle of the blistering sun. The sadness is not the trauma; it's the not knowing. Refugees can hope to return home, but they wake up in the morning, still homeless. Their life is a life of waiting.

I spoke to two of the most inspired boys, and asked them to think of how they might integrate creativity into their lives. Although very excited, they replied: "But we have no brushes or paint." This is a serious problem in the camp; the lack of basic materials. For many of these children, war has been the status quo and their suffering comes in the form of boredom, in the middle of nowhere-land. They are cursed to sit endlessly in the waiting room outside the door of war.

I was struck by how this traumatized community was full of repression, frustration and depression. The focus was not on the future but on the past. Many of these children had been taught that forgiveness only comes through martyrdom. Constructive building is difficult when the focus is on directed discontent. For example, when a child misbehaved, all would point and yell "Da'esh," the Arabic word for ISIS (Islamic State). What will happen to these Syrian refugee children? Many neighboring countries fear they will become like the Palestinians, never able to return home, yet never able to integrate.

I was honored to witness the energy and hope in the eyes of these children. They longed for an uncomplicated childhood, and were surprised by my attention. I asked the local Mercy Corps translator, Bassam, why he thought this part of the world had so much violence. He looked at me and replied "Islam. Not the true or real Islam, but the distortion and perversion of it." As I absorbed his words, my thoughts were interrupted by the boom of a UN bulldozer and the calls to prayer from a blue tower. When we asked the refugee children how they were, they responded in Arabic, with "Humdi'allah: Thankful are we to God." This gratitude forces hopeful appreciation, and becomes the norm.

As I was watching a man drag his tiny daughter by the ear across the desert, screaming all the way, I noticed a boy sitting quietly by the corner of the canvas, painting by himself. He was painting a truck with a missile launcher on top, and next to it, a boy holding a kite high in the air. One might ask: "What is the impact of art in a situation of dire consequences and a lack of basic necessities?" If one child can find inspiration and be able to deal with trauma in a more reflective way, then it is a release of what has been experienced, and a potential catalyst for a next step.

The morning began bright and early. We were met with excitement and the high-pitched songs of teenage girls, ready to begin work on their mural. We ended up jumping together to the beat of the language. When looking at these girls with their flashing eyes outlined in eyeliner and their bright hijabs accented by the blistering white of the dessert, they looked as if they were from a movie. Their smiles exposed lip-glossed lips, stretched over rotting teeth. One girl, Rooba, reminded me of Greta Garbo, a 1930s film star, ready to bedazzle the world. The reality is, these people were simply born in the wrong country at the wrong time, and the humanity of each child must always remain at the core of decisions, even when made on a large scale. At times, it can be inevitable that people become numbers, statistics, sectors and strategic goals in graphs and charts.

I walked into the structure designated as the Adolescent Friendly Space (AFS), past the dusty and torn sandals piled at the entrance. The girls were sitting quietly in a circle with a baby in the center. All eyes turned to me and the baby was handed to me without a word. The green-eyed leader of the AFS pointed to the mother; a 13-year-old child. I looked at the girl clad in purple, while the baby gazed up at me with an expression of serenity. The child-mother stared at me with eyes of silence. Teenage girls are often married off at a young age for a price. I would never know this girl's story, but as I returned the baby to her, I forgot all I had ever known about the innocence of childhood.

I grabbed the paint that was left from the end of the day and went to the guarded entrance of the compound, joined by a couple of the girls. On the corrugated metal wall, an image of a blue sleeping mother swaddling a baby emerged in a circle, the water of the earth. The mother levitated above a shadow, her feet in a triangle pointing down towards the earth. The painting was a dedication to the mothers in the camp, and to the child-mother whose baby had looked up, with the eyes of a tiny prophet, holding the promise of a future generation.

# India

*Shanti Arts in Action Program, Foundstrument Soundstrument and Mural Project: Give a Hand Foundation, Vidya Centre, Artolution, Okhla Phase I, Indira Camp, South Delhi.*

My first experience of India was driving from Delhi airport into the night. As we drove the wrong way down a bustling, one-way street, red traffic lights seemed to be irrelevant, a thing from my past. There were rusted holes in the floor of the taxi and the driver was wearing no shoes. We just missed a man pushing a dilapidated, ancient wheelbarrow of cell phone adaptors, among the trash-eating cows.

As we drove, pollution was everywhere. The thick air of Delhi was like a mist. Roadside trash fires burned underneath the congested electrical lines up above, and streetlights showered clouds of dust in cones of light. The small particles of everything in the city entered my lungs like a wave of small, crawling creatures.

India is not a place to be romanticized. We stopped in traffic, and I saw a small group of men gathered around a fallen motorcycle. A man was lying on the ground in a crimson oval of blood that encircled his head and body on the dirt-covered street. The man was dead. This was stated very simply by my driver, who looked on calmly at this everyday event.

As we continued to drive, people flooded the darkness like fish in an aquarium of soupy dust. At a traffic circle, with a bustling cycle of constant action, I arrived at my destination, in a neighborhood named Lajpat Nagar. Trees covered the front of the building and it felt like a haven among the honking and over-populated urbanism.

On the first day, as we entered Okhla Phase I, the largest slum community in Delhi, we were greeted by smiling faces and curious stares. Outside the walls of the center were busy streets with cows, rickshaws and brightly clad people. However, inside the center it was tranquil, with the faces of each child who had seen worlds within worlds.

We had brought with us, as a gift, half of the canvas comprising the international exchange mural, originally created in Jackson Heights, Queens, New York, by 15 local young painters. The canvas had been intentionally painted in two halves, with messages written in Spanish on one half, which later went to Peru, and Hindi on the other half, which came with us to India.

We presented this half to the children in the Vidya Centre in Indira Camp, Okhla, as a permanent gift to the Centre. Videos and photography of the group from Queens were then shown to the children. A conversation was ignited about what the exchange mural would be, to take back with us to the kids in Queens. The idea arose of a mural of conversations between two men and two women, one on either side of the Indian flag, written in different-sized letters in Hindi. These were painted over a colored ground of different tones of green. A traditionally patterned mountain range, river, sun and trees also emerged.

More than 20 participants worked on this piece over three days, and the mural was presented at the Shanti Arts final performance. This included the canvas mural, two large-scale wall murals and a foundstrument, with music and dance choreographed and created by the children. Over 100 kids gathered in front of the mural displayed for the closing ceremony.

Half of the canvas mural made in Jackson Heights, Queens, greets everyone who walks into the main entrance of the Vidya Centre, in Okhla, Delhi. The other half of the mural that went to Peru was collaboratively painted by a community in Callao, Lima, Peru, and this international "canvas conversation" mural now resides in the Joseph Pulitzer School in Queens, New York.

The second collaborative art project with the Shanti Arts in Action was the creation of the foundstrument, which comprised a multi-stage process. The first stage was the collection of trashed materials from the local trash dump. The second was cleaning and painting all of the objects, and the final step was to assemble all of these objects into a single sculpture designed to be played as a single percussive, interactive sculpture.

When the painting of the objects began, each object took on its own life, and the goal seemed logical to the children, who focused on pattern-making in teams. Participation was enthusiastic, from the youngest to the oldest. The tactile experience of individually painting random objects as part of a larger project was significant. It was a strong unifier for youth of all genders, who are traditionally divided. The task of having to completely cover seemingly ugly discarded industrial trash in beautiful color was sublime. It was meditative, therapeutic and satisfying.

Construction was the next step in the process. I knew we would need a drill, and enquired if there was someone who could lend us one. I was told the neighboring industrial shop in Indira Camp might have one we could borrow. We walked over to this tiny hole-in-the-wall shop, where even the air felt coated in black motor oil. The dirty but smiling industrial men gladly agreed to help, and pointed to their "drill machine." I looked down at the dirty floor to see an oil-encrusted hammer-drill. The cord was attached with raw wires to a car battery, with an open live cable. There was no power switch, but instead a taped wire light switch. This was then attached to a metal welding generator. There was no power plug, and the machine had one speed, drill hard. I thanked the men, and went back to the center with drill machine in hand.

We gathered all the young sculptors to hear the instructions, and the interest heightened about each stage of the construction process. The foundstrument process is composed of many smaller techniques, which work as a single collage of sculptural assemblage. Each of these different stages requires different skills, and different amounts of time, strength, dexterity and focus. Due to this, I knew that the pre-adolescents and teenagers would separate by their interest levels. However, I did not know how this would manifest. All the boys and girls were gathered around, riveted by how all of these painted objects could come together in a single sculpture.

Silent attention reigned over the young sculptors as the wire-cutters, handsaw and drill were shown. Through simple demonstration I explained how the objects could be drilled into, and then attached with plastic zip-ties and wire to the painted poles and wood. I then demonstrated how we were going to attach the frame. All of the participants nodded their heads in excitement when asked if they understood the process. Immediately, the girls and the boys separated into different groups, with different roles. All the girls grabbed the objects and set up an organized workstation where they attentively put zip-ties through all the object holes. They organically assembled different stations where one group of girls put the zip-ties into the objects and a second group attached them to the giant painted tree branch. As the seemingly random placement of objects began to take shape, there was a great enthusiasm to make sure that every object collected was attached to one of two sticks. As the girls sat in two perfect sets of seated-ovals, their quiet resolve brought a smile to my face.

As the girls were calmly working together, the boys took a very different formation. One group went to cut the important pieces of wood, and the other to assemble the skeleton of the foundstrument creature. I went to an area off to the side with three of the older boys, and demonstrated how to use the 65-rupee (1 dollar) handsaw. After making eye contact with each of the boys, with a head nod, I entrusted them with the task. As the boys got to work, they created a threesome with self-appointed responsibility, where two boys worked on either side of the wood, like little lumberjacks, while the other boy held the wood further back.

The other group of boys was eagerly waiting, laughing and tickling each other. I showed them how we were going to attach the central frame, and how to hold the pieces of wood firmly. They jumped around it, and put all their might into collectively holding the pieces of brightly painted, found wood together. Every eye was on my hand as I put the drill machine up to the pink, yellow and light turquoise striped wood. One of the boys needed to turn on the light switch wired into the drill, to be able to activate it. A different set of boys was holding every object that needed to be drilled, with ten hands per object, all safely out of the way. As I demonstrated how to use the drill, each boy was given a chance to try the construction tool, and the tasks switched hands fluidly.

Luxman was a boy unlike any boy I had ever worked with. Although quiet, his enthusiasm for constructing objects was remarkable. He was able to use the drill like a magician. Something special happened when metal was brought to wood. Midway through the project, Luxman came in with a rag covering his face. Considering the horrific pollution, it didn't seem a surprise, although none of the other kids had done this. The rag fell down once, to show huge gashes across his entire face, as though his face had been smashed in. I was immediately concerned that there may have been a severe issue with domestic violence of some kind. When I asked the center head, he explained that the boy had been attacked while sleeping by a large howler monkey. It had bitten him in the face—a petrifying reality for many children sleeping in uncovered areas.

As Luxman healed, his excitement for the foundstrument was palpable. He continued to pre-drill holes throughout the sculpture. Another group of boys was set on the task of creating the head of the creature. As they started to wire the different sections together, the visible manifestation of bringing a trash "being" to life triggered incredible engagement. Each attached object, further spurred the imagination of what other objects could be used to create facial features.

After looking at the progress of the foundstrument's head, I realized that more objects were needed. We rounded up the troops and assembled a group to go out into Indira Camp. There was a controversy over whether the girls were going to be allowed to come. Throughout the project, the primary theme for the murals and performances was violence against girls and children's rights. Javed, the traditional and custom-following director of the center, was not a fan of the idea of having all genders going out into the community together. However, when his wife Khosum was asked, she thought it was a good idea. To uphold the values we had been discussing, we made a push for the eager girls to be able to come out into the community for our final trash-picking run. Karla, Artolution's director of the play and dance, agreed to come to provide female support.

As we entered the first piled recycling area, or Kibati Valla, three burly and dust-encrusted men sitting around a trash fire looked at us and all shook their heads in unison. When asked why, they told us to leave immediately. Our primary translators, Punkaj and Kevin, explained they were dealing in illegal objects and were probably using the place as a front for black market drugs. As we continued, we came upon a slightly larger Kibati Valla, next to an open sewage stream and a dirt road. We needed to use some extreme haggling to keep the price at a reasonable amount for the rolling chair bases, metal buckets, fans and even a rusted bicycle wheel—a commodity hard to find in these parts. After we called the director of the children's center and had him talk to the junk dealer, we were able to settle on a fair price. The 20 kids each grabbed everything they could with both hands.

With an aura of victory among the group, the boys and girls began to sing, dance and bang on the objects with the fervor of a celebratory extravaganza as we walked back from the trash dump. The people in the slum community looked at us as though we were crazy, and this was an encouraging communal component to the adventure. The children walked through the streets with a sense of pride, an accomplishment of simple joy and absurdity. The percussive banging erupted into a parade with Hindi singing and dancing, the objects waving in the air like a real-life Bollywood movie. This improvized celebration, led to the entrance of the Vidya Centre, and all the trash instruments were thrown into a pile next to the skeleton of the creature.

Within two hours, everything that was collected was cleaned and covered in thick patterned layers of color, according to the sounds of the objects. The boys who had been building the head were overcome with imagination as they sorted through to create the elements of the face. All of the participants chose locations to put these colorful musical organs within the larger composition of a living musical creature. Progress was rapid, with the girls having an emphasis on attaching things, and the boys putting objects onto the larger frame.

Javed and the kids joked about how funny it would be to have something like a car door on the piece. I was able to arrange for a friend, Rohan, to be able to take me to Mayapuri, the largest industrial trash zone in Delhi. Rohan explained that this was one of the most polluted and littered areas of the city. As we drove to the outskirts of this super city, we parked and adorned breathing masks. We began to haggle for a good price with a slew of hardened vendors; we found a kind man who agreed to sell us a crimson car door, an industrial fan and a complicated plastic-molded piece for a reasonable price. As we drove back to Okhla, the community center's entrance was surrounded by an illegal rickshaw "parking lot" run by the center's guard. We unloaded the new materials and his three sons grabbed the door with looks on their faces as though the rusted car door was gold. Luxman, the middle child, brought his younger brother out and they began to bang on the door, along with the other objects, with glee. The guard, a weathered man with a long white mustache and red head wrap, nodded his head in silent approval.

When it came time to paint the door, Khulsum, the center coordinator, said she wanted to lead the painting of it in a traditional Indian textile pattern. A couple of girls joined her and within half an hour, this rusted red door became a beautiful artifact, which drew the praise of the whole center. After lunch, the intense process of trying to attach this beautifully painted door needed to be left to only the most dedicated. Three girls rose to the occasion. They were willing to sit with industrial wire and attach every hole to the built frame—an impressive task, considering how the role of women physically building is viewed in many parts of traditional Indian society. As I watched these three long-haired girls calmly doing an exceptional job, I couldn't help but smile.

Finally, we needed to add the magical wands of the project: the drumsticks. We were able to get the smallest girls into a circle where they painted each stick with spiraling colors. They almost looked like a knitting circle of tiny girls. The sticks were then put on a board to dry. We then drilled holes into each stick with some of the older boys. A group of three boys were given instructions how to take metal cable and smash connectors into place in order to hold the stick solidly to the foundstrument. Each group had their role, and once complete, we brought the sticks to the sculpture.

This foundstrument creature was built between two trees in front of a tall concrete wall with a metal fence along the top. Each of the cables was looped around the iron fence, and the connectors were smashed into place using bricks. We needed a strength test, so on completion, each cable needed to be able to have two kids pulling with their entire weight on it, and only then would each drumstick be solidly attached. In total, 18 sticks were attached.

When the sculpture-making was coming to a close, one of the girls quietly approached me, and asked if she could use the drill. She was the only girl to take the initiative to ask, although all the girls had been invited, and it brought me joy for her to conclude the project. She held the drill machine in her hands, accented by her ornate traditional scarf and bindi. As she clasped her finger around the trigger, the whirr of the machine brought a smile to her face. Luxman helped to guide the drill, supporting on the side, and I stood back and watched. They completed hole after hole together and we collectively attached a series of wooden boards, painted by the younger children, to the base. On completing the last board, she put the drill down, and uttered a simple, "Thank you, sir." A big handshake concluded the session, as she walked away out of the gate and down the chaotic road into Indira Camp.

To conclude the day, a sweet and smiley boy named Ajit, who was traditionally trained in Hindu religious percussion, began a complicated hand-banging technique on the ornate car door. We all watched in amazement as his hands quickly darted around the door like an old master of the tabla. It was a melodic rhythm that showed the calm side of the foundstrument.

On the final day of the project, all the participating kids were very enthusiastic to play on the new giant creature. From behind, this gigantic creature dwarfed the children, looking to be the size of a sitting giant. This giant now sits among three giant mural-covered walls, and an environment that gives context to the stories, which have surrounded the Shanti Arts Project. The first mural tells the story of a girl's journey through the challenges of Indian society, to the empowered image of what the children want to see for the future treatment of women in their country. The second mural depicts a boy and a girl with torches lighting a fire. This fire is coming out of a book with kids sitting around it in a circle. One of the children has their hand raised, symbolizing the importance of education in a place where child labor is common. They are both sitting in a river composed of waves, each painted by a different child, displaying the importance of children's rights in this community. Through paint and sculpture, the story of this experience transformed the space into an interactive story.

The final performance of the children included a play about gender issues and children's rights, a series of dances and a series of short speeches given by the facilitators. Before the speeches, each of the facilitators was blessed with a wreath of flowers and a red dot between the eyes, with a small flower. The finished piece was received with gratitude and love. After the play was complete, the finale was the playing of the foundstrument. However, after the finishing dance, the children were unable to contain their emotion, and they rushed up to Karla, all crying about the completion of the project. This sent the whole group into an emotional whirlwind, where they swarmed around the three facilitators with hugs and tears. Caught up in the motion of the experience, I was unable to facilitate the foundstrument playing as expected. But with the subtle movement of the crowd towards the base of the foundstrument, I was able to make a single beat with the drum, and the crowd erupted in a symphony of percussion. One of the older boys led the group in what sounded like a slightly Latin Reggaeton beat among traditional Hindi music playing from the loudspeaker. The joy of the music brought children of all ages together in celebration and the magic of percussive expression.

After the celebration was complete, many of the kids could not bring themselves to leave the reality we had created together. Going back to their "normal" lives was a difficult process for many of them. They gathered around as we packed up our gear, Luxman, Ajit, Punkaj and many more. I brought all of the most dedicated participants around in a circle, to make some concluding statements about the foundstrument. I explained that objects may come off or break, and even some of the sticks could split apart. Attrition is part of the foundstrument, and it was important that they keep it alive by fixing anything that breaks. I also told them that we were going to donate all of the tools and extra materials to the center for them to use so that they could keep their sculpture living and in good working order. The emphasis was that it was theirs. They built it, and they were the ones who would continue to bring it to life. I explained that this included finding new objects, and keeping it as a constantly growing creature to maintain its percussive health.

The group all nodded their heads in understanding after translation. I made sure to make eye contact with each individual, so that they understood the importance of each statement. There was a quiet and intense acknowledgement of this final conversation, which was imparted unto the disciples of the future life of the Okhla foundstrument. This last comment was a critical part of the process as it set the seed for future action. Rather than viewing the project as complete, it is a spark for unlimited addition and growth based on inspired interaction and resourceful creativity.

I have never encountered a more emotional goodbye in my entire life. Having ten teenage boys surround me in a group hug, all crying, was a revelation. I felt my shell of conditioned hardness softening to the point of breaking with the overflow of emotion. Rather than staying on the outside as an observer, I chose to let the emotions in and sweep me away in a wave of overwhelming acceptance.

I could not help but wonder what it would be like to be a child who gets to interact closely for two weeks with foreign artists, transforming the space they go to every day. What happens when this bubble of creativity leaves, and one is left with the reality of life? What happens to the boy who has the glimmer of a professional dancer in his eye, or the girl who could be a world-renowned sculptor if born into another world? What shifts have been made, and how can this be tracked? Long-term follow-up contact with the directors, participants and coordinators of the Vidya Centre will help us discover some answers.

There will inherently be a certain percentage of very talented kids in any group. The key is to provide the opportunity for trans-disciplinary expression. This allows the children who have strengths to shine. If one can utilize different techniques of engagement, the opportunity for encouragement and validation grows. This project allowed children to express themselves in a variety of modalities, which magnetized different children. The key is to create a final conclusion, which brings all of the different elements together into a single cohesive culmination. This project did this in a way that can act as a model for future planned projects.

Many of these children's families were surviving on less than two dollars a day. By the standards of international geo-political theory, this would be constituted as poverty. However, physical poverty and emotional poverty are different from one another. The children of this community were emotionally rich with open acceptance, emotional intelligence and self-expression, which is innately suppressed in many other parts of the world. This engagement manifested as a special celebration and emotional connection that I believe is unique to this special place.

# France

*Calais Jungle Refugee Camp Mural: Artolution, Pikey Wrongstockings, and PArt of Us.*

The Calais Jungle Refugee Camp in France is a series of approximately nine informal encampments, the major site located on a former landfill. These camps arose spontaneously, formed by migrants from many countries wishing to attempt to enter Britain illegally from France, on lorries, ferries, cars or trains. In 2016, when we were working there, conditions were poor, with no formal accommodation, and typically with no proper sanitation or washing facilities. Food was supplied by charity kitchens. Eventually, approximately 10,000 migrants were evacuated from the encampment and it was closed.

During our project, there were no organized, official non-governmental organizations working in the camp, and there was no real security when a difficult situation arose. This brutal refugee camp existed right along side a "posh" housing development and an industrial factory. There was a constant threat of the French military raiding and beating up the inhabitants and burning large spaces of the camp, leaving everybody homeless. A gigantic wall was built to keep the refugees in and out. With ethnic divisions prevalent, people were on edge and were easy to set off. Women and children stayed out of sight, and only adult males were free to walk around. Cigarettes were a way of trading and dealing with the constant stress.

Around the outside of the camp the French countryside was very green. It was a strange perspective to see two people, in pristine, head-to-toe polo outfits, riding perfectly maintained horses, as they left their gated home, to walk along the camp, next to the most severe poverty in the country. Adjacent to the refugee camp, there was a hill with the silhouettes of dark men standing alone, underneath the shade of the trees, in a dispersed line. Each of the figures was in the traditional pose of the contemporary world, with hands grasping a phone, and eyes glued to miniature screens. But there were also many attempts at eye-to-eye contact, the longing for interaction of people fleeing war, and looking at each other. They also looked up to the giant industrial tower, with smoke from the factory's chimney in the distance.

The possibility of danger was present throughout the art workshop, so all the participants were young men, as virtually no women were on the shanty streets. Male frustration ran high. All of the Sudanese men spoke Arabic, and were very excited to be greeted in Arabic, which I had learned when I was working in the Middle East. This was a challenging project, with a lot of raw emotion evident. Two boys took my photo and got into a massive argument about who got to look at it; they almost came to blows before I managed to separate them. As the project began, an Afghani man, face covered with a khafia, stole a bucket of paint, brushes and a roller from our project. I went after him, telling him we needed the materials for the mural. I got them back from him, but he grabbed me hard by the shoulder and screamed "Run away" over and over. He started to follow me until I was back in the view of the mural painting group. Then he turned around and walked away. One day, a deaf and mute man became very angry because someone had painted over his painting, with the words "One love, one blood." His response was to be very angry with me, and blame me for his discontent, and push me. His issue was with respect, and it took a lot of negotiation to convince him I had meant no offense. By having an extensive conversation via text on his mini-cellphone inside the tent enclosure of a local Sudanese man, we made slight amends.

But there was huge joy too, especially from the Sudanese population, who painted many images of hope and of their homes and animals. Many of the Afghani men painted their names and flags— nationalistic symbols in red, green and black. In the mural, a giant red swastika was painted in the center, likely referencing tribal traditions in Sudan. A very tall Sudanese man then intricately painted a Star of David in the center. He said it represented Israel. I asked him what he thought about Israel. He responded that he did not think highly of Israel, but unexpectedly felt a need to paint this.

As I walked around the camp, I was called Rasta, which stuck as a nickname. There were mixed responses to me, being from the United States. However, many residents also wore shirts from New York, and New York Yankees hats. There was an emphasis on handshakes, hugs and physical affection, especially as I am a man willing to have social conversation with people of all strata of refugee society. The refugee men and boys were extremely excited to interact with the project, and had a positive response when eye contact was made and the local language was attempted—Pashtu, Dari or Arabic. On one of the days, I had a silent conversation with a deaf boy from Eritrea, through painting an abstract painting, mark by mark, going back and forth for a half-hour through colored forms as a mode of communication. The smile on his face was incredible. The next day I saw him with bandages on his arms, hands and back. He explained that he had been stabbed and beaten. The look on his face was of a pained and silent resilience.

The people in this camp were truly memorable. There was a small Afghani man who took his time to meticulously draw a perfect flower on the mural. Each mark he made with dedication. He showed signs of being on the autism spectrum or having survived serious trauma, or both. His green eyes were sunken deeply into his face on either side of a hooked nose, and he alternated amiable smiles with looks of deep worry. Another man who had had to flee was an applied mathematician, trained in Eritrea. Many of the men were highly educated, just born into the wrong situation.

Two 13-year-old Afghani boys painted with me daily, and talked about their four-month journeys, including their perspectives on language, culture and life. One of the boys had a lot of aggression, which he took out on the nearby punch bag directly after painting. Sometimes, it was difficult for me to get the attention of the children, because of the local football games and other activities. But the most dedicated painters made a big effort to be involved in the wall-painting process. They started by laying down the background. Then all the participants began drawing. The design concept arose, and it became a gorilla, with the body of a tiger and a full dragon emerging from its back. Inside were images of hometowns, huts, shacks and trees.

One day, I had a very intense hour-long conversation with K. He confided what it felt like to be treated as an animal, with food and shelter in a cage. He told of his experience of coming to France from Sudan. He spoke of being beaten by the French police, and that he would have hoped for fair treatment of people in the camp. He also spoke of the importance of how he was raised, with his indigenous beliefs. He felt discriminated against, being neither Muslim nor Christian. K said he saw how hate had come with many religions, and talked about how many of the people in the camp "hate the Hebrews" and talked about killing them; and yet they had no idea they were interacting with underground Jews on an everyday basis. Ironically, there was an orthodox rabbi and his wife working in the refugee camp without any of the refugees knowing. They were putting out the subtle signs of being Jewish and were trying to create a kind of "summer camp." One of the camp members was singing "salam," in the place of "shalom," to the traditional Jewish summer camp melody. He then followed up with "One Day" by Matisyahu on the guitar, with all Muslims surrounding him, not knowing the origin of the tune.

One night, we had dinner at Abdul's house, a shack made with loving care and attention. We ate beautiful Sudanese home cooking that his mother had taught him to make over an open fire. David, an Ethiopian man who fled with his wife because of political persecution, told us of how he had lost his baby during the seven years of trying to find asylum. The baby had been lost under a bus while trying to cross the Libyan border. He explained what it was like to be put in slavery in a work camp in Libya during his imprisonment there, and how they were able to escape.

It rained in the camp. The grey gave an aura of depression. Trash fires would burn in the dumpsters. But the children were captivated by the Hapi meditation drum, and some were addicted to its sensation, and could not stop themselves from playing it non-stop. Many of the children just needed simple, supportive contact, in a healthy way—testament to the resilience that children can embody. Many of them did, however, exhibit serious signs of abuse and trauma. We used the paint as a medium to express anger, from mark to mark, with major movement of our entire bodies.

The kind-natured way of the Sudanese population was touching. The men put a huge effort into learning English and French—one of the outlets and opportunities to productively work towards a future and heal from their trauma. Marco and Demarko, a Kurdish refugee and a Nigerian migrant, created a school for the children and it grew slowly with the help of volunteers. Marco said he wanted people to feel welcome in the art project. He asked if we could write "We Love You," in gigantic orange letters at the highest part of the tallest tent, so that all who enter could see the words So I climbed to the top of the tent and painted the words as large as possible. The words pointed in the direction of the French police who were stationed there 24 hours a day.

Although work on the mural progressed well, there were elements of uncomfortable situations that arose in the camp. For example, the Afghanis were known to be the most violent in the camp and they ran a kind of mafia. Once, they told me that all of the problems in their country were the fault of the British, French and the Jews. They had no idea about me being Jewish, and didn't ask any questions about my opinions around their political ideas.

I met a man named Ahmed who was from Syria, who told me the story of his fleeing the Assad regime, who were looking for him. His 11-year-old son had been tortured, his arms burned, cut and mutilated because his father had previously served in the military. There were stories about how life was better in France in the camp than at home.

When the children had the opportunity to paint, they went wild with the color in a very aggressive way. Using the color as a way to take out visceral emotions and communicate raw feelings on the wall helped relieve them. Squirting paint directly out of the tube was a way to express frustration. When paint or brushes were available, there was a huge need for ownership, and they became a representation of owning something tangible. There was also evidence of destructive ways of painting, and the intentional use of paint to destroy what other children had done. Paint became a source of power, but showing signs of aggression wherever possible through paint could be seen as a healthy form of acting out in large-scale expression.

Two young Syrian boys, for example, came to paint, both with significant energy. They had very assertive tendencies, and were adamant they needed to spray paint. When they started, there was a flurry of using the spray frantically and watching the paint come out of the can. Then when they started on the large wall, they put a huge amount of time and effort into creating a simple yet poignant image of an iconic home and a child.

I brought out Tra, the puppetry "paint creature," and when it came out, the general reaction was one of aggression and immediate attack. Many of the children had to try and remove Tra's face-covering, to see who was inside (although I was able to avoid the attempts). There was a large amount of hitting and violent behavior towards Tra, and a group mentality became the response. In the front of the "classroom" tent, some of the children were too afraid to be close to Tra. There was mixed imaginative response, with some not able to believe that Tra was real, and some letting themselves fall into the magic, taken to a whole other world.

Music also took the inhabitants of the camp to another world. For example, the depression of months and months of waiting had a heavy affect on Moosa, the local hip-hop artist. As we discussed the impossible nature of his situation, he spoke of how hopeless his life felt. His facial expression would shift from intense pain to happiness, and back. He took the opportunity to play the Hapi drum at the project, with his expression moving between tears and curiosity. With giant scars across his arms, face, mouth and hands, his hands slowly played the drum.

Each displaced person's situation had deep-rooted similarities, while also having their own unique conflicts. Whether it was the mandatory conscription of Eritrea, or the ongoing wars of Afghanistan, or the Taliban of Pakistan, or the civil war in Sudan and Syria, violence was the common challenge that drove all the inhabitants of the camp to the northern tip of France.

For the men, waiting became a way of life. Many people were in a haze of frustration. There was the strange irony of seeing people whose homelands had been colonized by Great Britain begging to go to the country that had planted the seeds of conflict in their countries by dividing up the lines. The problem of displacement is eternal.

Everyone had dreams. K, for example, wanted to become a humanitarian aid worker, to become educated. Rashid, was an incredibly talented artist. Moosa rapped about his journey, his struggles and his life. From the beginning of the first day till the last, he brought music and meaning to a gathering based on the arts. Painting, music, dance and storytelling all began to form new memories, which were voiced by the men of the camp.

The arts grew in the camp, reflecting how important a collective creative outlet can be for the traumas of displacement and stagnation that have spread across the world, even when camps are temporary. Since we departed, the camp has been burned down and disbanded by the French police. All the murals were burned and destroyed. What is left are the relationships and the memories that came from this transformative segment of time.

## Greece

*Samos Refugee Camp Mural and Foundstrument: We Are One Collective, Calais Action, Friendly Humans Samos, United Nations High Commissioner for Refugees (UNHCR) and Artolution.*

This refugee camp on the island of Samos in Greece is ironically known as "the Paradise Prison." It is carved into the rock of a mountain. As I looked out onto the emerald Mediterranean Sea, the incredible view was sliced by barbed razor-wire that cut across the landscape.

The heat was stifling, and people milled slowly about. There was a strange aura of quiet during this project. At the time, the camp was officially run by international organizations, with offices inside shipping containers. However, there were very few humanitarian aid workers to be seen, even during the standard 9–5 day. There were huge questions as to what was actually being done here.

As we walked through the rows of haphazardly strewn tents, containers, fences and circles of wire, we came upon a series of tents, burned black. A massive riot had previously erupted between two violent sects, causing the destruction of many of the buildings, primarily in the center of the camp. It seemed that, from our discussions regarding the current issues, the systemic problems of this camp largely came from the inability of the international agencies to work together with the local authorities, and with the difficulty of functioning within the slow, relaxed pace of Greek island time, amid severe conflict-ridden adversity.

Yet as is the way of children, they all ran up in greeting. Many had massive scars across their faces and arms. Colorful humor penetrated everything, cutting through the darkness. For example, Majida, the teacher with whom we worked, cracked a smile when I told her about my work on the Jordanian/Syrian border in Za'atari and Azraq Refugee Camps. She said, "Oh, its much more dangerous here. Here, you have to deal with me!"

The small makeshift school she had started was ill-equipped to deal with the hundreds of children in the camp, but she did all that she could. Many people had been waiting to leave the camp for four or five months, when originally they had thought it might be four or five days. The local people living on the island of Samos would ask me, "What can we do to help?" This was an incredibly different response from those living around the Calais Jungle Refugee Camp. There, in France, we had been forced to hide our work from the public because of xenophobic retaliatory actions. But here, the Greeks were in a far worse economic situation, yet they had a deeply rooted sense of mutual co-existence, especially for such a small island, so ill-equipped to handle the number of refugees arriving.

There were constant ironies and paradoxes in Samos. It is a developing vacation island, and almost-naked European couples could be seen riding their Vespa scooters directly across from the refugee camp, where religiously garbed Muslims stood, completely covered. There was the paradox of local luxury, yet there was no water in the taps at the camp. When it came, it was dirty water, which gave children hepatitis. In this environment, eternal waiting—for help, change and resources—became a way of life. No matter where you went, people were waiting. Some had become stateless, others were the stateless of the stateless people, such as the Palestinians fleeing from Syria.

Yet the collaborative partners on this project, Pru from Wales and Saleh from Ireland and Palestine, stated that they had never seen the children so attentive and silent as during the art project. Once again, the Hapi drum attracted the squinting eyes of the children. On the first note, it was as though silence overtook the chaos of the camp. When asked for their visual stories, the children made many drawings of many boats and journeys lived. Images of houses—that iconic and eternal symbol of "home"—began to spread across the mural.

An older girl, Jana (meaning "Paradise" in Arabic), came up and started speaking to me in fluent English. She was Palestinian, but she had never actually experienced life in Palestine. Actually, she had never lived outside a camp, as she had been born in a Lebanese refugee camp. Under her pristine white hijab was an incredibly sharp mind ready to take on the world. When I asked what kinds of dreams we needed to put on the mural, she exclaimed with a smile her dream of becoming an astronaut. As we began the mural, she relished the opportunity of being the official translator. She provided instructions to the others for the painting. With honor in every syllable, it was she who explained to the older, middle-aged men exactly what to do.

At the end of one of the long days, I walked down the narrow Greek street, arm in arm with a smiling woman in a white hijab, bantering away about the ways of the world. Majida was a Palestinian woman, fleeing from Syria, who had the wry wit of an aged sailor. The tourists stared at us, this strange, paint-covered pair. She shared with me the wisdom of her grandmother, who said there are only five kinds of people in the world: those who were animals, who lived from day to day; those who were trees, who took from the world and then gave back; those who were stones, who never let anyone in; those who were children, who saw the world with wonder; and lastly, those who were artists, who made life a reflection of itself, and who searched for meaning every day.

As with the other art projects in other camps, a huge amount of preparation time had been dedicated to the logistical organization of mural and sculptural materials, and most importantly how to distribute them, specifically in this environment where even the smallest piece of string was of value. The paint had its own value of ownership, which was an opportunity to emphasize sharing. As each day began, the children waited attentively. Just the process of bringing out the objects needed for painting was an endeavor full of excitement and curiosity for the children.

With such large numbers of children involved in the project, the problem of how to spread our attention equally was magnified, especially amid adversity. Normally in the camps, people are grouped into sections, by language, culture or family structure. However, in art projects, it is different. All people can participate at the same time and this was a very unique sensation. There were also opportunities for the genders to mix. There was, for example, a moment when a Pashtun-speaking Afghani man painted with an Arabic-speaking Palestinian-Syrian teenage girl. They painted in unison, two different sides of the same image, watching their two brushes move as one—a situation that in many other contexts would not have been deemed appropriate, and would have been considered to be a contravention of a cultural, age and gender divide. Yet through painting the front wall together, the entire paradigm of what is "allowed" was "allowed" to shift.

Some of the children could be quite disruptive, yet one of the most violent children showed huge concentration while painting the dumpster, making polka dots as a form of healthy expression for his aggression. After a long day's work, we gathered underneath the olive tree, sitting on an abandoned mattress, with the UNHCR tarpaulin above us. The heat of the day slowed down our interactions with one other. But the heat was a great opportunity to capitalize on the calm needed for meditatively painting patterns.

Over time, the children put such a huge amount of faith in me that large-scale art could accomplish something mysterious and exciting, despite trauma. The truth is that attention given to any child is an essential part of learning how to interact in a healthy way. "Sheshera" was the name that befell me from the mouths of these children; they called me "tree" because of my hair, which resembles tree branches.

One afternoon Mirvan, our local Syrian partner, had spoken about how it had been a terrible day—he and his wife and baby had been denied asylum yet again. As the trash was laid out in the blistering heat of the sun, he started painting simple yellow circles on every object. Circle after circle, he painted in meticulous patterns. This sense of meditation is a way of being part of something larger, while dealing with the personal problems inside one's head. He voiced how painting made him feel at peace, even though it felt as though his life was "falling apart in purgatory."

We started one of our days with a conversation with three women from Africa: Eritrea, Sudan and Ethiopia. The lead woman was known as "Mama Africa." She told us that where we had been painting the day before was where they prayed, and that they didn't want us working there. Pru, the local facilitating partner, let me know that this was a small Christian minority who felt oppressed and marginalized throughout the camp. Because of this, any kind of conflict or ethnic tension needed to be avoided. They were only in that spot in the morning, and the rest of the better part of the day the location stayed empty, but these were the kinds of compromises that needed to be made in order to avoid anyone feeling marginalized.

After the mural came the foundstrument. The Samos Found-strument was unlike any before it. It expanded very quickly, and the intention was for it to greet every person who entered the refugee camp. The involvement of the adults was critical, especially the teenagers, who with every sound of the drill showed immense excitement. There was a girl with a massive bubbled abrasion on the front of her face who had been an incredibly active participant, her enthusiasm growing every day. I saw her go to her two-person tent, which she shared with her entire family, underneath a concrete block overhang. Her mother later came up to me and asked if she could use the fluorescent orange duct tape to fix one of her only objects—a broken and torn purse.

A chubby, disruptive Afghani boy walked up to where we were calmly putting together the foundstrument. His first entrance was by shaking my hand and trying to kick me in the groin. He had a water gun in his hand. All I could see were the guns that had killed the family members of the people in the camp, the millions displaced because of the slaughter from guns and bombs. I told him he could not participate with the gun. He became angry and threw a tantrum. We gathered around to calmly end the session and as we sat down, all of the little girls began to chant "Sheshera," my Arabic name for tree. Yet the chanting was not just repetitive. It was melodic and constantly shifting tonally.

Throughout the foundstrument process, we collected trash and recycled objects from the island with the children. Three of the children were dedicated to using files to get rid of any metallic sharp edges. The filing was a fascinating role for the small children to play, as they were actually able to concentrate for a long time on the repetitive motion of moving the file back and forth. The other kids fixed a huge amount of attention on putting all the zip-ties into the correct spaces, which held the most important elements together.

There was an immediate sense of gratification, when the giant head was being built. Older teenage girls in hijabs, little children and older men all helped move the foundstrument head into place, bringing people from different strata of the camp into a single forum. We became a single team. When it was raised into position, the foundstrument became a "living" creature.

We were able to cut plastic pipes, which when hit with mismatched and discarded sandals allowed each pipe to make a melodic sound in different tonal ranges, with a resonating base, producing an orchestral rhythm in front of the barbed-wire enclosure. The gigantic butterfly wings on the back of the body of the gorilla were made of giant metal stars and snowflakes. Old lampposts created the octopus arms. The robot-like head had a car rim arising from the top with a massive organ of a technicolor mouth.

Then the Greek police arrived. We were called into the police office where we were interrogated and had our documents taken. Despite our five days of work on the art projects they decided to tell us that we didn't have permission to be able to finish the mural. We told them that we had already been working with the community since the beginning of the week, but they refused to listen, even though we had permission from the first responders, the municipality and the non-governmental organizations. They brought in the head of the police, who knew that what he was saying was wrong but said he was just following orders. They intentionally wanted the camp to be as negative a place as possible to force people to leave. They refused to rebuild the fire-bombed center of the camp, and they would not let us finish the mural. Despite feeling crushed about the mural, we continued to build the foundstrument. At the end of the night, as we were packing up the gear, two of the boys offered a name for the creature. They wanted to call it "Mapsoop," which sounds very similar to "mapsut," which means "wonderful" in Arabic.

On the last day, we arrived at the camp and there were people of many different nationalities all gathered around the foundstrument. They knew something special was about to happen. We were able to set up a music speaker, playing Pakistani music, and the whole group burst into dancing—Kurdish, Syrian, Palestinian, Pakistani and Afghani—the dancing of a lifetime. The music and the banging brought people together and became the common language. The music corresponded to the percussive playing of the foundstrument. One man, who had just arrived the night before from Afghanistan, experienced this as his first impression of the refugee camp, and his excitement to see this was palpable. He hugged and kissed me and told me that he loved me, and that he had never seen anything like this before in his entire life. He then went and trimmed all the zip-ties with a wire cutter, and was eager to contribute in any way that he could.

Without any hesitation, the children understood how to complete the sculpture. Three girls from Afghanistan came, and immediately understood how to use the zip-ties to solidify all parts of the sculpture. Anything that fell off was re-attached with more durability. Every piece of the foundstrument came alive.

This day was the epitome of all that I live for. To live life in this way—to the ultimate—is humbling, and takes some experiential digestion.

The police had previously given us a brutal warning that if we continued to paint without permission, we would be arrested. They had stationed guards at the wall and were very strict with this absurd rule. Yet on the final day when we arrived, nobody was stationed there. I decided to risk it and finish the mural myself. This risky maneuver brought the project into the world of street art. The adrenalized sensation of illegally painting the outside of a refugee camp took the pressure of the project to a powerful level. I frantically moved across the wall and interwove black and white lines through the complex story—between the boats, the story of displacement from home, to the future question of a new life. As I ran back and forth across the wall I connected images of flowers growing from boats; houses on fire in their home countries; airplanes bombing their villages; mass migration on small boats; boats tipping over with people dead in the sea; the arrival at Samos; the dreams for future life; doctors, astronauts and teachers; simple concepts of home, with an underlying message of a longing for continuity.

Dripping with sweat, I was able to complete the work to its best in half an hour. Overcome with the feeling of closure, I moved the paint and started to take photos. I then walked up to the foundstrument, built on the hillside. As I walked up, I heard a scream from behind and saw the police shouting at me to come down to the mural. My heart sank, and I prepared myself to be arrested or accosted. "You are not allowed to take photos inside the camp!" he told me. With surprise and relief, I agreed calmly and he nodded his head in smug approval. With a sigh of relief, I went back up to the foundstrument, and we got all the children seated around in a circle calmly.

I thanked each of them for their participation, with the understanding that this was the end. We did a final musical meditation, and the eyes of each of the children closed. I looked into their faces and saw the calm that existed in each of them, even if war and displacement had ripped their lives apart. After we took a series of breaths in and out, we slowly opened our eyes, and I explained how we were going to calmly go and play the foundstrument. They slowly stood up, and we gathered around and had a call and response back-and-forth conversation that grew into a cacophony of sound. I nodded at Pru to lead a small workshop, while I went behind a Greek olive tree to transform into Tra, the puppetry paint creature.

As Tra slowly came out into the scene, he looked at the giant foundstrument in awe. This time, instead of genuine fear, there was a surprising response from the children. They all ran towards Tra with huge hugs, one small child after another, with arms outstretched to grasp and hold around the neck for an extended period of time. Tra shouted, "Let's jump" and started to prance around the foundstrument while singing "Boop boop be ba boop!" As they danced, others banged and whirled about the giant creature in the center. Tra led the children to jump in a circle, spinning and dancing around the sculpture in celebration. As the children gathered around, the pulsating colorful brain came off the top of its body, and I (the human) emerged.

There was a feeling of surprise among the children, because they really had allowed themselves to go deep inside the world of their living imaginations. Yet me coming out of the creature changed the magic. It made it real to them, because emerging from this strange otherworldly being was that wild and goofy face that they had been working with for the past week. The smiles were huge, and surprisingly quiet. The only words that I could say, looking at all of their transfixed and glimmering eyes, were "Thank you, Shukran."

I told everyone they needed to get into a line to all get a surprise gift. As they all clambered into a misshapen yet perfect line, I went and grabbed the surprise from my backpack. One by one, I handed each child an Artolution card, which could be exchanged for a hug. This triggered different emotional responses. The first boy flung himself at me and clung around my neck huddling against the body of the creature. The boys tended to hug more than the girls. After each exchange was made, a card for a hug, there was a blanket of calm. Everyone got the same special piece of a memory.

I gazed across the small crowd of children, and over their heads I saw something alarming down the hill. I saw the police officer looking at the mural, and pointing across the piece and taking photos. This was the Greek police officer who originally reported the mural painting to be a "wall infringement" to the top ranks. I then saw him point at me.

The world of magic was cut. I was afraid of being arrested, an hour before my departing flight. I said that I needed to leave immediately. We threw everything in the car in a frantic frenzy, with the children crowding around us. They did not understand why the energy had changed at the drop of a hat. As I was getting into the car, the children swarmed towards me. As I closed the door, they were banging on the windows with smiles. As we started to pull away I made eye contact with Majida, who mouthed from the distance a heart made with her hands above her head, "We love you."

We pulled away, the children running alongside the car with dust spilling from the back tires. The Greek policeman was pointing at the car, but I still needed to pack up my gear. I told Saleh to go back to the camp and tell all the kids we were working with to meet me at the bottom of the camp to say goodbye, where the police would not be able to see us. I quickly packed up all my tools. We went to the bottom of the camp to be greeted by Majida, Adnan, Saod and Guan, all with smiles strewn across their faces. I got out, and was immediately locked in hugs. Majida told us right away that three police cars were searching for us. Pru also explained that a young policeman, our only advocate in the precinct, made a simple yet poignant statement to the illegal completion of the mural. He said, "It looks like you found a solution."

As we drove off, I saw the young boys walking slowly down the street, making the sign of a heart with their hands above their heads. I put my hands in a mirroring position at the back of the windshield as we drove away down the winding Greek road.

Radical action through imagination is one of the most powerful weapons in healing the devastation that wars wreak across the world. The foundstrument is the only major addition that the children of the refugee camp will be able to make to the environment that they have been forced to live in. Many times, children have no autonomy concerning how their space looks, and with what they can interact. The arts can act as a catalyst, and the way that I, as the facilitator, interact with the population is reciprocal. When I put my positive energy into the environment, I receive just as much, if not more, energy in return.

Physical contact is also a quintessential part of making connections that transcend cultural lines. Handshakes, hugs and shoulder pats were abundant in the camps. The amount of affection was huge, which was surprising considering the amount of physical violence between the small children.

There was one boy who was particularly violent, and I witnessed multiple occasions where he would provoke another child, and then let out a huge amount of aggression on the other kid. In the final Hapi drum meditation he refused to be involved. And yet, when Tra the puppetry paint creature came out, he was one of the children affectionately hugging. As each child lined up to get their Artolution cards, he was the only child to come up and kiss me on the cheek. This may seem like a minor gesture, but the adults who lived in the camp could not believe that he was willing to show this kind of positive affection and they had never seen anything like it before from this boy.

There was another boy who took two cards instead of one. This could have been an attention-needing behavior; however, he really did it so he could come back up to me and return the second card, in exchange for a second hug. This kind of need for positive attention is really an integral part of the work. This is especially true when children may have severe neglect, parents in shock, overcrowding of siblings or no parents at all. This is part of responsible, positive, community facilitation.

I feel that the work that we do around the world—community-based, public action founded in fieldwork—is a model for the future of this discipline. Art and art education can be implemented in a trans-disciplinary way on the ground around the globe. The Samos Refugee Camp Project can be seen as a model for the integration of percussion, sculpture, drawing, painting, murals, meditation, conversation and collaborative storytelling, stemming from a facilitated collective action. An interactive, giant creature is built of recycled materials and it becomes a physical part of the landscape. Digital communication is then maintained on the ground with local facilitators on an ongoing basis. This tracks the progression of the meaning of a piece through the day-to-day interactions, interpreted through an educator on the ground, continuing to work around the foundstrument.

I will never forget Hamadi, a wild-haired little four-year-old boy, who was the youngest of a family with many siblings. His mother had to go to the hospital earlier that day because of an emergency. On the last day of the workshop, he came up to the foundstrument and grabbed one of the attached sticks, and started to uncontrollably bang on the objects on the foundstrument. The aggression in his face was a release of his frustration. He had no other way of coping. He looked around expecting an adult to tell him to stop; yet we all stood and simply smiled. The fact that nobody yelled at him encouraged him to let it out. Pound after pound of energy exploded out of him. I am told he continued to use the foundstrument to let out his experiences through music, interaction, play and healing through ongoing creative expression. Unfortunately, the police have tried to remove the sculpture and there is still ongoing debate about what will be happening for the future of the life of Mapsoop, the refugee sound creature.

I have drawn several conclusions from this work over the years. When looking at these stories holistically, the constant across each of them is the joy and engagement facilitated through participatory expression. By participating in the painting of a mural, each collaborating young artist becomes linked to all the other communities involved in the international Artolution community-based public arts network. This dialogue transcends language and uses hand-created imagery to share a voice with those who may never have had the opportunity to connect. When this kind of discourse is directed at populations in conflict and displacement, art becomes a social catalyst for communication and humanization.

How will these communities remember their creation? What is the difference made to their lives and can they grow from this work? What is the impact and how can these projects evolve into sustainable models? Each one of these projects is only the first seed of influence. The true social impact and chronological significance lies in the ongoing interactive narratives, which I hope will develop over time. The intention is that the principles, stories and experiences expressed throughout the murals will continue to live on within the participants and communities. This is especially true when the mural continues to live publicly in the location where it was collaboratively created.

## Syrian/Jordanian border, Jordan

*Azraq Syrian Refugee Camp Mural and Foundstrument: International Rescue Committee (IRC), UNHCR and Artolution, Trauma-Relief Workshop, Azraq, 2017.*

We worked for over a year to try and get back into Azraq, the same refugee camp we worked at in 2014, to educate local artists to be able to develop ongoing programming. Through the IRC we were able to make it a reality. Azraq had not changed, and still felt like an open-air, barbed-wire enclosure on the moon.

I came across Mahmood, the same boy I worked with three years earlier. It was a moment of humbling joy. He had not been able to leave this camp-prison for four years. Mahmood is a remnant of a war that has been raging, and his family is stuck in a time vacuum.

The unending, white, sheet-metal shacks feel as though they are out of a sci-fi movie, or a concentration camp. Unlike the past projects, this project was out in the camp itself, not in an enclosed community center. As the children wandered aimlessly in this moonscape of a setting, the wind caught their hair and covered them in a thin coating of dust. There is nothing to do here, and there is a world of waiting ahead of these children. The silence of the barren desert is the norm in Azraq.

The question is: what are the implications for a child who spends the majority of their life in, or is born into, this environment? How does it affect their development? When the children were asked about what the images were that would be most representative of their lives, they spoke about the importance of music as a sign of resilience and what keeps them going through their lives. They wanted to have an image of an oud player with birds coming out of the instrument, holding letters to be delivered to Syria with their messages to the future, and a girl sailing paper boats made of their hopes and dreams back to their homes.

As I was painting with the children one day from up above on a ladder, I looked down behind one of the walls and saw something very jolting. I saw a girl with special needs tied to a wheelchair, making grunting sounds, her face covered in flies. She was dripping in sweat, with her eyes rolling around in her head. It really triggered me to think about the difficulties, not just for the children in the camp, but also the children with special needs without any services. I asked about this and was told "It was life."

The children in Azraq are aggressively emotional. Anything they can do to show affection, every tiny morsel of attention, has endless value. They climbed all over me, they made sure that you know that they want to be known. Being an outsider, in itself, has a specific quality that makes the children interact with certain disbelief. Spending the time to make simple eye contact, or singing and painting together slows everything to a halt. Taking that time has a significance that is beyond words. It is the concentration of acknowledging that they are human.

Children are born in this camp and people will die in this camp, and the war continues. Our translator told us that some of the caseworkers were surprised at the way we were interacting with the children. They explained that we were really human. They continued by stating that we really seemed like a bizarrely accurate version of humanitarian artists, and that we treated the children as if they were people rather than just children. This was something unique, new, and they wanted to learn more.

When departing along the dusty road, there were two silhouetted children amid the white landscape who had gathered random bits and pieces and had built themselves a miniature fort in the middle of the desert: random crates, cardboard and rotting fabric tied together. I watched as they ran in and out, played and crawled through the misshapen doorways, and I smiled. It was evident to me that creativity can never be squashed no matter what the circumstances. It is a resilient flame that can eternally burn among the most ferocious of winds.

## Conclusions

The stories in this chapter are the beginning of a body of field-research. The intention behind these projects goes far beyond any single interaction or single analysis. In the long term, these projects, when viewed together, are a network of community-based public murals working towards a greater movement in cooperative social dialogue. These scenarios revolve around the relationship between family, culture, geography, violent conflict, trauma, ideology, religion and communal creativity. When a piece of community collaborative art is made with the intention of being shared with a global audience, the engagement of the participants increases. Expressive participation through large-scale painting and sculpture makes engaging in dialogue accessible, and accessibility is the nucleus of Artolution's mission. The social practice of building relational capital is formed through adaptable interactions. Because of this, flexible and empathetic understanding is fundamental when facilitating each of these diverse public art-making experiences.

Tangible and lasting public artifacts continue to tell stories every day, and it is storytelling that is the great unifier, a shared iconography that crosses ethnic and cultural divides. Storytelling runs through the creative lifeblood of each of these children, whether they are Muslim, Christian, Hindu or Jewish. Each child's voice can make a difference to the whole mural, putting the displaced, underserved and marginalized participants into a forum of artistic dialogue with each other. Creating visual statements through a public storytelling process has an ingrained therapeutic quality.

Shuman (2005, p.5) examines the social relations embedded in stories and the complex ethical and social tensions that surround their telling. Through her analysis of narratives, she explains that stories and creativity are the child and adolescent's natural medium for self-expression and group expression. The vehicle of narrative expression can come through a paintbrush, drumstick or conversation. These particular stories point to the value of facilitated educational experiences. However, building cooperative resilience starts with acknowledging where the communal trauma and struggles have originated. The visual process encourages children to express thoughts and concerns for which there are no words. In the Azraq Syrian Refugee Camp, for example, when the boys got to drawing, "the images were full of violence and the ravages of war. There were planes dropping bombs, tanks shooting rockets, people with bloody limbs missing, people dying, people being killed, and images revealing a longing to return to Syria, in spite of the war" (see Azraq Refugee Camp narrative earlier in this chapter). These images can initiate the cathartic release in a group setting of feelings, traumas and frustrations (Smilan, 2009, p.81).

Some of the images are apparent and show the trauma or issues, while others are demonstrated through the conversations surrounding the mural painting. For example, the mural painted at the YMCA in Jerusalem during the 2014 Gaza War was a process that involved Israeli and Palestinian children communicating through paint with one another. One of the Palestinian teenagers explained that, "As a Palestinian teenager, I am afraid to leave my house and go into West Jerusalem" (see Jerusalem narrative). He explained how devastating the war had been, and that he hadn't told anyone about his fears. Yet, during the mural process, he felt comfortable talking about his internal fears openly with *the other*. Cooperative resilience is based on the idea that accessing shared traumas through conversation can build the relationships between the members of a project relationally, with genuine empathetic dialogue. Rothschild (2006) and Shamay-Tsoory (2011) break down the different types of empathy to include cognitive empathy, emotional empathy and somatic empathy. In this case, the arts act as the stimulus for the creative perspective of empathy and to access a freedom and mode of expression that did not previously exist.

The arts can develop physical, cognitive and emotional adaptations, as current or future responses (Coles, 1998, p.94). This concept is very powerful when applied to creative storytelling as a tool to help children manage future conflicts and traumas, as preventative measures, as ways to work together and as ways to learn from one another. In the case of the Azraq Syrian Refugee Camp in Jordan, the question was asked to the group of adolescent boys, "What do you want to see for the future of your lives?" "The answer was a question, 'How can we rebuild Syria?' Together, they decided on a simple hammer, a school and a forest of planted trees—basic human desires for the rebuilding of a lost home and a lost life" (see Azraq Refugee Camp narrative). The conception of envisioning their future, amid serious adversity, became the goal of the mural project.

Community-based public arts can create a civil-social gift, infused through the content and participation (Jenkins, *et al.*, 2009). When the act of public sharing is utilized to facilitate conversation in traumatized communities, the intention is to provide an opportunity to transform spaces and people's experiences, and expand the participants' conception of themselves in the world. Public artistic expression has many different modalities of engagement with the audiences that view and interact with the work in the future.

One of the most important capacities of community-based public arts can be their ability to address urgent social issues. In the al-Am'ari Refugee Camp, the theme of gender-based violence was requested by the local principal of the school. She specifically wanted this subject because it was a prevalent problem and she used the arts workshop as a way to discuss this sensitive and difficult issue. "After this topic was presented to the teenage girls, their drawings displayed serious signs of violent abuse as a commonality among the girls. Images ranged from women being beaten, faces with bruises and blood, subservience, and women kneeling in prayer among the cactus of waiting for change. However, along with this darkness, a butterfly emerged, pulling a chained house out of the camp with the chain snapped in two" (see Ramallah narrative). This allegorical series of stories became a way to discuss common traumas that local taboos may have suppressed. The issues grew into a story, which was transferred onto the wall of the local UN refugee camp girls' school as a larger statement to an audience inside and outside their local environment. They all demonstrated excitement that their work would be discussed and shown to people in other parts of the world.

Jensen (2001) discusses how the participating young artists are able to represent their transformed memory directly through the arts activity. Community-based public arts can serve as tangible storyboards of multi-dimensional traumatic events, expressing the un-visualized or un-verbalized memory associated with a trauma or conflict (p.3). The teacher's reaction to this adaptable and intentional process was an expressed desire for these kinds of opportunities to grow. "The strongest part of the project was the response of the art teacher and the principal. Both stressed a desire to make this model of collaboration sustainable, and to continue painting the whole school" (see Ramallah narrative). The public discussions of the girls became an example for the participating UNWRA refugee camp teachers and administrators. The project focused on the statements of the girls, as a voiced response to their experiences of living in the al-Am'ari Refugee Camp. The way that the participating girls and adults perceived the finished piece became a beacon of reclaimed power and a source of pride to be shared with others. Excited responses from teachers and administrators can be professionally and technically very influential.

Throughout the diverse settings of these narratives, there is an emphasis on utilizing community-based public arts to understand how to "play" out or express feelings and emotions in a context of supportive play materials and positive relationships (Frost, Wortham and Reifel, 2001). The narratives point to unique ways of addressing conflict and trauma through the arts as a gateway to coming together and defining what is important to share with others. In the ALYN Hospital in Jerusalem, where both Israeli and Palestinian parents live with their children, a mother exemplified this through her contribution to the mural. In reaction to the severe and inflicted brain trauma of her child, she created a "violent scribble, tearing at the center of the paper. The scribble inside the drawing of a child's head was a single bold word, 'FIX'" (see Jerusalem narrative). This reaction was a public release from the perspective of the mother, on behalf of a shared trauma between her, her child and others in the hospital of different cultures. Her sadness was translated through the visual statements she made, as a form of release for an issue that her child was not capable of expressing and she needed to share with those around her. Holt (1967/1983) discusses how people have a natural desire to master control over self and environment in the learning process (p.86). These narratives observe and describe the facilitation of the holistic process of having the children, and communities take control of the content and art-making process directly and express issues most important to their lives. Participatory public arts thus become the gateway for discussing greater issues, and releasing energy in a healthy forum.

Taking control through paint or creative activity is an act of communally motivated empowerment. In Okhla, the story of one specific adolescent girl discusses how a facilitated creative experience can help to transcend social boundaries, and relate to traditions outside of one's own. "She was the only girl to take the initiative to use the drill, although all the girls had been invited… She held the drill machine in her hands… As she clasped her finger around the trigger, the whirr of the machine brought a smile to her face. Luxman helped to guide the drill… They completed hole after hole together and we collectively attached a series of wooden boards, painted by the younger children to the base. On completing the last board, she put the drill down, and uttered a simple, 'Thank you, sir.' A big handshake concluded the session, as she walked away out of the gate and down the chaotic road into Indira Camp" (see Delhi narrative). Although simple, this narrative is an expression of the ways that this sculptural process can take a locally stigmatized subject of girls participating in a traditionally "male" job, and transcend it. This workshop was able to take this girl's enthusiasm to participate and turn it into an act of facilitated boundary breaking. Looking across the narratives, we see that there is *emancipatory potential* for the art to stimulate dialogue in sensitive places and across cultural taboos (Mienczakowski, 1995; Park-Fuller, 2003).

There are a few essential ingredients necessary to this kind of work. Robi Damelin, Parents Circle Families Forum Israeli spokesperson, stated to me, "Healing and reconciliation can only happen with a good sense of humor" (see Beit Jallah narrative). The emotionally sensitive nature of working with trauma demands consideration of how to adapt across a wide variety of settings and responses. Working in this field has varying behavioral responses, and the educational tools for creating a healthy space for public expression demand adaptability. Parents Circle Families Forum Palestinian spokesperson and director, Mazen Faraj, made a final statement of essential importance about how flexible support functions in the reconciliation mural workshop for communication outside comfort. He said, "Thank you for thinking of us, many don't. You have helped these women find themselves" (see Beit Jallah narrative).

I would suggest that facilitating a successful project requires the following techniques: establishing a supportive atmosphere of discursive response; encouraging freedom of a healthy creative dialogue; affirming and reflecting the participants' feelings; showing respect for the child and community's ability to solve problems; setting out flexible guidelines; allowing the arts to evolve at a comfortable and fitting pace; and establishing shared responsibilities (Rogers, 1942).

This question of *how to facilitate* was reflected in a conversation with a boy named Muhammad in the Azraq Syrian Refugee Camp in Northern Jordan on the Syrian border. He explained a desire to continue to paint and create art across the refugee camp for the future, and to tell his story to the world. He voiced a frustration that, "We have no brushes or paint" (see Azraq Refugee Camp narrative). Muhammad brings up an essential point to logistical reality and the need for structures to be put in place so that facilitation can exist on an ongoing basis.

Imagining a better world and life is an ever-present motif throughout the narratives. Underlying hope and wanting to learn amid adversity are rooted throughout the narrative explorations. Although varying geographically and culturally, the concept of learning through imagination can be viewed through the lens of active play through physical materials publicly and cooperatively. Smilan (2009) explains the potential of this concept in her formative article "Building resiliency to childhood trauma through arts-based learning." She argues for establishing an environment for learning processes and reconciliation through play and the creative arts; artists, teachers and facilitators can guide authentic explorations that empower children organically (p.383). This concept of play employs the power of imagination towards public health and learning. The differences between learning and health tread a fine line in this work.

Visualizing a better world is part of the healing process. A fascinating example of this occurred in the Shoafat Sector C Palestinian Refugee Camp in the minimally regulated "no man's land" between the West Bank and East Jerusalem. Before the project began, the municipality of Jerusalem had warned me that the imagery would potentially be violent and full of hate. Yet, after a day of artistic expressions, the Palestinian coordinator "voiced to me her immense satisfaction that, in this otherwise extremely politically charged location, the statement here was of the children's imagination for a better world" (see Shoafat Refugee Camp narrative). In spite of the political rhetoric of the region, these children chose to make hopeful political statements.

This is exemplified by the universal nature of imagination across boundaries. In "Imagination and aesthetic literacy," Maxine Greene (1977) discusses how essential the use of imagination across the arts and arts education is, in order to make their significance "really real" (p.15). The reality needed for a piece of art to be influential through imagination is captured here, where the "abandoned factory-turned-children's-school now has the shimmering world of the children's imagination welcoming them each morning" (see Shoafat Refugee Camp narrative). This physical reminder brings a *very real* reminder of the value of imagination amid adversity, and is a very specific trait of learning through imagination. Before this mural was painted, there were no communally made public displays of imagination. In this challenging environment, imaginative play with color became a mode of communication beyond words.

It is difficult to know fully what kinds of trauma the participants in these projects may have been through, or what they may have experienced during the projects. We will never truly know the effects that the arts may have as they continue with their lives. But we can infer something from the al-Am'ari Refugee Camp in Ramalla. "As the painting neared completion, four girls refused to stop, embracing every last second of the experience. Before finally departing, one of them started speaking quickly and radiantly in Arabic, translated by her friend. She said, 'I feel like I have found myself through the paint!' With the nods of the other three, the girls walked back to the refugee camp" (see al-Am'ari Refugee Camp narrative).

The finding of one's self through the medium of paint becomes an experience of identity, as a felt experience of being part of a larger group co-experience. Opening a process of creative identity formation can become a characteristic of learning about one's self. Studies in the field of participatory arts have shown that active participation in the arts leads to improved self-concept and sense of control over one's life. (Guetzkow, 2002; Lynch and Chosa, 1996; Seham, 1997; Weitz, 1996; Williams, 1995).

Community-based public art-making can be viewed not only as cognitive learning about self and other, and as emotional learning, but also as a physically therapeutic quality. At the ALYN Hospital in Jerusalem, a rabbi and father of a girl with severe spinal cord and brain injuries was visibly moved by the experience of the art project. "With tears in his eyes, the rabbi, in traditional black and white, came up to me and confided a story... He said, 'My daughter has moved her arms more in the last hour painting than in the last six months combined.' This is what the blessing of art can create" (see Jerusalem narrative). The physical reaction of the rabbi's daughter demonstrates the power of being motivated to participate as a physically therapeutic action, in the cooperative mural painting experience. The imagination involved in making even a single mark held major significance for both the child and the parent. The father was able to learn about the power that art can have in the life of his daughter, and the daughter was able to see the inspiration she had in herself that needed to be released. Through the process of participating in an imaginative experience of expression, the arts were able to help her go beyond her physical trauma and learn about her own potential and the founding pillars of her resilience.

Learning and health are deeply connected in informed community-based public arts, along with the recognition of shared experience. There is much value to this process that includes reconciliation of similarity and difference. In the Parents Circle Families Forum reconciliation mural, one of the bereaved Palestinian mothers chose to work with an older bereaved Palestinian grandmother. "[They] chose to paint a tree divided into two branches; one branch: Israeli, one Palestinian, coming from the same base. Both had leaves falling, symbolizing that both groups had lost lives, yet came from the same roots" (see Beit Jallah narrative).

In this case, the power of metaphors and stories become the vehicle for discussing a shared trauma through poetics, hope and reflective imagery. The allegorical experiences of the participants cooperatively develop a shared memory where characters, plot lines, roles and constructive making occur (Jung, 1968, p.412). Hicks and King (2007) contextualize this visual culture of sharing and communication through describing the arts as an important discipline for meaning-making and processing. The local children and adolescents in the Okhla community voiced that "I didn't know what I wanted to do in my life. Now I feel like I want to do something important." The visceral experience of seeing one's actions manifest as public pieces of art makes difficult ideas of dreams and aspirations seem possible. This concept of achievement has substantial *futurizing* value. Kulsum Farooqui, the local Indian community center coordinator in Okhla, Delhi, wrote a long letter after the completion of the project, stating, "This project made a mark in their life. It will be there in their minds *forever*… This was a wonderful program, which brought them together. They learned to work in a team. This project really made a connection between the visiting artists and kids, which will remain forever."

Ellen Dissanayake (1999) describes art-making *as the making of special* (p.103). When creative facilitation is translated through a special *civic occasion*, the doors open to dealing with some of the most difficult and stigmatized issues in a community. If we look to the stories of gender violence in Delhi India (and Ramallah Palestine), or the traumas of living as a Syrian refugee in Jordan or Turkey, these are not issues easy to discuss, especially publicly. Yet, expression and the feeling of participating in a monument, memorial or celebration become infused into a process of taking experiences and imbuing them with artistic value. Ideally, this can be a tool to discuss and, it is hoped, lead to transcending conflicting societal, social and mental health boundaries (Stuckey and Nobel, 2010, p.246).

It is important for this work to be promoted in intensive environments. There is the need for art education to move into the community, especially in places where there may not be art education to begin with. The artistic significance lies in the future of bringing children and communities together in grassroots, institutional and collaborative approaches to narrative. When addressing common traumas, the capability of the arts to provide a forum for commentary and public storytelling is unique. These narratives all point to the need for societies to have a sounding board of the problems and hopes of children, adolescents and adults through public visual expression, which has the potential to grow through different facilitators and types of programs. However, longitudinal follow-up would provide a greater insight into what has happened to each piece of art, and what is needed for the practice to continue sustainably. The most critical issues about doing this work are the importance of balanced relationships in the power dynamic between participants, the facilitator, the community and the piece of art itself.

Working in this complex field within the continuum of cultural expression between the "developed" and "developing" worlds also acknowledges an ever-present and underlying narrative in an organizational context. It is important to acknowledge group dynamics when facilitating a project. Any person facilitating any kind of expressive program in such environments needs to place priority on being understanding interpersonally across cultures, while simultaneously seeking to understand the larger perspectives and needs amid adversity and displacement (Dryden-Peterson, 2006, p.392).

This work has relevance and application for educators, artists, practitioners and facilitators. Art therapeutic and educational methods have been documented to be effective in addressing trauma and psychosocial needs (Smilan, 2011). However, painting murals and assembling public percussive sculptures is a unique and emerging technique in the field of education in emergencies and development. The process of working through traumas at community and group levels for refugees and marginalized learners is a field that is still growing and being explored. An informed and ethical practice needs to consider each of these components. Participant-centered perspectives have a range of meanings, and each one requires that the practitioners be versatile and adaptive. The genuine empathy that it takes to listen and assess the needs of each individual is as important as balancing the group dynamics. The arts have a catalyzing role to play in the future of building bridges across disciplines through education, expression, healing and engagement around the world. When addressing trauma, the arts can provide a unique forum for commentary and public storytelling.

On every mural and sculpture we facilitate throughout the globe, a small word is painted on the lower corner. This word seeks to bond all the cultures, communities and participants together through the creation of an evolution, revolution, solution and resolution within the arts. That word is "Artolution."

## Chapter 8

# STORIES FROM CANADA AND SRI LANKA,

### with Survivors of Ethnic Conflict, Religious Intolerance, Tsunami and the Effects of Globalization

*Paul Hogan and the Butterfly Peace Garden*

## Pigeon pie

The biggest weapon of mass destruction is the human heart. I didn't know that when I was a kid growing up in Windsor, Ontario. What I knew deeply, intuitively, was that the world is a magical place, no matter how frightening it sometimes seems. What gives it its magic is a combination of good and bad things teetering precariously on the abyss of human combustibility, ready to blow at any minute. You never know what will happen next.

Shadows and light. We have to steer our way through them without a clue where we're going. I got my compass from good people—my mother and father, the nuns at Notre Dame de Bon Secours primary school and the priests at Assumption High—but their curriculum didn't include magic, apart, of course, from Holy Mass and other ecclesiastical events that entranced me as an altar boy but also excluded me, encrypted as they were in Latin and inscrutable hieratic protocol. We didn't have smartphones back in the 1950s but I think that's what I was looking for—something unfathomable I could carry in my pocket to confound on demand the wily coyotes of this world, including everyone from Mother Ignatius my piano teacher to the Pope himself.

Not coincidentally it was one such coyote, my uncle Roy McPeak (Mac to us kids) who introduced me to the magic I yearned for. Mac was an ex-World War Two United States Army war veteran, a tall amiable Texan who loved my Aunt Kay with a passion she worked hard to keep in check. What spilled over went to us kids. He used to take us with him sometimes when he was on his sales rounds all over the city of Detroit, but it was the nitty-gritty downtown areas he seemed to favor, particularly down around John Road and Brush, the tenderloin you might say.

To this day, I don't know what he was selling but that was long before crack came along so I'm pretty sure it was harmless, and more along the lines of cleaning products or aluminum siding. Once we got down in the hood, Mac would park me with his friend Zeke Zauder and disappear doing business. Zeke had a little magic shop that became my "rabbit hole." He would unveil one illusion after another and I knew the last thing in the world I wanted at that point was to be disillusioned. Astonish me Zeke! Magic me! That's all I wanted.

Franz Ezekiel Zauder—Zeke—became my mole, an undercover role model. I wanted to be a magician like him, a scrappy little guy who'd taken more than his share of flack but had the perimeters secured now with accordion shutters on his shop windows, triple locks on the doors and chutzpah going all the way back to the shtetlekh (Jewish communities) of eastern Poland. He always knew exactly what to say and what to do. Nothing surprised him. Nothing scared him. He was my main man but also a big secret. With magic there were lots of things you kept hidden, including your sources. I'm only revealing this now, as a 70-year-old man, because Zeke is long gone with his stories, his store and the city I remember as a ten-year-old boy, all of it burned to the ground in the riots of July 1967.

The patter would start when he'd pull a colored silk out of his sleeve, followed by another, then another. And he'd say:

"OK, Paulie, what color is the next silk?"

And I'd say, "Pink?" and it would be pink.

"And now?" he'd say.

"Yellow?" I'd guess, and it would be yellow.

Then "Black." And it was black as midnight coal.

I wondered where they came from, all these silks, and how he'd get the colors right. I tried to throw him off when I got to know him better and was less intimidated by his sometimes surly manner, as if I was just another annoying kid and not the promising apprentice I considered myself.

"Zebra stripes?" I'd say. "Ladybugs? Pizza birds?" When things got routine I tested Zeke's steel.

"Nice try kid, but no more silks today. Maybe Friday. Get Mac to bring you back next Friday and I'll see what we can do."

So I would get Mac to drop me back during his rounds the following Friday but by then Zak would be on to other things, like doves or dice boxes.

"Do the dove again, Zeke," I pleaded after seeing him do it once, and he'd say, "Can't. We don't do doves in Detroit. Just pigeons. Maybe you got doves across the river in Canada but we just got pigeons here, and hawks, of course. This is the United States of America, you understand."

"No hawks, Zeke, I'll take a pigeon. Do a pigeon." Zeke got up and shuffled into the back of the store where he kept his heavy stage gear and came back with a pie fresh from the oven.

"What's this?" he asked, like I'd never seen a pie before.

"What do you mean, what's this? You think I never saw a pie before? My mom makes them every Sunday morning and we have them for dessert all week. With ice cream."

"Is that so? So what kind does she make?"

"Everything. Blueberry. Peach. Pecan. Apple. Raisin sometimes, but I don't like raisin."

"Any particular reason you don't like raisin?"

"They're too small. The raisins. Seeds get stuck in my teeth."

"Here, let me give you a raisin to believe."

The pie was changing shape in his hand, bubbling and boiling like lava and there was a sweet, fruity aroma in the air. Zeke whipped out a zebra striped silk, covered the pie, gave it a snap and…whoosh… a pigeon flew out of the door and parked on the gushing fire hydrant across the street. Zeke closed the door and handed me a raisin.

"OK, I believe. What happens to the pigeon?" Zeke cut me short.

"No problem," he said. "That's Laureen. Nice girl. She doesn't wander far but it's hard to coax her back though, once she's out with the boys."

"Let's get her back into the pie now, Zeke, in case we get hungry later."

"That's what I'm telling you, son, there are issues. She stays out a night or two and you never know what's going to happen. Mean streets out there. Pigeons in the park all strung out on bennies and bingo. She might not make it back till tomorrow."

"So what's the problem?"

"I'm trying to tell you. Magic is a complicated game. There is a lot of backstage business."

"Like what?"

"Like tomorrow's Saturday. She can't go back in the pie. I'm not permitted to work on the Sabbath."

"But how much work can it be putting a pigeon back in a pie, Zeke?"

"You'd be surprised. Anyway that's not the point. The whole idea of the Sabbath is to see if you can be quiet and do nothing—and I mean nothing—not even put a pigeon back in a pie. Let God do it all. Just once a week, mind you. Not much to ask. Very sensible really. The rest of the time we're allowed to interfere with the world as much as we like. After a few thousand years of that, look what we got."

"What we got, Zeke?"

"Pigeon pie, Paulie, my boy. A fine mess, that's what we got. Which is why the world needs magicians. 'Cause we specialize in doing nothing, so the really important things can happen the way they're supposed to. That's real magic. You know what I mean?"

"Sorry, I don't understand."

"Not many do, boy, so don't be sorry. Now let's get down to business. You buying a trick or not?"

"I can't Zeke, your tricks are too expensive. And my mom thinks magic is a waste of money. I can't imagine how many papers I'll have to sell, cars I'll have to wash, lawns I'll have to cut, brats I'll have to babysit, how much snow I'll have to shovel…"

"All right already! Your mother's pretty smart. Tricks aren't worth a fiddler on the roof's fart. But stop whining. If you want to do magic, the first rabbit out of your hat is attitude. That's it—your first trick, and it doesn't cost a dime. You need the right kind of heart if you want to do the impossible. All for naught or not at all is what I say. Everything's easy after that."

"You mean, do the impossible once and everything's a snap after that?"

"More or less, until the next impossible comes along. But don't sweat it. You got the goods. You just don't know it yet. So I'm to going teach you."

"I don't know how I can pay you, Zeke. I'm just a kid."

"Never mind about the money, Paulie. OK? Here, I'm going to give you a trick to show your mom. We'll see how it goes from there."

He pulled a rose out from behind my ear. A yellow silk rose. He showed me how to crumple it up and make it disappear and come and go from nowhere in a stunning array of rainbow colors. Then he handed me the rose.

"Take this home and try it on your mom," he said. I did but it didn't work. First time it fell into the pie batter and made a mess. Mom scolded me. Then she laughed. She washed it off and told me to keep trying. I tried it again and again every Sunday, regular as Mass, standing on the stool beside her as she worked the pie dough, till finally I got it, more or less, right.

As long as I thought of myself as Harry Houdini I stayed motivated and bought as many tricks as I could over the next couple of years. I stored them in a sturdy apple crate I painted crazily for the purpose, not realizing at the time what it was I had in my hands. It was the original "Out-of-the-Box Curriculum" that was later developed in the work I did with art and survivors. With that yellow rose and the box of tricks I was firmly in charge of leading myself "down the Garden Path," which is what I did later with others through the expressive arts. Nothing stood in my way for the next 60 very odd years except my wavering attitude and, in Sri Lanka, military checkpoints, visa renewals, diplomatic posturing, a bit of mortar fire here and there (most of it out-going) and, oh—how could I forget?—the famous Boxing Day tsunami of December 26th 2004.

In the summertime, neighborhood kids would come to watch me perform magic in the garage. Dad had to move his new two-tone blue

De Soto so my sister, Fran, could set the stage with faded floral drapes and a potato sack scrim. She would prepare herself to get sawed in half. I was a clumsy kid so most of the time I flubbed the tricks but in so doing, I learned an even more important art, one that came to play an important role in my future career as a traveling magician and confidence man—patter. You've got to know how to baffle them with your bushwah.

No matter how badly you flub a trick, if you can turn it around and make kids laugh, you score a huge hit for humanity, or so I believe. Their hearts are wide open when they laugh and they believe anything you say. If you help them get an education on top of that, keep them healthy and get them to take care of one another and not pick up the guns and drugs their masters sell on the street, well, they may not have won the race, but at least they're in it.

## Crickets in the camel's tent

So much for Detroit—its mystery, its magic, its murder rate and the fact that it was my "sipapu" or place of emergence into a much bigger and more violent world than I could ever have imagined as a kid. Not convinced that I wanted to have any part of it, I moved to Bali in 1969, before there was an international airport with 20 million sun-screened buzzards from Europe and North America arriving every year to pick paradise clean.

I lived there for 18 months in cheap rooms, one right after the other, each becoming more tenuous and threadbare as money ran out along with the memories and myths that sustained my original reasons for migrating to the far shore. When the expanded Ngurah Rai International Airport opened at Denpasar in 1970 I left Bali and never returned. The last place I lived, before deciding to build a villa of my own, was invisible—a ghost house you might say, which set me on a new trajectory. It belonged to the king of the village of Mas whose name also was Mas, which means "gold" in Balinese. Mas was my patron, a visiting professor of gamelan[1] at the University of California, Los Angeles (UCLA): witty, soulful and mildly skeptical of the dubious goals of Western development but indulgent and kind nonetheless, a romantic who cherished young poets and artists of angelic sensibility who wandered his way. He offered me the house he had used for secret assignations when he was a dashing young prince astride his 1951 Vincent (motorbike). I gave him a rough sketch of the house of my dreams, which he then commissioned to be built in his ancestral village on my lavish budget of 40 US dollars.

You couldn't see Djakorda Mas's pondok (romantic hideaway) from the adjacent paddy fields, the sole point of entry for which was a gate disguised as a bramble bush. Once inside you made yourself as polite and small as could be, moving about with Balinese aplomb, the scale of the architecture requiring recalibrated, proprioceptive skills and decorum. It was a decisively different time and space from downtown Detroit, yet I felt I was getting closer to be where I wanted to be and I definitely felt more at home.

The pondok was scaled to the size of the dwarf gargoyle standing guard on a pedestal inside the gate. The triple-thatch roof gable opened out onto the rift valley below Gunung Agung, lord of the mountains and home of the gods. Underneath the bedroom love bower was a lotus pond trilling with frog song at night. It mirrored the incandescent blue sky by day while the garden echoed with temple gongs and Majapahit[2] mantras. Waking up and falling asleep there was an uninterrupted reverie.

Often, a very slight old man, a pedanda (Balinese Hindu priest), appeared sitting cross-legged on a flat stone pedestal in the pond wearing a saput poleng—the high priest's black and white checkered cloth— bound tightly around his chest. He chanted over the hibiscus and blessed the frangipani blossoms scattered on a silver tray while flicking them in four directions, with the last flower offered to the mountain. Always the mountain. Everything began and ended with Gunung Agung. Once the flower and rice offerings were made, the silver plate reflecting the sky in God's eye was wrapped up in spun silver and gold cloth and returned to a basket of ritual implements. The pedanda straightened his back, composing his sarong and saput. He adjusted his turban with the flare of red hibiscus tucked behind his right ear, sat stock still and returned what remained of the day back to the gods. I closed my eyes when he closed his and when I opened them he was gone.

Daily the yard at Mas's pondok was swept in interlocking spirals by the gargoyle's grandmother, Ibu Rai. She entered the yard silently before first light to kindle fire and make coffee. Later Gusti, her grandson, arrived, bearing sticky rice in banana leaves along with freshly picked mangoes, snake fruit and bananas for breakfast. Gusti and I became instant friends the day he showed me how to mulch the fruit up into pulp, pour it over the rice then sweeten it with a dollop of Panda milk. He begged me to take him to the house I'd built in the woodcarver's village at Mas. Considering the 40 bucks I paid for my hovel in the hills to be excessive, he wanted to see it with his own eyes.

In some respects, Gusti was right. That house, dubbed Cricket Castle, proved to be more expensive than I anticipated, skewing my finer instincts for savvy property investments for years to come. But the experience of meeting the little "crickets," the Balinese kids who lived in the woodcarver's village nearby, was worth every penny, and the house itself was far more beautiful than anything you get in downtown Detroit these days, or even Toronto and Vancouver, where modest bungalows on sterile patches of concrete go for millions of dollars.

Cricket Castle had wings and flew through uncharted worlds of imagination accompanied by devas and apsaras (Hindu angels) who guided its progress home. After this house, nothing could compare—neither the Singing Fish Cottage on Kallady Lagoon where I lived during the war years in Sri Lanka nor Monkey's Tale Centre in Pioneer Road, Batticaloa, my abode during more peaceful times.

The castle was plain and simple. It came equipped with a front verandah and a cane chair for the master. Open the door and you were inside the one and only room, which was wall-to-wall platform bed with storage space underneath for packsack, sandals and painting supplies. From floor to ceiling the room measured five feet at its apex so there were two basic postural possibilities—lie down or crawl. Size wise, if you can imagine a child's backyard playhouse in an upscale part of a Canadian city you're already two or three times too big. Scale it down a bit further, and picture a suburban model of the same kind of playhouse, which is significantly smaller but probably bigger than Cricket Castle. Or imagine a birdhouse built for Batman and Robin's son, Ricky, but the birdhouse can't be up in a tree. Bats and Bobby don't want their kid to have the reckless kind of life they had as childhood superheroes. His playhouse has to be safe and sturdy on the ground, but the memory of flying should linger. Now maybe you've got the picture.

I know my house sounds miserably small but there was one saving grace—it had wings. In a typical stroke of Balinese genius, Cricket Castle came equipped with a clever system of ropes and pulleys, which raised and lowered the woven bamboo walls providing ventilation on demand. It also created a whole new form of village entertainment for the cricket children who gathered day and night to watch a visiting alien tinker with his downed UFO (unidentified flying object) while adapting to life in their village—and this, years before Netflix! I was an instant box office sensation!

It was hard being a hit 24/7 in real time, so I often packed up and retreated to Mas's pondok, and let the crickets have their way with the house. God knows what they got up to, but after a while, I'd miss them and come back home. I found evidence of small woodcarvings and palm leaf offerings tucked under my pillow or tied with coir twine to a spray of bougainvillea arranged in a tumbler on the verandah table. Sometimes a single frangipani blossom had been pinched into the door latch or a firefly lantern left by the door for night journeys through the jungle.

At first the crickets would run away and hide when they saw me coming, pretending nothing had happened while I was gone. I'd make a fresh jar of lemonade and wait on the verandah for them to reassemble, which I knew they'd eventually do, especially if there were refreshments on offer. One by one they'd skitter down the path, or straggle in small clusters of brother, sister and baby bump-on-hip, scrambling for front-row seats in the shade of the jack tree, piled up on one another, pumped and primed, ready for show time. That's when their big smile-a-thon would begin. I felt so welcome and so necessary to their well-being, which was patently absurd since they'd somehow managed without me for thousands of years. They were a mythic race of child immortals, as avid to know everything about me as I was besotted by them.

They came to see me every time I returned, because they just simply had to know how I was doing, what I was going to do next and, more to the point, what in creation brought me there in the first place in the back of their back-country village in Bali with my downed Sopwith Camel house that I couldn't stand up in without cracking my skull.

There was also the matter of the nearby coconut trees that bombed the shack in the rainy season when winds were high, ergo holes in the roof and a wet bed. The kids didn't mind a little puddle here and there in the house. They knew it would be this way because it was always this way where they lived. From the minute the camel spread its wings and opened its doors to the crickets, the kids were smiling. They were ablaze. When you have 20 or 30 kids clinging on to one another in your front yard first thing in the morning, all smiling sunbeams, guess what you do? You smile back. That's what you do. Automatically.

Anyway, the crickets knew from the start that my house, like my heart, belonged to them—entirely and completely, inside and out—though I was allowed to play there too, as long as I included them in the playbill. Within a couple of months, the house returned to their exclusive remit, but meanwhile I had become their friend, manservant, cook, student, teacher and slave, forever loving and loyal.

I will never forget them. They were my inspiration, and muse, my guru. I taught them to make art, which was a bit presumptuous of me, given their pedigree (and mine), and they taught me to make offerings to placate the people or the gods through their surrogates, the trees, the clouds, the mountain or the sea. It was our private conspiracy, sealed in improvized ritual, accompanied by silly song and dance routines. I was an avid student of their spontaneous wisdom. Everything I learned about future "gardens of peace" for kids in zones of conflict started with these Balinese kids.

Some nights, Gusti would light a fire and we'd listen to the gamelan and drums riffing in the distance. When the kids went home at dark, Gusti and I would follow fireflies over paddy field trails in quest of magic. One night we ended up at a Wayang Kulit "shadow" play deep in a forest clearing. Everyone, young and old, huddled on the ground just the way the kids did in my front garden, but for once I was not the show. It was Rama and Sita and the demon king Ravana who had the stage.

A fire pot hung behind the screen, and to begin with, there was some kind of leather puppet, more or less the shape of a tree, leaning against the screen. Waves of gamelan thunder crashed through the clatter and chatter of the assembling audience whereupon Gusti solemnly took my hand in his. The leather tree wavered and slapped the screen. It changed size with the undulations of the wayang master's voice and its proximity to fire pot and screen.

"What is that tree thing, Gusti? What it's doing, slapping the screen like that?"

"That is the tree, Po, the One-and-Only-Tree in the world."

"Really? It looks like a big…well, you-know-what."

"That's exactly what it is. A very hungry you-know-what."

"Looks spooky to me. Aren't you scared Gusti?"

"Not really. Spooks are everywhere here. Best concentrate on the deva."

"But suddenly she turns around with fangs and sagging tits. Where's the beauty? Gone…bingo! Or bit by bit, without noticing." Another deity streaked past. "My God! What was that?" I asked.

"Not sure. Must be Ram."

"Ram? Is he a comet? Or asteroid?"

"Sort of. He's Sita's husband."

"So where's she?"

"Ravana's got her."

"Where?"

I could see Gusti wanted to watch the show and was growing impatient with all my questions. He turned and looked me in the eye. I thought he was going to do the Detroit thing and tell me "shut yo fuggin' mouth." But not Gusti. He did the Balinese thing. He smiled.

"My dear friend, in Bali either you get it or you don't get it. You know? There's no in-between."

"Sorry," I said, and nodded. I was beginning to get it, a little, but for me it was all in-between. True, nobody seemed to know what was going on, but it was definitely all going on, and would continue to do so at a more and more furious clip until suddenly, it stopped, full crescendo. Just like the gamelan orchestra stops. And then, almost inaudibly, it started up again.

## Intravenous rainbow

It was the spring of 1983 when my friend Nancy Brown was diagnosed with an autoimmune disorder and admitted to the hospital. She asked me to take over the art classes she taught children at Toronto's Hugh MacMillan Medical Centre[3] while receiving treatment.

I said, "OK Nancy, for you I'll do it, but I have no idea what to do."

"Oh," she said, "I'm sure you'll think of something."

I agreed to help in spite of the fact that I knew nothing about teaching and very little about art. I was also allergic to doctors and hospitals in any form. But I remembered my little crickets back in Bali, and I knew they had already taught me everything I needed to know to appease the aesthetic appetites of the children in the rehab facility. I leafed through my dossier of serviceable alter egos and found Dr. Smock, inventor of both the BaffleGab Chamber (BGC) and Intravenous Rainbow Therapy (IRT). Here's the ticket, kiddies. Ready to ride?

Dr. Paolo Smock considered the charts and sighed. Looked like rough seas ahead, fair to frightening with terrifying intervals. Appointments heavy in the BaffleGab Chamber this morning—pretty steady, one right after the other, till noon. Two kids with upper limb amputations, Zoltan and Abu, war zone injuries from unexploded ordinance they picked up while playing in Bosnia—they would be painting with their feet. A hyperactive asthmatic boy, Thurston from Jamaica, with the concentration span of a gnat but the voice of an angel. I'll coax him to sing "Easy Skanking" while he jives around the room flinging paint at paper taped to the walls. Maria Elverez, an eight-year-old cherub from the Canaries who liked to show photographs of her grandmother's stone-hewn cottage dangling from a cliff in Tenerife—spina bifida, paralyzed from the waist down. She comes in a wheelchair, so that means moving the paint table. Brewster with cerebral palsy—emotionally up and down like a yoyo, but pretty good on the crutches now. Last but not least, feisty little Theo, a post-op, crank casualty from Regent Park who paints laying down on his gurney, which means moving everything in the art room out into the hall temporarily. It's a hassle but Theo's a diamond in the rough. We'll do it for him, no problem.

Whoops! Almost forgot. Last appointment just before lunch, Gord the master gob-lobber. Gob-lobbing is a technique which utilizes a Tourette's patient's uncontrollable limb spasms to degrade the predictability of the painted surface of any art work by releasing cannonades of color delivered at high velocity in erratic, unpredictably timed volleys. Just because the paint will be flying in all directions at the apex of treatment does not guarantee Gord will hit the target or come remotely within range. However, one bull's eye will do the trick. Then lunch.

We were at a critical juncture in the BaffleGab procedure. To be honest these were my first actual field studies. I had no idea how it would go with Nancy's kids, but if I have one indispensable piece of advice that covers all such occasions it's got to be the Zen dictum "Only don't know, go straight!" I scribbled it on the blackboard first day as a mnemonic cue from ground zero.

I remember opening the door to that art room and sagging like a limp lily in the summer sun. Such a horrendously small, square, sterile cell! How could anyone expect these kids to re-invent their lives from this torture chamber, be it ever so well intended? Better they sit out under a tree planting tulips or playing Parcheesi, but of course that was only a summertime option. I couldn't believe how depressing it was. I sat on a stool at the art table and bowed my head in prayer. There must be a God in heaven, I said. I will ask him. He answered in a heartbeat.

"Don't be a chump, Paolo," He said. "You are a doctor. A professional! You need a stethoscope. A smock. Minimum. And you need to mix your paints, starting with black and white. After that, colors. Remember? Now ask yourself: what would a proper doctor in your position do? He'd get up and do the right thing, that's what he would do. Right now. OK? So do it!"

I picked up the phone and dialed the nursing station, explaining my predicament and asking for ten sheets, a smock, a stool and a stethoscope. I had trouble making myself understood.

"Whose stool specimen do I want? No, no! You don't understand. Not a stool specimen. Just a stool, you know, with three legs. And a stethoscope. Don't forget the stethoscope. And may I please have a proper nametag so the kids can identify me? God knows who they think I am. I'm Dr. Paolo Sandreno-Hapsburgeo Smock, MD (psych), FRC psych (UK), BGT psych (Zurich). Should I text that to you?"

"That won't be necessary, doctor," the nurse demurred, "I'll take care of it." Within an hour, I had seven sheets and a tag that read, "Dr.

Shmuk." That's right! That's what they sent. No initials. No degrees. No stethoscope. Nothing And they spelled my name wrong!

The first principle in dealing with architorture in any form is to alter it so it becomes more conducive to happy thoughts. This is called Decoration for Self-Defense. I had a long way to go with DSD in that art room but first thing I did was get rid of the circular table that took up most of the floor space. I folded it in two and rolled it out into the hall until further notice. Then I hung a circle of sheets 12 feet in diameter in the center of the room. Suddenly we were back to bindu, which is the only place to be at the outset of mission impossible. Simply defined, bindu means, "nowhere you've ever been before but somewhere from which you've never strayed." It also means "zero." One of the principal push points of the BaffleGab Sequence is that everybody gets to be nobody going nowhere for a while, which is the default setting for human existence after all, so it's very user friendly and gets amazing results.

Before the kids started rolling in I went over the list of materials on hand and made certain we were ready. I called for a scrub nurse, and who should turn up like a bad penny but Ms. Frith, the same smug little bug who had prepared my nametag. We incanted the litany of the color spectrum from red though violet, intoned various sizes and weights of paper and card stock, enumerated brushes of various sizes with handles of varying lengths, positioned bowls of black ink at the ready, cut soda straws to a range of lengths, reminding ourselves to blow not suck, during the actual procedure.

"Is this how we do it, Dr. Shmuk?" Nurse Frith asked, demonstrating classic BaffleGab blowback technique. "Yes, Nurse. Perfect! Now forget all that because we'll start today by assessing the collective story world of the ward."

"So I should prep the Shadow Tableau then, is that correct?"

"Exactly, Nurse Frith. You must have trained with Belchmier in Berlin? You really know your stuff!"

"Yes doctor. During the blitz. I'm ready for the worst!"

"Excellent! So here's how the BaffleGab Shadow Tableau works. I light a candle and place it on the Siberian shungite altar placed here, precisely in the center of the room. You turn off the lights and I disappear behind the sheet. When you hear me ring the bell you can admit the first patient or, in this case, two patients—I think start with Abu and Zoltan first, A to Z sounds good."

Nurse Frith turned out the lights and we were ready to proceed. The initial interviews took over a week to process but proved to be a classic Phase (I) BaffleGab intervention. Donning neoprene scrubs and goggles I turned on the respirator and rang the bell. Abu and Zoltan appeared. I instructed them to blow out their candle. Then I lit mine. It went like clockwork from there.

"Did you have any dreams last night boys?"

"Wet or dry, doc?"

"Let's start with dry."

"Saw a bird with no wings trying to fly."

"Saw a newborn baby with wild wolves all around it."

"Saw a highway of diamonds with nobody on it."

"Saw a black branch with blood that kept dripping."

"Saw three men in a boat—looked like a mango."

"Saw a rainbow IV in the gown of teacher Brown."

I worked feverishly to keep pace with them. Everything they told me I drew in rapid-fire calligraphy on the back of the sheet holding a candle in my right hand. By the end of a week the scrim was full and we had the story of the Intravenous Rainbow, be it only in black and white. There were plenty of colorful details still to be added, and a lot still depended on luck. Would the Mango Boatmen come and deliver the rainbow to Nancy's room at Toronto General? Would the rainbow fit in her room? Would the hook-up adaptors between Canadian and Serendib intravenous devices fit without leakage? Leakage was definitely a no-no. In fact, leakage could be fatal. So no leaks please, I prayed, especially with the Russian patients. This could create an international incident. Russians and leaks: not a good combination. But what was Shmuk worried about? The Mango Boatmen knew their job.

We worked for a week after that, making the collage story into a full spectrum, six-panel tableau, which the hospital proudly displayed on its walls. The day we finished, Nancy was discharged from Toronto General. She was at home sitting in her garden. I called her and told her what all happened while she was away. She was speechless at first. Then she overflowed like the water in her birdbath.

"Oh Paulie, you won't believe this but when I got home this morning and looked out the kitchen window there was a rainbow hovering over the birdbath in our backyard. I went outside and watched it fade away and disappear. I felt as though it moved inside me. Inside my heart. Inside my cells, you know what I'm saying? When it was gone, a dove appeared out of the mist where the rainbow had been and bathed herself in the water, a pure white dove. The water overflowed. I closed my eyes and it flowed over me. When I opened them, she was gone. I knew I was better. A complete cure! Ready to get back to work."

Back at the rehab center, Nancy convinced the board of trustees to hire me to collaborate with the kids and some downtown artist friends of mine, namely the Chong,[4] to create the Spiral Garden, an idea for which we'd already drafted plans. The board pulled back. Certain donors, principally the Ministry of Health, called for a review of the BaffleGab Chamber and Dr. Shmuk's credentials, or else no disbursement of funds would be forthcoming. Can you believe it? Oh ye of little faith! The kids all knew the Intravenous Rainbow worked and they loved it, but some of the medical staff remained skeptical. They looked down their noses at Shmuk's brilliant clinical record, dismissing his work as quackery, like something a duck would do if some dolt criticized his waddle. They seemed to think it was bad for kids to be exposed to "witchcraft" in a reputable medical establishment. Shmuk shrugged his shoulders.

"One person's witchcraft is another person's wisdom," he said, leaving them to make the final decision.

## Mystery plays: apparitional theater of the Chong

Within the concrete canyons of the spreading necropolis of Toronto, a many-faceted "mystery" plays through the Chong: a people, a dream, a memory contained and nurtured over the past 20 years through the rituals and ceremonies, migrations and passages, and now the iconography of a serpentine mural.

Too elusive to be a subculture, too Pythonesque to be a clan, Chong plays in the shadows (collective and individual): appearing suddenly like an unexpected apparition and stirring up a certain fertile strangeness outside the Palaces of Dry Reason.

Always in flux, Chong moves like a river, like the whorls of a fingertip towards the center of Mystery.

Bypassing the temples built to the Shopping God and the TV God, Chong opens other possibilities for play and prayer.

Chong spirals slowly towards the heart, home and harmony of the senses whole and holy, to inspire the children and the child within.

In a culture of fragmentation and dismemberment, Chong remembers the positive dark, the forgotten and outcast Yin, the holy Crow sent from the Ark on a long journey of prophecy.

Connecting with all other peoples of prayer and playfulness, all who dare the night migrations of the soul in this arid time, Chong is both quest and question marking time, masking time, moving time out of the linear familiar and into the deepening spiral, the root that taps new wine, the juice of being.

Chong honors the mystery, shedding the old like a skin to keep on moving, dancing to the earth beat on the long journey home.

I became involved with the Chong in the 70s, when apparitions mushroomed in the back alleys around Spadina and College in downtown Toronto. The phenomenon had its roots in the Umbanda rites of Brazil, Hopi Kachina dancing, Balinese processional theater,

Wile E. Coyote, Road Runner and Looney Tunes. Chong people came from many diverse cultural and ethnic backgrounds—black, white, brown, red, bronze and gold—strangers from all over the planet whose parents or grandparents had settled in a place the Aboriginal Huron people called "Toronto," a word in their language meaning "the meeting place." We were artists and artisans, city sanitation workers, writers and poets, taxi drivers, housewives, single mothers, dancers, acrobats, musicians and a French chef.

We met as strangers and became friends, but since we were also the remnants of a gone world, ghosts as it were, we appointed a King (King Ha Iti Iti), a Queen (Queen Isabella Maria Kataragama), a Bishop (Bishop Chong) and an Abbot (Holy Abbot Owlbird) to steer our course through the real world. During the next 20 years we performed their Ghost Dance, hoping it could magically alter the course of a comet streaking toward us, a comet projected from within the citadels of our own earthly powers.

"Keep on dancing," the elders instructed us, "and the good times will come." So that's what we did and, sure enough, the good times came. We made music and parties and miracles and love on the rooftops and in the warren of lanes behind their dwellings from the early 1970s through the mid-1990s. Our name, derived from a Taoist maxim, "ping ping chong chong," translates as "Doing the ordinary in a marvelous way, doing the marvelous in an ordinary way," which is what we aimed for.

In his encyclical of 1982, "De Feritate Humanorum,"[5] Bishop Chong described Chong before it had a name as "complete political anarchy circumscribed by a punctilious form of mass ritual behavior called MegaShock Decorum." Chong identity and sense of mission evolved with time. The genuine underlying intention of our performances and the amount of effort it took to pull off "spectaculars" were not always evident, but it was there from the beginning: the comedy, the coherence, the continuity and the caring about community that characterized all endeavors. Chong was so dedicated that Bishop Chong jokingly referred to our practices as a form of homeopathic fascism.

Though our motives and skill sets may have been mixed, we shared a unifying sense of hope in the apocalypse. Something went seriously askew with the world we had inherited after World War Two. We were all damaged goods, a generation traumatized by the extent of violence and brutality visited on mankind in the 20th century. Hitler's meth-saturated stormtroopers were defeated, thank God, by our heroic fathers but it cost us dearly, for many of them never returned home to us. Yes, of course they were shipped back but somewhere in the mid-Atlantic, possibly while passing through the Bermuda Triangle, their souls were replaced by the "Father Knows Best" clones of the 1950s—Senator Joe McCarthy and his kind at the House Un-American Activities Committee in Washington being typical of this button-down breed. Along with Senator McCarthy, a new fangled political class appeared in America, which seemed to care about nothing but making money and waging war, one and the same thing for the military industrial management team.

In the 1960s, my generation responded by going bonkers with peace, love and grooviness. Hippies and draft dodgers took to the streets, parks and public squares directly challenging the patriarchal psychosis of the time, unmasking and unmaking the speed, superficiality and sterility of a corporate culture that, to this day, carries on with war through destroying the environment, human imagination and human relationships, using the latest technology to hasten the process. Towards what end, we wondered? Don't ask. Don't tell.

Chong apparitional theater followed three principles: 1) each performance was offered only once; 2) it was performed with no motive for gain; and 3) it was performed for those who saw it by happenstance and was intended as a gift to the people and to God. We lived monkish yet sybaritic lives of voluntary simplicity, avoiding media and cultivating an aesthetic of unknown-ness. Our theatrical events had a hit-and-run quality, eerily prescient of the terrorist tactics of today but never with the intent of doing harm; quite the opposite in fact. So, for example, when there was a citywide garbage strike one summer in the 1980s, the Chongalong guerrillas suited themselves out in black garbage bags and piled up in rotting heaps of refuse on Spadina Avenue. At around 8am and again at 6pm when people trudged through summertime's slime and stink on their way to and from work, a costumed percussion band known as the Machingo Society would materialize from a lane behind the Toronto Dominion Bank on College Street, whereupon the garbage would jump up and boogie back to life.

Like Buddhist suttas, Machingo Society incantations remind us that all phenomena exist because of causes and conditions. When the causes and conditions for them cease to exist, they also cease to exist. Simple enough. But who among us is willing to commit to this kind of simplicity with its deeper implications? It implies that we are all connected to one another and have to take care of one another and do something about the garbage we make in our terminal pursuit of freedom, security and happiness in the la la land of our doomed planet. Machingo wisdom counsels moderation and equanimity. Don't be sad, the Machingo men and women chant, this is not a permanent state of affairs. Nothing is. "If all the sorrows in the world your heart besiege, don't be grieved, just say it will all pass away."[6]

At the end of the day, the musicians would shepherd their flock of ghostly garbage bags back home, thus relieving the world of a little litter and perchance getting a smile or two along the way. Each performance was unique. Seldom did they happen more than once, but there were many such shows along the way. They had names like "Night Migration," "Vas y Donc pour Une Cake," "Bag Lady Prosperity Dance," "Bishop Chong's Book of Hours," "The Hieroglyphic Animal Crackers," "The Womb Bomb/Bomb Womb Ceremony" and "Snowball's Chance." The last of these rites, "Rat Plaza Reunion," was intended as a "de-obsession" of Chong cults wherein all artifacts related to apparitional theater were publicly incinerated in the plaza behind HRH King Ha Iti Iti's palace on Huron Street in the King Lee Apartments.

Being part of a Chong parade was like dreaming you are dreaming, and that in your dreaming you fall into to a swollen river and are being carried along by the torrent, God only knows where. Rat Plaza Reunion especially had this feeling because we all understood it marked the end of our brief but brilliant civilization. Sixty-four Chongalongs processed through the back alleys of Spadina on June 21, 1992 for four hours bearing the relics of our collective history. We trained hard for six months for this operation and suddenly there we were, in the river. It was an occasion of initiatory significance that carried people away from each other's company to distant places in their lives. Intuitively we understood the role separation and loneliness would play in our lives as we aged and the world became less hospitable to our kind.

Jack Kerouac was right: "All life is a foreign land." The party was over. We sensed it like rats on a sinking ship. Yet Rat Plaza Reunion had a festive atmosphere, rather like an Irish wake, with its liturgical climax coming in the "Shake the Snake Awake" ceremony. We raised our arms and shook colorful snake staffs at the sun setting behind the old synagogue at the corner of Cecil Street and Hotelvilla Lane, saying farewell once and for all to childhood's beautiful nonsense. "The snake had shed its skin to find the snake within."[7]

In hindsight, this ceremony marked the beginning of a new era, a revolutionary turning outward towards the real world—to the war zones in Sri Lanka and the killing fields in Cambodia—while simultaneously cultivating deeper roots of mysticism and silence. Some of us had signed on to help Nancy Brown conspire with the kids at Hugh MacMillan Rehabilitation Centre[8] creating the Spiral Garden. This was the children's gift to us and, reciprocally, it became our gift to the world.


## Spiral Garden

The Spiral Garden would never have happened without a fox spirit joining forces with the Mango Boatmen and Joe Carasco, the landscape gardener at HuMac. Nancy Brown mistakenly thought she had an agreement with the administration for an outdoor children's garden after Dr. Shmuk's infusion of intravenous rainbow spirits flowed into the center, but it all fell through at the last minute.

The garden "dance" was predictably unpredictable. There are always gaps in communication which should be taken as a given. I've learned that the spirit is in these gaps if it is anywhere at all, but you have to be patient and receptive if you expect to learn anything, and you must also be willing to accept prophetic, as well as not usually profitable, advice. You learn to stop and listen in silence to the spirit in the gap—in the liminal space between words, breaths, thoughts and the blink of an eye—until it becomes second nature.

Something else complicates my understanding at this point: when it comes to the "poiesis" of the Garden Path (the creative process mediating practical and poetic possibilities in a garden space) nothing moves in a straight line. The Zen dictum to "only go straight" when in doubt is a teaching riddle or koan which can best be understood as an instruction to follow your deepest intuitions. If you listen to nature, to crows bargaining for position on a park bench, to kids explaining where the moon goes in the morning after it sets, to a star caught out in the rain, to dogs chasing rabbits in their dreams, you will discover how stories spiral endlessly on from one vortex into another. Some people find the flow of constantly shifting perspective impossible to manage. They're much more comfortable with log frame analysis and strategic planning than being led down the Garden Path by Dr. Shmuk—which is what happened when Nancy asked HuMac for the promised funds so Joe and I could carve a spiral pathway into their back lawn and get busy building wheelchair-accessible planters, ramps, sand traps and a bamboo water transportation system. Rome was not built in day. Neither was walking on water or getting this garden growing. It was the spring of 1983 and flowers were bursting into bloom. Meanwhile, the Intravenous Rainbow kids were languishing in their wards staring glumly out the windows into the Would-be Wanna-be Garden, while HuMac admin dithered, waiting for a decision from the board. Nancy called an emergency meeting with the Mango Boatmen and the kids. The Boatmen recommended inviting Mother Fox from her lair in the ravine for a consultation.

I walked on site early the morning when Joe and I were scheduled to start work and there she was, bold as brass, silent, sultry, full of subliminal suggestion, Madame Fox. I didn't see her come or go. She sat there looking curious but calm, self-contained and totally unconcerned about our predicament, her eyes roaming back and forth from Joe to me, as if to say, "Aren't you the lovely couple?" She smiled at her team: Joe with his wheelbarrow, me with my notebook. I realized the spot where she was sitting was the precise tip of the spiral and center of the garden universe as projected in preliminary drawings. The sun flashed as it came over the treetops and she lit up like a tongue of flame. "Get your mojo, Mr. Po Jo," she said. "Now's the time! Don't let silly details stump you."

Joe cranked up his rototiller and we sliced a spiral pathway into the dew-damp ground. A few days later, while we were waiting to be arrested, the money came through. We followed this spiral pathway as day follows night for many years thereafter, always relying on the wisdom of Mother Fox to help us dream our out-of-the-box dreams.

Perhaps it's my Celtic background, but spirals are an obsession with me—spirals, and labyrinths. Both are pathways that compress a journey into a small space. They are ancient symbolic devices going back to Neolithic times, perhaps earlier. Although we don't know why early people drew them, we have discovered, in drawing and walking them ourselves, that they have power to soothe the anxious soul and provide direction for someone who is lost. They encourage empathy because they require us to travel outside our own experience, expanding our frame of reference. They help us to see that our entire time in this world is spent in pilgrimage from one sacred moment to the next without going anywhere. We are grains of sand in an hourglass turned at random by the humorless hand of fate.

The word "path" and the word "empathy" resonate with one another. When we embark on a journey of healing or redemption, along the way we are bound to experience regret, confusion and fear. But if we persevere we will find friends who accompany us, at least for a while. Eventually the path leads home where another journey inevitably begins. Friends notwithstanding, there come times when we must walk on, facing very difficult decisions alone. To reach our destination we must turn away from it and enter the way of unknowing. This is the nature of the Garden Path.

> We shall not cease from exploration
>
> And the end of all exploring
>
> Will be to arrive where we started
>
> and to know the place for the first time.[9]

There is great wisdom walking a spiral or labyrinth, exploring it not only underfoot but also within our breath. By inviting children to come and go from the garden every day by way of this spiral pathway, we were helping them find the way back home to their hearts and know themselves perhaps for the first time. By accompanying them we also grew and healed in places we never knew we were broken.

The first summer began with the artist Melanie Tchaikovsky, a thrice-removed, twice-replaced great grandniece of Pyotr Ilyich Tchaikovsky, the Russian composer. I followed Mel's musical intuitions as we broke ground and started laying out the site with inspired input from the teaching and medical staff of HuMac and another inspired soul, a Chong landscape gardener by the name of Laura Berman. Laura perceived the garden site as a "woman," her head and hair the rows of plants and flowers, her right hand gesturing in towards the heart, her left arm sweeping out to include the whole world. Come Canada Day, July 1, 1983, neighborhood kids were invited to join in, so the Spiral Garden became fully integrated with specially abled children from the hospital, physically normal children from the neighborhood and superannuated Chongalong superstars all interacting.

At first the program spanned two months only—July and August—like a summer camp, but eventually it expanded from mid-May until Halloween. The difficult part was scheduling kids for the garden between their medical and therapeutic appointments and learning what they could and could not do given the physical challenges they faced.

More and more Chong artists and graduate students from the Ontario College of Art and the Nova Scotia School of Design came on board as the program expanded year by year. A second garden, called the Cosmic Birdfeeder, opened in 1994 at the original Bloorview campus. There must have been over 25 artists and volunteers working at the Spiral Garden itself by the time I moved on in 1994. They were graphic artists, painters, mimes, puppeteers, musicians, costume designers, fabric artists and sculptors. And, oh yes, a story-teller. I found Professor Trölldust (aka Norman Perrin) headfirst in a recycle bin at Ecology House when I went there one day to find out what, if anything, ecology might have to do with a garden like ours. We were just beginning to understand in those days that the whole environment thing was a misnomer. There was no "environment." It was all one thing with no inside or outside really, and all of it was interconnected and interdependent from top to bottom. What you push down here, pops up there. There's no getting away with anything.

True, we human beings are the delinquents in God's greater plan. We are also the dreamers. And with time, by sharing our dreams through art, we might moderate our delinquent tendencies, since dreaming is what ties all mankind together. Dreaming aloud is a ritual art form usually enacted on consecrated ground, places like the Asklepeion on Kos in ancient Greece, and indeed, the Spiral Garden during the late 80s in Toronto.

We developed a sophisticated method for generating stories that linked together all the various creative centers on site, from the potato patch to the Legend House, to FIASCO (Friends In Art Seeding Creative Opportunity) and the hinterlands of the Hoo-Chee-Poo World.[10] Story was recognized as the hidden structure and unifying principle of the garden. Very often, if not always, the seeds of a story or theater extravaganza lay in the myriad of images being generated around the garden at any given moment by children playing.

At one level, the idea was to get these images to cross-pollinate and proliferate. At quite another level, we wanted to capture and contain them in stories, theater, processions and parades. There was a third countervailing force whereby we encouraged the children to fully enter and accept their own bodies and there take a firm foothold through play. This was the tricky part, because we knew that at some point they would have to put all imagination away and stand fast simply in who they were. No more Hoo-Chee-Poo, which had become a wish-fulfilling gem for many of them. Just the hard truth of their maimed reality and what we could do together to make it work for them.

They played with paint, clay, fabric, twigs, leaves, wood offcuts, binding twine, baling wire, balloons, mud, a bit of make-up and the words of a song found on the wind or composed by the cricket living in the creaking axel of the teeter-totter (seesaw). His chirps in concert with the rhythmic up-and-down squeaks of the teeter-totter could provide the basis of a percussion interlude and line-dance by the Wunday Society of the Harvest Festival.

A site-specific method of mythography developed in the Spiral Garden provided the database for our collective memory. The Story Stone technique developed by Professor Trölldust (once I had extracted him kicking and screaming from the recycle bin) is now a standard part of the Out-of-the-Box Curriculum. It has proved over time to be an enduring and effective way to introduce young people around the world to the living theater of their imaginations.

It was in the spring of 1994 I was invited by Dr. Robbie Chase and his colleagues at McMaster University's Centre for International Health to join their newly formed Health Reach team to create a Garden of Peace modeled on the Spiral Gardens in the West Bank, Gaza, former Yugoslavia or Sri Lanka. My Balinese crickets piped up in chorus and I packed my bags and headed for Batticaloa, Sri Lanka, in the fall of that year.

The children and staff of the Spiral Garden minted a special edition of commemorative clay coins and filled a woven straw replica of the Mango Boat for my voyage. I was instructed to present them along with diplomatic credentials dressed in full crow regalia on arrival in Sri Lanka as the garden's "emissary." My dear old childhood friend, Jan Mackie, a costume artist with the National Ballet of Canada as well as the Spiral Garden program coordinator, made me an outfit to wear on my new assignment. It was the most resplendent crow I ever saw, so much so I was a little nervous it might make the Batti crows jealous.

This crow had it all: marvelous, fluorescent-orange, three-toed feet that attached to my ankles like spats with Velcro straps; a resilient lightweight foam beak (also orange in color) through which I could clearly view the ovoid world I was entering like a Mars Probe astronaut and, best of all, the most glorious multi-colored bustle a crow upstart anywhere in the world could wish to sport—a bustle that contained a secret weapon guaranteed to cut to the quick of any kid's heart: a whoopee cushion! Jan was way ahead of me on this one, having two mischievous lads of her own. If there's anything kids everywhere in the world understand it is the subversive nature of a well-timed fart. I used the technique with reserve, but to great effect in my mission to the war-weary children of Batticaloa, and they responded in kind by giving the Canadian Crow an honorific title that will go down in the annals of humanitarian assistance in Sri Lanka forever. I was knighted Katadi Aiya by the children, Sir Windy, and I could not have been more pleased had I received the Order of Canada.

## Always

Bishop Chong accompanied me to the airport. He lifted the tea cozy miter off his silver mane and rested an arthritic old hand on my shoulder. "This may be the last time we meet, my son. You are going to war. Our one and only Chong volunteer. I'm very proud of you but I must say...worried."

"Don't worry about me, Your Remnants. You know I'll be back."

"Certainly you will, but remember—by the Three Ages is mankind's trajectory in this world determined. Frankly, I'm confused where we are in the cycle right now—whether it's going up or down."

"Down like a lead balloon, judging from all reports."

"Quite so, but one can never rule out serendipity, my son, especially when you're on your way to Sri Lanka, which happened to be called Serendip in the time of the ancient Persians."

"Serendipity: look for one thing, find another. Is that it?"

"Correct. Allow me to tell you a story. In ancient times there were three princes, sons of the great King, Giaffar. These three sons came to represent the Three Ages of Man that govern our lives: Silly, Stupid and Senile, and Giaffar put equal faith in all of them. Each ruled for seven years and then yielded to the next. To this day the system holds."

"So what does that have to do with me and the price of paripoo[11] in paradise?"

"I'm coming to that. According to my calculations, it turns out that you will land in Serendip exactly at the dawning of a new age of Silliness, in fact the silliest age ever and possibly the last. This is most auspicious for you!"

"Really? How can this be auspicious if I may ask?"

"Well for one thing, everyone will throw money at you now. That can't be bad, can it?"

"Not at all...I guess...so how does it all play out then?"

Bishop Chong tilted the tea cozy on his head at a rakish angle and regarded me fondly. He then spoke as though he was no longer in the room, his homiletic reverb on full volume. He became "Moses on the mountain" right there at Pearson International. It could have been embarrassing but no one paid him any mind, thank God.

"I can't tell you everything, my son, but I will tell you this. For seven years from 1994 to 2001, you will be in *Silly* mode with kids and clowns in your ascendant who make the Butterfly Peace Garden a reality. Then from 2001 to 2009, you will achieve a kind of *Stupid* serenity as money and offers pour in from around the world. You and the garden will be famous: your 15 minutes of fame, so to speak. Around 2010 the impact of the stock market crash in 2008 hits you, money evaporates into thin air and the garden implodes. For the next seven years from 2010 to 2017 you are completely and incurably shattered, a *Senile* zombie roaming in the wilderness."

"Silly. Stupid. Senile… I get it. Doesn't sound promising. Maybe I shouldn't go."

"Oh no, no, no! Don't be silly! Besides, what choice do you have? It's your fate. Do you remember what the Rubaiyat says?"

"I remember one verse, I think."

"Which one?"

"The Moving Finger writes; and, having writ, Moves on: nor all thy Piety nor Wit Shall lure it back to cancel half a Line, Nor all thy Tears wash out a Word of it."[12]

"Exactly! Your goose is cooked before you pop it in the oven. Do you want to know the rest?"

"Yes, uh… No! My flight is here, I better run!" I grabbed my bags. The Bishop accompanied me through Departures. I wasn't listening to his rant anymore but I could hear what he was saying. Swept along in the fluctuating tides of intercontinental transit I studiously ignored every word.

"Senility isn't bad, my son. I've been there for years, none the worse for wear. You don't need to carry a shepherd's crook and wine skin. That's what I do, but rest assured, you will steer your way quite competently. Do you want to know how?"

"No."

"No? How can you not want to know how?!"

"I like not knowing; the element of surprise. I like that."

"I'm going to tell you anyway. It's my duty as your bishop. After the Butterfly Garden, you retreat to a cave on the Mekong in Isaan, and write an account of the children you met in Batticaloa called *Small Wonders*. No one hears from you for a while. You disconnect, dissociate—despair, actually—immersing yourself in the fog of your own failure. Post-traumatic stress disorder? Who knows? No reason for it really, because you actually made it through the course fate assigned you when you met those kids in Bali and Batticaloa. And you give an honorable account of the times in your muddle of Mud Mountain Journals: *Cuckoo in the Jam, Blood of the Mango, Nightfall of Coconuts.*"

"Which, of course, never see the light of day…"

"A mere detail, son… Well on in years you return to Canada with a box of toys you drag around in a daze, attempting fatuously to demonstrate the magic possible in every moment, like your friend Zeke did back in Detroit when you were a kid. But the world will have moved on and it won't be long before global warming takes its toll with raging wildfires devastating huge tracts of forest in the Americas, glaciers melting down in Greenland, coastlines disappearing, desertification, wars for oil and water, refugees at the gates of Rome, Paris and Berlin, fascist backlash, total corruption at the top, and all the rest. Self-help gurus babble away on fatuous talk shows, parliaments dissolve while politicians take to the treetops twittering from aloft. Down below people consult their smartphones for direction, streaming to supermalls to shop, and church to pray for peace or Armageddon, very often confusing them for the same thing…"

"With respect, Your Remnants, it looks like I'm busted before I begin. But how do you know all this, anyway? None of what you say even happened. Or ever will!"

"No, it will. It will, my laddie. It will! I swear by my pectoral cross. But don't be discouraged. The toys you bring back? They're precious and beautiful and the legacy of war children around the world, a gift to us—the people who give them the wars. And I hope you're hearing what I say and take it on board, because…" he turned and stopped dead in his tracks… "This is it. We won't be meeting again. Not in this world. You must be bone-headed, my son, and believe in the toys and in yourself. Bone-headed! Got it? Meaning single-minded, like a diamond drill bit. That's the key."

"This is the final announcement. Passengers for Cathay Pacific Flight 721 to Vancouver and Hong Kong…"

We embraced, and my dear friend Bishop Chong burst into tears, then bent over in a spasm of uncontrolled laughter. Then the tears again. Just as suddenly as he started crying, he stopped, advancing purposefully in my direction with a twinkle in his eye.

"I just remembered something. Omar Khayyam had another line besides the one about the fickle finger of fate that made him famous."

"I bet I know the line you're thinking of," I said.

"I will give you a prize if you do," he said. "It's all you need to know in this world."

I told him what I knew without doubt. "Be happy for this moment, for this moment is your life." He lowered his shades and put them in his pocket. Nodding slowly, he raised both arms above his head thrice like the Great Auk of Om, then placed his hands gently on the crown of my head.

Closing his eyes, he whispered in a barely audible croak, "Kiss my ring… I'm out of here."

"What's my prize?" I asked, bowing to kiss his Bisbee blue[13] episcopal ring made by King Ha Iti Iti himself in the seventh year of his reign.

"I shall remain with you, Bonehead," he said, lowering his hand. "Always."

"Is that a promise or a threat?" I asked, but he'd already pixelated and vanished into the crowd.


## Butterfly Peace Garden of Batticaloa

Father Paul Sutkunayagam is a Jesuit priest from Batticaloa, Sri Lanka. When we first met in 1994 he was attending a conference at McMaster University in Hamilton as a partner in the Health Reach project. When he returned the following year, we visited the Spiral Garden together. He was totally enthralled and expressed a keen desire to establish a "garden of peace" in the war zone where he lived. He had witnessed the suffering among young people there and understood only too well how their marginalization fed into a self-perpetuating cycle of ethnic hatred and violence.

As time progressed, Father Paul and I were able to consolidate a partnership with Health Reach and make concrete plans for a peace garden in Batticaloa. He and I worked very well together. He was my mentor, my new Bishop Chong. Everything seemed to click effortlessly into place.

When I asked him, during a planning retreat on Majestic Island in the Kawarthas, what he would name this garden, without a moment's hesitation he replied, "Vanathithipoochchi Samathana Pongka"—the Butterfly Peace Garden.

Father Paul is a psychologist with a background in philosophy and theology so he may well have understood that the word "psyche" in ancient Greek can translate either as "soul" or "butterfly." I can say the idea of butterflies being emancipated souls pleased me in retrospect. Butterflies are delicate yet resilient creatures. They come in many sizes, colors and shapes, specks of iridescent dream fragments blowing and drifting through our turbulent lives, there to remind us of the passing of beauty, the passing of time, the passing of life. In Father Paul's context of the Sri Lankan civil war zone, a butterfly would land, either on the open palm of a child's hand, or in the cup of a moist morning flower, or on the barrel of a sleeping soldier's gun, with the same lightness of touch, curiosity and insouciance. It moved through the world haphazardly in a pattern of inscrutable dance no human mind could configure or guess at.

By the time I arrived in Batticaloa, Sri Lanka in 1996, an estimated 60,000 to 70,000 people had been killed in the north and east since the escalation of the conflict in 1983. The civilian population was caught in a vice between a variety of government and pro-government forces on the one hand, and anti-government forces on the other. Harassment, intimidation, extortion, torture, killings, disappearances, kidnappings, assassinations and a range of human rights abuses were common. Ethnic-cleansing campaigns had destroyed relations between communities—Muslim, Tamil, Buddhist, Christian, Hindu and Sinhalese.

Batticaloa District had come to be known for its bomb-making and suicide bombers—one clear indicator, along with the high suicide rate, of hopelessness among its young population. Not surprisingly within this context, contact between children of different ethnic and religious communities had diminished and there evolved a corrosive culture of segregation and violence. It was in this soil that the Butterfly Peace Garden took root.

The garden was an oasis of imagination and creativity in eastern Sri Lanka that brought together artists, peace workers, ritual healers and children from various ethnic and religious groups, to nourish the spirit of healing and peace for generations to come. It became a small zone of peace dedicated to "earthwork, artwork, heartwork and healing" and a symbol of hope and inspiration focusing on the inherent rights and needs of children. Amid the horror and hopelessness of war it gave them a fresh opportunity to discover their creativity and potential, affirming that, in their own hands, hearts, imagination and intelligence they could find the seeds of peace and the possibility of shaping a new world together.

The war ethos of violence and destruction was replaced with gentleness and creation in the Butterfly Peace Garden. Both those aspects of the child which were wounded and those which remained resilient were addressed. By seeding the inner garden within their hearts as well as the outer garden of earthly experience with equal imagination and compassion, children healed and became healers in their communities.

## Oasis of poiesis

What made the Butterfly Peace Garden different from other work with war-affected children at the time was the miracle that happened within its half-acre perimeter by those who experienced it—some 25,000 children from the time of opening on September 11, 1996 up to its 15th anniversary in 2011. Though this number may appear insignificant, what made a radical difference between the garden and other programs was the primary operating principle of "presence in poiesis as the practice of peace," where peace is viewed as a balance of inner and outer forces.

The only way to connect with the moving elements of the garden, out of which its healing springs, is to empty oneself before the mystery and attend to its revelation moment to moment from the ground itself, by engaging in the making of living art, through imagination, story, painting, music, song, dance, ritual and theater. There are no bystanders in the creative process. Both children and animators are immersed in the garden poiesis. What this requires is bringing one's personal creativity to bear in an encounter with the unknown. Out of this encounter arises a confirming experience of the process through which creative intelligence works in the world.

There is a force that moves within a group, an individual or a situation that is distinctly "other" and not subject to outside control. It flows through our lives like a river. We can be refreshed, renewed, reborn by immersing ourselves in it, releasing ourselves to its flow. The opening of oneself to this creative intelligence through a combination of silence and exercises of the imagination brings with it a new kind of confidence in handling life situations, which of their very nature include contradiction, conflict and chaos.

As space opens up, new configurations of energy constellate that allow one to move into healthier ways of being. The ultimate goal of this transformative process is an enlargement of imagination for all those who participate, both adults and children. Balance, a sense of well-being and, indeed, blessing can be generated through contact with the deep ecology of creation. The universe in its emergence is neither determined nor random but creative. By aligning ourselves with this creativity through the gift of art we experience healing in our lives.

To be clear, poiesis is not a panacea. It merely opens psychic space so we can deal with our everyday situations from a more positive perspective—nothing more, or less. Through the cultivation of relationships of trust, through the sustained presence of friends walking a perilous path together, and through the primacy of its child-driven logic, the garden creates and de-creates itself continually.

In essence, it becomes a space where children "heal" themselves, and sometimes those wounded souls who work for them. This might be called "collateral healing" or it might be called a "blessing," for in offering themselves to creation rather than the destructive forces they encounter every day the children directly empower the Blessing Way of the Garden Path.

"Every practice in the garden's sanctuary, every song sung, story told and ritual enacted, every expression of creativity is a blessing and an offering."[14] Central to the idea of the Blessing Way is ephemerality, impermanence and a kind of questioning that goes along with it. Why be unheard to one another; why hurt one another in this fragile, fleeting butterfly world? Better to bless, to open, to love and enjoy being loved. This is the path of replacing self with other, of giving and taking, letting go and letting be, which helps us to see more clearly. "Il s'agit de voir tellement plus claire de faire avec les choses comme la lumiere."[15] Or it is necessary to see things more clearly; to do to things what light does to them.

The Butterfly children kept the light shining during the darkest times in Batticaloa. Though the children's imaginations were bruised by years of brutality, they were far from dead. Garden "animators" offered their many skills as artists and musicians to woo the children back to the wonders of collective imagination. The Butterfly Garden belonged to the children, plain and simple. All you had to do is read the signboard at the gate to get the picture. "If you consider the world of God, it is the world of children. If you consider the garden of God, it is the garden of children. If you consider how in the world we ought to live, then pay a visit to the place where playing are the children."[16]

## Awash in enigma

It was a mystery from day one. I arrived in Batti disguised as a humble crow detective, much indebted to the comedic genius of Inspector Clouseau, the French sleuth savant. Wherever would we find a place to cultivate our garden? How would we convince wary and war-weary parents, teachers, religious elders and community leaders to trust us with their children? What about getting kids to and from the garden? We had very limited funding beyond seed money from Health Reach, which turned out to be less than expected, so how would we keep the garden going once we got started? And where would we find local artists with the right trickster spirit to animate the garden?

One by one the problems became challenges, and the challenges, once embraced, evolved into transformative events through the dream process of the Garden Path—and serendipity, of course. Human beings are essentially "dream beings." What ties us all together beyond color, religion and culture is our capacity to dream. It is a form of play in which everyone delights, given the chance.

We combed Batticaloa District to find a place with the right combination of physical, spiritual and political quantum to cultivate a garden. We required accessibility, arable land, water, shade and security, not to mention police, army and ministry clearance at national, district and local levels as well as the tacit approval of the rebels. Very often, Tamils did not feel safe on Muslim land and vice versa. The issue of ownership was fraught with contradiction. In our garden tradition, the land must be "ceded to the earth," at least ceremonially, if not legally, before it can be seeded in the hearts of the children. That is, the sacred mission of the garden must not be usurped by whoever holds legal title to the land for private gain—a tall order in a country such as Sri Lanka where land issues are very much at the heart of the ethnic violence.

Our search for space ended when Fr. Paul and the Jesuit order decided to donate their own land behind St. Michael's College for a period of ten years to the children of Batticaloa in order to establish the Butterfly Peace Garden. This land, which had been a monastic garden for decades, was neglected during the war and had become an impromptu playground for children from the vicinity. World University Services of Canada (WUSC) donated a bus to the garden for the nominal fee of one dollar. From out of the blue, representatives of a Dutch development organization, HIVOS (Humanistisch Instituut voor Ontwikkelingssamenwerking or Humanist Institute for Cooperation), visited the garden and agreed to support us for a period of one year, with the condition that longer-term support might be possible given the strength of the fledgling garden's performance during the trial period.

The Butterfly Peace Garden of Batticaloa became one of HIVOS's exemplary partners for the next 12 years, a felicitous arrangement on both sides. This partnership led to collaborations with other international organizations such as the Canadian International Development Agency, the Canadian Red Cross, the Canadian High Commission, the Royal Netherlands Embassy in Colombo, WUSC, War Child Canada, the German trade union syndicate Arbeiter Samariter Bund (ASB) and the German Organization for Technical Development (GTZ).[17]

The garden had a ripple effect in the country. Responding to the emergency of the tsunami, in 2005 I invited two Sinhalese artists, Chaminda Pushpakumara and Nalaka Ranasinghe, to train in the skills of animation with the Butterfly Garden.

They later opened two centers for contemplative art—one in Colombo (Step-by-Step Studio) and one in Negombo (Crippled

Crow Centre for Contemplative Art)—and assisted me in the design, installation and programming for Kalabala Bindu Garden in Hambantota, a facility for tsunami-affected children of the south, supported by ASB. Their collaboration continues to this day with the Monkey's Tale Centre and WUSC in reconciliation-based Peace Puzzle[18] projects in the south.

The attitude of an ideal garden animator is fundamentally summed up in three words: openness, awareness and spontaneity. It is a matter of learning to dance with the moment. One of the initial challenges was how to find such people. I quote in part from an advertisement that was published on March 3, 1996 in the Tamil newspaper *Virakesari* when we were seeking facilitators or animators for the Butterfly Garden. It was a most unusual ad for the times, in that it requested applications from all communities—Hindu, Muslim, Christian, Buddhist—for a children's program aimed explicitly at promoting peace in Batticaloa:

> Cultivation of imagination in oneself and other is a key objective of the Butterfly Peace Garden. This requires that all the animators be in touch with their own imaginations, that as a regular practice they cultivate the arts in one form or another. The dedication to their art should be open-hearted enough to include children and the creative processes of nature and other adults. This open-hearted, creative, joyful spirit takes precedence over official credentials as childcare workers, teachers or play program facilitators, be they ever so impressive. At the Butterfly Garden, the child is the teacher. Her images and stories become the structure around which all the Butterfly Garden will unfold. An animator in the Garden programs must be willing to follow the child's lead. S/he should be a good listener and observer, skillfully interacting with the delicate and mysterious processes of garden and child…

After an extensive period of search, interview and audition we found the animators we needed. They were very special people, not only because of their skill sets but even more so because of their sensitivity to the children. They possessed a deep personal familiarity with the war where most of the victims have been non-combatants or civilians. Some had to stand helplessly by when loved ones were arrested under the Prevention of Terrorism Act in conjunction with emergency regulations, never to return home again. Many had lost loved ones or even been forced to watch when family members or community members were publicly tortured or killed. Yet their greatest strength, which they demonstrated to the children's unflagging amusement over many years, was comedy.

## Komali Theater

The Komali (clown) Theater of the Butterfly Garden was based on stories the clowns themselves made up, or stories the children created in the clay at Mud Mountain, most of them fables strongly imbued with a sense of irony and black humor. Komalis were essentially contrarians— they did everything the opposite way to the dominant culture.

The essence of the clown mind is always backward. He is a trickster. A contrarian. Whatever people are doing in one direction, the clown does in the opposite direction and that is usually funny. But it is also serious, because the clown is offering a critique of the predominant view. So if everyone else is walking forwards, they will walk backwards, and if everyone says "yes," they will say "no." This is consistent with modes of Chong Apparitional Theater and Spiral Garden parades. In the case of the Chong, the clowns ridiculed the corporate/consumer combination that regards people as products in their soulless monopoly game. In the Spiral Garden, it had to do with differently abled children. Where they might be considered dispensable in some segments of society, the clowns would show them as the equal or better of anyone else. Clowns always switch perspective around.

We worked very hard at this in the Butterfly Garden, where there was an elite Clown College run by Professor Kungilliyam (Professor Firebomb, aka Thuraisamy Naguleswaren). Children learned how to make scripts from scratch and bring them to life. Nothing was taboo. There were some scenes that spoofed abduction, torture and terrorism, subjects that were very sensitive and politically silenced at the time.

Everything was original—story, costumes, staging, music and dance routines—and everything was unabashedly over the top, influenced by ever-popular Bollywood and Chennai films, which everyone adored in Batticaloa. Since each cohort of children came for nine months there was plenty of time to work up routines. The most popular characters from one season often returned in the next, much as they do in a television series or soap opera.

The comedy, story and improvisation tools of the Komali Theater expressed themselves in three different forms at the Butterfly Garden: 1) weekly performances of the works-in-progress at the Mango Tree Theater, every Thursday afternoon; 2) end-of-the-season operas where popular characters and situations that appeared during a nine-month season reappear in a final musical spectacular; and 3) parades, which run the gamut from runway fashion shows to the kind of extravaganza a clown might conceive of for Red Square, if somehow they managed to persuade the Politburo of its political merits.

Komali Theater united all the other art forms practiced in the garden, from writing and acting to painting sets, making costumes and props, composing and performing songs and dance. The garden was an improvized temple of dreams for children whose faith in themselves was broken by war. It was both a public stage and sacred space where dreams were renewed and young dreamers revived. No one was left out of the process.

The Butterfly Peace Garden is also the source and inspiration for the Out-of-the-Box Curriculum, a komali curriculum and seed kit of Garden Path wisdom, now available in Sri Lanka and Canada. Its practices draw on years of trauma treatment experience in an active war zone where children from conflicted ethnic and religious groups are given an opportunity to discover their original unity simply through being who they are as playful human beings.

## Time out for a tsunami

The day after Christmas in 2004, a massive tsunami made landfall at Maruthamunai about 30 kilometers from Batticaloa town. From there it proceeded to sweep the entire littoral of Sri Lanka leaving immense destruction in its wake. The Butterfly Garden responded by focusing its logistical and creative energies on bringing relief to children in its locality where 280,000 people were displaced in one morning.

I wrote a series of reports on the effects of the tsunami over the next three months, informing friends around the world what had happened to us. Here are excerpts from three of those reports.

## JANUARY 2, 2005: BUTTERFLY PEACE GARDEN—TSUNAMI REPORT 2

Twelve days have passed since the tsunami swept over Sri Lanka. So much is happening, so fast—a rip tide of events with ripple effects throughout all sectors of society. No one has a handle on this. Everybody's guessing.

… The earthquake is over but shoreline communities are trembling with aftershocks of social mobilization organized by government at various levels and non-governmental organizations with help from the UN and disaster management teams from Europe and North America. Communities at ground zero are coming to grips with a vastly altered reality. Things will never be the same. But just how different will they be?

… There are worries that heavy-handed social engineering at this point will result in the loss of local culture for coastal communities. Some see an opportunity for peacemaking across ethnic lines. Others fear the aid effort will become politicized, fueling new conflict scenarios with money siphoned of into military re-armament. There is genuine concern about the outbreak of diseases such as cholera, typhoid, malaria and pneumonia.

… Although many horrifying tabloid-style reports have surfaced in the press concerning people, particularly in the south, taking advantage of the situation for personal gain— stealing children, stealing homes, stealing relief money intended for victims—the experience in Batticaloa has been orderly with few exceptions. Even the LTTE,[19] the Sri Lanka army and the Special Task Force[20] are reported to be cooperating in the Batticaloa and Ampara districts.

… It has been at once humbling and empowering, this tsunami. No matter how besieged we are, we now know we are not alone. We are digging through the rubble and amidst all the grief and horror; we are finding our heart, our common humanity. We are finding the energy and commitment needed for renewal, reconstruction and rehabilitation buried there in the ruins.

## FEBRUARY 1, 2005: BUTTERFLY PEACE GARDEN—TSUNAMI REPORT 3

One month ago on Unduvap Full Moon, out of the clear blue, this tsunami arrived and took Lanka in its embrace. For a brief ten minutes from one seaside town to the next, it had its way with her, tearing the resplendent coastal raiment to shreds and shaking the island to its core. It was rape, by someone you know and trust. Someone true blue and treacherous: the sea. This tsunami killed up to 40,000 people and displaced about a million in Sri Lanka alone. Three-quarters of these are in the north and east.

… We are adrift in irrationality. Nobody can find time or space enough in their lives to deal with the grief that eddies all around. We are too busy picking up the pieces and beginning again. If the tidal wave of water was 20 meters high, the wave of sadness sweeping across Sri Lanka reaches the moon.

…. Before the wave there were 5500 people living in Navalady and Pudumuhutuvarum, less than 5 kilometers from where I live. Of these, there are 1400 survivors. Fifty percent of the deceased were children. We secured permission from the District Secretary to bring these children into the Butterfly Garden from their temporary settlement camp at Methodist Central College. There are many things I will remember about that day but three recollections come readily to mind along with many mixed emotions.

First there was the enthusiasm of the children, their thirst for play. They descended from the bus and tore through the garden like a little tsunami, such was their joy and delirium. They shouted and ran everywhere climbing trees, dancing on tables, chasing the ducks, touching everything with their eyes, their fingers, their unrestrained curiosity. The pelican, from his perch on the bullock cart, cast a wary eye on this uncivil intrusion into his tranquil domain. Every inch of terrain, every member, part and particle of the garden, including all its people and places, was surveyed, slotted, secured. "You are mine," the children seemed to be saying. "You belong to me!" Within moments of arriving, they completely possessed the garden, and for the rest of the day they used it with the anarchic bravado of children playing in their own backyard.

The second thing I remember is being lifted off my feet by a boisterous mob of these kids sometime mid-afternoon and carried from the garden minaret to the kuthu merlai[21] where I was unceremoniously dumped in the sand with kids dancing wildly around chanting, "tsunami, tsunami," as though it were ring-around-the-rosy. I laughed with them, but I was a bit shaken by their frenzy, and astounded by the nerve it took on their part, the freedom they must have felt. Many other adults were carried off in this spontaneous outburst of tsunami-inspired mischief, even visitors unknown to them from Colombo. This must be therapeutic, I remember thinking, as I dusted myself off. It must be good for them, though no therapist I know would ever be so bold to prescribe this ritual as a collective nostrum for children suffering from tsunami trauma.

And the third thing was Sassi and Ganesh, two boys who seemed to forget themselves in the interests of the younger children. What quickly becomes apparent when you see these kids en masse is that many adult caregivers are so grievously assaulted by their own losses that the surviving children in their charge are left to fend for themselves. They tend to congregate in packs and decide on their own agenda. Among them are boys and girls who stand out as leaders. Though their hearts must also be broken, though they too are homeless and adrift, they somehow manage to overcome the misery attendant to this catastrophe and look out for the little ones.

… Imagine this for a moment. A boy of seven is running from water which is bearing down on him from above. He comes to an inlet on the lagoon where a dhoni (small catamaran canoe) is drifting. He realizes that if he can only climb aboard there is a chance he will survive. He tries to hoist himself up but the boat is in motion, already being driven from the shore. He loses his grip, slips and falls in the muck, and frantically tries again. His hands are slippery with mud. Suddenly, seconds before the water hits, he is lifted from behind by a stranger who shouts in his ear. "Hold on boy, here we go!" There is so much confusion he barely understands what the man is saying. Then the water hits. The boat is propelled skyward and carried aloft to a calm patch of water mid-stream in the lagoon. All the boy knows, when he gets his bearings, is that he is adrift without a paddle. The turbulence has stopped. He is safe for the moment. But he is not alone. Coiled at his feet is gleaming black snake who also sought refuge in the little canoe. Together they drift to their destiny, companions in a narrow, and temporary, victory over certain death.

By March 2005 we set to work creating a standardized kit of "toys" called the Butterfly Garden Medicine Bag, which we brought to tsunami-affected kids in the villages to help restore their courage and confidence. I describe the idea of the "medicine bag" in a report at the time. It was to become the inspiration and prototype for today's Out-of-the-Box Curriculum.

## MARCH 1, 2005: BUTTERFLY PEACE GARDEN—TSUNAMI REPORT 5

These "toys" in our Medicine Bag are just that—toys— meaning the kids play with them just to have fun, but they are also therapeutic tools originating in or adapted specifically to the therapeutic approach of the Butterfly Garden. Each in its own way helps restore balance and confidence in the children affected by trauma and practitioners who assist them. Playing with the toys over an extended period connects both child and animator in an ongoing healing relationship. Like the garden itself, each toy is a mnemonic device that, when linked, makes the Butterfly Medicine Bag's potential much greater than the sum of its parts. It is a microcosm of the garden.

… Although the toys of the Medicine Bag are accessible to a broad age range of people, effective treatment depends on understanding the kit's full potential. Those who use it need training and, because of this need, a Batticaloa-based training and treatment center is conceived: the Garden Path Centre for Contemplative Arts and Narration.[22] The curriculum and services of the center revolve around the Butterfly Medicine Bag, including Meditation, Mystery Painting, MettaMapping[23] and other toys of the Garden Path. Young men and women, alumni of Garden programs, are trained there to become animators and facilitators in trauma treatment.

## War within war without end

There are places within ourselves that serve us well and which are of the light. These we celebrate. But there also darker places or personae within that terrify us, and which we'd rather avoid and not expose to others, for fear of censure and exclusion. "Ourself behind ourself concealed should startle most", was how the poet Emily Dickinson put it.[24] But what would happen if we chose to befriend ourselves? Befriend the other? Get real?

The adventure in learning we embark on when we follow the Garden Path Out-of-the-Box Curriculum brings with it both the soothing light of the tropics and the jagged shadows of a war zone. It exposes us to our own vulnerability but tempers the hard truth with the unqualified love and tenderness of the children who are its progenitors.

These kids whose lives had been overturned by chronic illness and disability (in Canada), communal violence, war and tsunami (in Sri Lanka) and genocide (in Cambodia) found it in themselves to meet and rise above their suffering at the Spiral Garden, the Butterfly Garden and the Mango Tree Garden—Garden Path sites all of which followed the principle of "presence in poiesis as the practice of peace." The Out-of-the-Box Curriculum is essentially the gift of these children to the world. They are its guarantors. Their innocence is its impeccability.

The fundamental intention of this curriculum is to bring us home to our humanity in its myriad manifestations, both dark and light, and to do it as gently as possible, accompanied by the spirit of the children of the Garden Path. In a metaphorical sense, we journey back to another garden, at the time when Adam and Eve were eyeing the apple. The dove is watching. The crow is watching. The serpent is watching. God is watching through the mirror of his people. The story unfolds like a movie, which we watch while acting it out ourselves. For the most part we go about our daily business unconscious of the archetypal drama we are enacting and the dream coiled up there in utero. We are dutiful, patriotic citizens but somehow we are entranced—seldom questioning the relentless march of progress, that anxious and anonymous accelerator that propels us from behind. We seem indifferent, if not oblivious, to the fact that we are being manipulated, and we are being watched. Maybe it's time to stop, take a good look at ourselves and take back control of our lives.

We are all refugees, teeming back into the homeland of the human heart. We need humility, we need courage and we need creativity to befriend one another in the turmoil of today's world, just like those kids at the Spiral Garden, the Butterfly Garden and the Mango Tree Garden did in their time of affliction. We have traveled so far in the course of our evolution and become so confused along the way that we have forgotten the basics: we are made for love, and humankind is our family. The children of the Garden Path want to share their spirit of transcendence with us. They want to share their toys.


## A glimmer of hope

Out of the blue, a little poem fell into my hands the other day. I was walking home in the early evening along Bloor Street in Toronto and I looked up to see the breathtaking beauty of Venus, the evening star. She was very bright, very close, and sparkling like a jewel. She seemed to be speaking. I stopped to listen and, as people bustled all around me, I heard what she had to say. "The twinkle in the star, the glimmer of hope, how lucky we are here, at the end of our rope."

Many people talk like this now. Even Stephen Hawking says the human race has a hundred years left at its present rate of decline. In other words, the world as we know it will be gone within the next century. Why bother with the poor little children in the war zones? Why bother with anything? We've already trashed this planet, time to move on to Mars.

I think the star may be twinkling with another message, the same one that came to us during the war in Sri Lanka, from the kids in the Butterfly Peace Garden. When you're at the end of your rope, there's no more room for duplicity, your own or anyone else's. We are at the point now where true participatory democracy remains a vague possibility but not without public education and massive mobilization of collective will. Maybe it's time to return to the streets the way we did in the 60s, and during the Occupy Movement, with town hall meetings and teach-ins to inform ourselves of the options at hand as they narrow by the day. We must likewise return to the inner sanctum of silence, and imagination within, for sustenance and inspiration.

"Against your better judgment, let's go and learn to walk on air,"[25] the poets declare. "Don't become mesmerized by the negativity all around." "Don't let fear paralyze you." Yes, there *is* fear in the air, but we have put it there.[26] We can replace it with courage, imagination, compassion and creativity. Work quietly, and create an alternative reality in all areas of life even under the most oppressive conditions; or I should say, *especially* under the most oppressive conditions, which is what we did with children in the Butterfly Garden for about 15 years, until the sky fell and donors universally pulled out, one after the other, during the financial meltdown in 2008. We don't blame them. We are grateful for the support that got us started and kept things going for more than 20 years, particularly the support and mentorship of our Dutch, German and Canadian partners.

Among the things we learned, were two important lessons: 1) we cannot rely entirely on external donors like governments and non-governmental agencies to carry us; and 2) we must use the resources we now have to fabricate the Out-of-the-Box Curriculum, and train people how to use it. We can begin to support ourselves by sharing what we have learned over the last 40 years following the Garden Path. The point is not to throw it all away. We will find ways to share it with people everywhere because what we've learned from the butterflies in Batticaloa cuts to the heart of a very modern malaise.

We have all this connectivity with our computers, smartphones and the internet. Yet people are more removed from one another than ever before. We inhabit a world our ancestors would have found impossible to recognize: seven billion people and an epidemic of loneliness. This is not progress. This is a terrible regression.

Part of the problem is that we grow up with education focused almost entirely on external values. We are not concerned about inner values. Because we are growing up with this kind of education, we have become very materialistic. The culture we have produced is primarily about buying, selling and promoting ourselves as a product. But we are not products. We are people, passing through a transitional moment in our evolution where we must hold fast to human values and recognize the interdependence of all beings or, as our prophets have warned, lose everything. "We must rapidly begin the shift from a thing-oriented society to a person-oriented society. When machines and computers, profit motives and property rights are considered more important than people, the giant triplets of racism, materialism and militarism are incapable of being conquered."[27]

We want the children we have met along the way, we want all children, to have hope in their future. Relationship and community are what nourish hope. There is a Tibetan saying that "Wherever you have friends, that's your country, and wherever you receive love, that's your home." We want to be part of that kind of world, and we believe the Out-of-the-Box Curriculum is a step in the right direction.

## The Out-of-the-Box Curriculum

There are ten toys in this first generation of the Garden Path curriculum. Some toys we invented (the Story Crow, the Story Snake, Mystery Painting, Mud Mountain and MettaMapping). Some we adapted from other sources (Kolams, Labyrinths, the House of Peace, Masks and the Amma Appa Game). All along the way we improvised and we invited others to do the same.

From July 2015 to December 2016, Master E. Kularaj, his studio assistant K. Thevakanthan and I worked on prototypes for the Out-of-the-Box Curriculum and field-tested them at the Monkey's Tale Centre with students from Eastern University and the Swami Vipulananda

Institute of Aesthetic Studies in Batticaloa. We also conducted workshops using the toys with trainees in WUSC's ASSET program.

The Out-of-the-Box Curriculum was first launched in Sri Lanka at the Monkey's Tale Centre in Batticaloa on October 2, 2016. It was later introduced in Canada at Toronto's Carrot Common on May 15, 2017. Plans are now being vetted to establish the Falling Sky Centre of Contemplative Art in Toronto (or, alternatively, in Hamilton or Ottawa) in order to implement the full Out-of-the-Box Curriculum within the refugee community.

The main teaching of the curriculum is this: We live in a moral universe in which ideas and actions have consequences. In the end, we get back what we give. This isn't exactly news but many people seem to have forgotten it these days. Our political and corporate masters work tirelessly to promote and reinforce this amnesia. The toys give us time to play and learn, and lots of space to get lost along the way. In fact, that's the whole point. Without getting lost, how will we ever find ourselves? But now is the time to wake up. The journey towards this destination, while undoubtedly the work of many lifetimes, forever unfolds in the moment at hand. Now is the time.

## 1. Kolams

Our rapidly changing world is a fearful place. No one knows whether or not the progress we have made will lead beyond reason to complete catastrophe. The creation of beauty is an antidote to fear, which itself is the natural response to not knowing what will happen next. Kolam drawing originates in India. It is a way of grounding ourselves through concentration on the breath. Because the world is moving so fast these days we make a deliberate practice of slowing down, clearing our minds and coming home to ourselves through engaging with these mystical diagrams.

## 2. House of Peace

The House of Peace is based on a traditional carpenter's puzzle adapted at the Butterfly Garden to illustrate the importance of bringing one's inner and outer lives into accord. Social and ecological harmony depends on people understanding that they do not exist in isolation from the rest of creation, nor are they sovereign over it. We are part of an intricately interwoven web of relationships embracing all beings. We are custodians and co-creators of beauty.

## 3. Labyrinths

Labyrinths are a playful and yet profound way of paying a visit to one's inner world at the point it meets and merges with outer reality. They involve ancient rituals that allow one to engage the soul's predicament, recognize its more or less knowable and workable parts, identify strengths and weaknesses both within oneself and one's community, recalibrate terms of engagement with outer realities and re-emerge more confidently into the field of action. We have identified four labyrinths—earth, air, fire, water—that lend themselves to different kinds of psychological environments.

## 4. The Story Crow

Though commonly considered shifty characters, crows are tricksters and sacred clowns who mirror human duplicity and self-deception in order to teach people the error of their ways. Were you to freeze-frame the chaos crows create around themselves, getting beyond all the squawk and talk, you might be surprised to discover a silent sage who is both observant in the seeing of things and clever in the saying of them.

## 5. The Story Snake

The two-headed Story Snake helps us accept uncertainty, honoring change and diversity, starting with our own ambivalence about who we are and why we are here. What is the point of all this suffering, violence and destruction? The Story Snake volunteers an answer, a host of paradoxical and impossible answers, in fact. The Story Snake brings different perspectives into the story circle using games that open us to complexity and transform us in positive ways.

## 6. Mud Mountain

The children of war zones pay a steep price for their elders' obsession with using violence to solve their problems. The greatest loss is the loss of their sense of beauty. Our ability to experience the world as mysterious and magical is dulled by habituation, particularly habituation to hyper-violence. Thus, there comes a time in life when we have to retreat up the mountain. Things are not right with us and we need to seek higher altitudes, and perhaps higher attitudes, where there is an opportunity to disengage from what passes for life below.

## 7. Masks

Masks are a means of exploring the question of identity. They raise the question of an identity more profound than one's ethnicity, culture, race and religion. Masks enable us to reach inside and touch a part of ourselves that is quintessentially human, opening up the possibility of understanding and embracing others who are different from ourselves.

## 8. Mystery Painting

Mystery Painting is a contemplative practice that combines silent meditation with art, story creation and dialogue. It allows us to give form to the unconscious energies and impulses that direct (or misdirect) our lives. Through cultivation of intuition and imagination, it allows us to better see what we care about, and leave behind that which smothers and ensnares us.

## 9. MettaMapping

MettaMapping unites people through their artistic creations. Painting, sculpture, installation, ritual and performance art from around the world inspire new images and stories in communities weakened by war, poverty, social marginalization and natural disaster. This image-based, non-sequential planning tool facilitates dialogue between people, enabling them to bridge differences through collaborative art encounters.

## 10. *Kuti Amma Appa Game*

The Kuti Amma Appa ("Little Mother Father") Game is a non-invasive accompaniment protocol developed at the Batticaloa Butterfly Peace Garden, with the intention of giving program animators a better picture of the participating children's lives and, even more so, to help child participants realize untapped strengths as heralds of healing and change within the war-weary world.

## The Out-of-the-Box future

On May 14, 2017, at the Carrot Common launch of the Out-of-the-Box Curriculum, Garden Path and the Community Counts Foundation announced the formation of a new coalition that offers tax credit for donors and logistical support for programs in creative process with youth in Canada, Sri Lanka and further afield using the Out-of-the-Box Curriculum. A brochure at the time elaborated a mission statement for the new Garden Path/Community Counts Coalition.

### *Mission*

Collaborating with a network of experienced artists, story-tellers, environmentalists, teachers, healthcare providers and community workers in Canada and abroad, the Garden Path curriculum offers training that awakens understanding and appreciation of creative process in young people, encouraging them to become catalysts for positive change in their communities.

### *Vision*

Inspired by lessons learned during 40 years of experience working with communities affected by war, natural disaster or disability in Canada, Sri Lanka and Cambodia, the Garden Path curriculum transforms dissociation and despair among young people into empathy and engagement with community renewal through practice and cultivation of the arts.

## Short-term objectives

- To establish the Garden Path/Community Counts Coalition in Toronto, Canada.

- To establish the Falling Sky Centre for Contemplative Art in Canada as a partner organization to Step-by-Step Studio and Monkey's Tale Centre in Sri Lanka.

- Using Mystery Painting and the Peace Puzzle as a point of departure, to inspire and instruct a core group of Canadian artist-animators in how to use the Garden Path Out-of-the-Box Curriculum in their communities, starting with a core group of Canada's Aboriginal people, its oldest inhabitants, and Syrian refugees, its newest arrivals.

- To consolidate the Garden Path archive at Falling Sky Studio.

## Long-term objectives

- To seed and support Peace Puzzle projects in Canada and Sri Lanka.

- To support the Sri Lankan reconciliation process through programs at the Monkey's Tale Centre, Butterfly Peace Garden and Step-by-Step Studio.

- To create a team in Sri Lanka that fabricates the Out-of-the-Box Curriculum and implements a training-of-trainers program at the Monkey's Tale Centre in Batticaloa.

- To create an affiliated team of Sri Lankan Peace Puzzle artists who are ready to go anywhere in the world to work with refugees using the Out-of-the-Box Curriculum.

## Timeframe

This is conceived of as a two-and-a-half-year pilot program which began on April 1, 2017 and will continue through to December 31, 2019. The project will be renewed with an expanded mandate in 2020 for a further five years with emphasis on skills enterprise development in Sri Lanka and training-of-trainers in programs in Sri Lanka and Canada in partnership with international donors.

## *Anticipated results*

At a time when it feels as if the sky is falling and the world is closing down in self-destructive politics we will continue to cultivate the Garden Path ideals of compassion, creativity and community in today's young people, so that they will shape a just and more understanding society tomorrow. Applying Garden Path principles, which have proven effective in times of war and natural disaster, we will inspire young people to embrace their future with wisdom and spontaneity.[28]

## Notes

1. The traditional ensemble music of Java and Bali, made up predominantly of percussive instruments
2. Majapahit empire—1293 to around 1500—a vast maritime state based on the island of Java and extending from Sumatra to New Guinea
3. Hugh MacMillan Medical Centre, popularly known as "HuMac" by the kids and staff when we were there, is now called the Holland Bloorview Kids Rehabilitation Hospital
4. Chong is a street gang of avant-garde Toronto artists
5. De Feritate Humanorum—*Concerning the Feral Nature of the Human Species*—Bishop Chong's only pastoral letter to his flock
6. The Apocryphon of Mother Ralphe—an early Chong inspirational text by a revered Chong saint
7. Leonard Cohen—a lyric from his last album, *You Want it Darker*. Cohen died on November 7, 2016
8. History of the Centre: http://hollandbloorview.ca/Aboutus/Welcometo HollandBloorview/History/ThelegacyofDrHughMacMillan
9. T.S. Eliot (1943) *Four Quartets: Little Gidding*. New York, NY: Harcourt
10. Hoo-Chee-Poo World—an imaginary realm mapped and maintained over the years by the children at Spiral Garden
11. Paripoo is lentil porridge, a staple dish in Sri Lanka
12. Omar Khayyam 1048–1131, Persian astronomer, mathematician, poet and philosopher
13. Bisbee blue refers to the turquoise that came from copper mines located in the vicinity of Bisbee, Arizona, now depleted

14. Lawrence, P. (2003) *The Ocean of Stories*. Colombo: International Centre for Ethnic Studies, p.15
15. Guillevic, E. (1969) *Selected Poems* (translated by D. Levertov). New York, NY: New Direction
16. Butterfly Peace Garden signboard verse is taken from *The Apocryphon of Mother Ralphe*, an early Chong inspirational text by revered saint
17. The GTZ has now been renamed Deutsche Gesellschaft für Internationale Zusammenarbeit (GIZ)
18. Peace Puzzle is an elaboration of mystery painting emphasizing teamwork in creative process—one of the toys from our Out-of-the-Box Curriculum
19. LTTE – Liberation Tamils of Tiger Eelam, a Tamil separatist organization fighting for the creation of an independent state in the north and east of Sri Lanka. It was defeated by the Sri Lankan military in 2009
20. The Special Task Force is a paramilitary wing of the Sri Lankan police
21. A kuthu merlai is a bamboo and palm thatch temple dedicated to dance and performance
22. This center opened in November 2005 and was later renamed the Monkey's Tale Centre for Contemplative Arts and Narration, the name it bears to this day
23. MettaMapping is an image-based method of strategic planning; from the Greek "meta," meaning the "big picture," and the Pali "metta," meaning compassion. The big picture behind Garden Path practices is to connect with compassion for oneself and others
24. Vendler, H. (2010) *Dickinson, Selected Poems and Commentaries*. Cambridge, MA: Harvard University Press, p.184
25. Seamus Heaney, 1939–2013, poet and playwright from Northern Ireland who received the 1995 Nobel Prize in Literature
26. Ben Okri, contemporary Nigerian poet and novelist
27. "Beyond Vietnam," Martin Luther King Jr., 1967
28. For Garden Path updates see www.thegardenpath.ca

## Chapter 9

# STORIES FROM CANADA,

## with Survivors of Cultural Genocide, Neo-Colonial Racism and Inter-Generational Trauma

*Dr. Sally Adnams Jones, TransformArta,*
*Expressive Arts Therapy*

I have great respect for trees. They have presence, patience and perseverance. As they grow tall, they slowly spread their roots deep and wide, dropping one seed in front of another. Quietly, they propagate their way across entire continents, creating vast forests in their wake.

Trees provide us with shade, shelter, fire and fruit, even the air that we inhale deep into our blood. Trees take care of us in the most substantive ways, and yet, their undemanding and ubiquitous nature make them invisible to us. Trees take no credit for their generosity and yet in my country, they are the supportive, unassuming backdrop against which every Canadian lives out their lives. I am not sure if my gratitude officially makes me a tree-hugger, however, as I also happen to carve trees. Trees have given me art.

Used by the indigenous people of Canada for thousands of years, trees are the traditional material for creating transport in the form of canoes, and shelter for communal gathering places. They also form part of a great legacy of powerful totem poles and masks hewn from red and yellow cedar. I was greatly privileged to train for a year with one of Canada's most respected First Nations master carvers, in the art of shaping cedar. This is my story with trees, and how I also came to understand them as instruments for the healing of people's souls.

In my capacity as an artist, and transformative educator, I was drawn to the carving studio of Simon Charlie, a Coast Salish elder, situated in an overgrown, rural woodland on Vancouver Island. Over the years,

Simon had gathered apprentices together to learn the traditional skills of his people, and one day I found myself standing with ten, young, First Nations men, as we watched a small truck, loaded with logs, back up towards us. As it parked, red cedar logs rolled off the back, dropping at our feet. The trees had been cut from deep in the rainforest, without any twist to their trunks, nor a single branch spiking from their girths. The student carvers were excited by this parade of cellulose perfection in front of us and we quickly appraised each one, like speed daters, searching for our unique log—the one that somehow might speak to our individual chemistry and imagination. Then, as we chose our match, we rolled our logs to a spot in the overgrown yard, and cleared a space for ourselves, to get to know our selected log. As I stared mutely at mine, I felt mildly queasy; I was overwhelmed with clumsy ineptitude when faced with the mystery held within my old-growth tree. Somewhere, gratitude opened up inside me for the lessons this wood would impart to me over the year to come.

Slowly, as we absorbed both the grace and the limitations of the cylindrical tube of our raw material, we tried to intuit what might be waiting for release. We turned our logs over, inspecting them closely from all angles. Hesitantly, we stood them up, caressed them, searching for any hidden defects. As we embraced their singular anatomy, we tried to "see" the possibilities of a future together over the next year.

I felt humility in the face of my tree and these great traditions of carving cedar trunks for totems and masks. As an artist, I was used to softer mediums: paint, canvas, clay, fiber. As a middle-class white woman, I felt under-equipped in the use of wood-cutting tools. I felt the self-doubt that my hands might fail me; the fear that my inspiration might abandon me; and the panic that my ability to shape wood might never materialize. "Failure" loomed on my aesthetic horizon.

At first the students, who were gathered by the Simon Charlie Society to reconnect with their culture and explore the healing available to them through this tradition, were uncomfortable with each other—ten strangers gathered from different parts of British Columbia, to learn the Hul'qumi'num tribe's tradition of art-making from one of its foremost artists, Simon, or "Hwunumetse'," as he was known locally. Simon was a man of great cultural stature in his community, having been awarded both the Order of British Columbia and the Order of Canada for his expressive totem poles that stood proudly, both locally and globally, and for his work in transmitting the cultural carving traditions to a generation of younger men, some of whom felt quite disconnected and directionless due to various experiences they had suffered in their young lives. They were here in the art program to heal from various traumas as well as to resurrect a culture on the verge of extinction.

> Since 1966, Simon had carved the equivalent of 22 logging truckloads of cedar logs. His totem poles stand in the Royal British Columbia Museum, at the parliament buildings in Ottawa, and are also in Washington State, Georgia, New York, and in front of the McDonald's Corporate Headquarters in Chicago. Four of his 20-foot poles are in Australia. His masks and other art works grace collections in South America, the United Kingdom, Finland, Netherlands, Germany, and Japan. In 1997, as part of an elders' delegation, he carved a totem pole with Maori carvers in New Zealand. (Caro, 2005)

Simon was prolific. He was also a gruff man, not given to many words, and the students were deeply respectful of his reputation. We awkwardly followed instructions, as we attempted to draw out our ideas, front, back and side in rough sketches, trying to think three dimensionally as we converted our ideas onto scaled paper. Simon and his assistant inspected our drawings for various possibilities, and helped us select a final direction. As an immigrant to Canada, I was careful to avoid appropriating any aesthetic from a culture that was not my own, while at the same time, allowing myself the deep privilege of learning the techniques and rituals of this ancient practice.

And so we began. Together, the group offered thanks for the gift of the great cedars that grow endemically on this land, and which were given to the Hul'qumi'num people for carving stories, canoes and timbers. Then we embarked on the sacred act of removing the cedar's bark, which has traditionally been used for basketry, clothing and the hair on traditional masks. We straddled the trunks, and began to strip the grey fibrous lengths, not by lifting it with our fingers from the bottom of a living tree, and then pulling the bark upwards as we walked away, which is the traditional method (Simon Fraser University Museum, 2008), but rather by using modern tools—a double-handled bark stripper with a curved blade—moving rhythmically with assertive gestures along the length of the prone trunks. At first, there was resistance from the protective covering, but it soon began to lift, revealing smooth, oily sapwood beneath. As we worked, twisted fiber piled around our feet, and the fragrance of grazed red cedar filled the air.

Once the logs were bare, we stood back and considered what could be revealed from within the naked trunks. We squinted; we stroked our chins; we hoped for revelation. I felt anxiety in my gut, and in my shortened breath—how does one express such a mystery, such a responsibility, such a calling, such an impossibility? As a group, we rode the wave of self-doubt together. Could we do justice to that which was asking to come through the wood with our novice hands?

Then, when we could stand the creative tension no longer, we picked up our safety glasses and ear-muffs, and ripped the starter cords on our chainsaws, wildly hoping to make cuts that might somehow match our drawings. The quiet day was suddenly split open by the abrasive roar of small engines, and our hearts startled into full tilt. Flooded with adrenalin, we felt the panic of cutting, and yet we committed to it anyway. Fragments flew through the air, as blades bit deeply into soft-bellied logs. Our guts curdled, yet excitement goose-bumped on our skin. Somehow, this felt like matricide, yet the raw power of being an agent of change invited us deep into the soft, buttery grain. We felt the exhilaration of the gas-fired tool running like a dangerous extension cord through our arms, as chainsaws bucked and kicked against knots within the wood.

I tuned in to the sound of the engines, listening deeply for any altered pitch or tempo—a clue to any resistance hidden within the rings, a density that could cause the blade to buck up into my face. Through terror and error, I learned that the grain determined the ease of the cut reflected in the sound. Slowly, slice by slice, I honed my log down to its essential essence. Then, finally, exhausted, I shut off the engine, stood back and raised my safety goggles. With a critical eye, I contemplated the skill of my cuts. Had I successfully subtracted enough negative space, leaving only the positive behind? Or did I need to take more?

Gratified to have made an impact on this tiny part of my universe, however small, I settled back with the others among the piles of sawdust, the sweet scent of cedar filling our lungs, and our ears ringing in the after-silence of the blades. This was our preferred way, to rest quietly following activity, feeling the vibration reverberating onwards inside our bones. We would drop below words, with only the occasional, understated jibe at another's progress. As we sipped our coffee, we began to warm to each other. There would be a wry comment given at another's expense, and we would respond with self-deprecating laughter, and a good-humored, retaliatory jab. With collusion and collaboration, came advice, proffered and accepted.

Finally, someone stood up, bravely committing to the smaller hand tools—the soft whine of the grinder, the exploratory scrape of draw-knives and the tentative chip-chip of chisels, which mesmerized us with their peaceful rhythms. From the old sofa and coffee machine, we were pulled again back into the solitary practice of art-making. We braced ourselves. We inhaled, we exhaled, we held our breath in our separate corners, and the work of hand carving started to unfold in earnest. Chop, chop chop. Chip, chip, chip. Zip, zip, zip.

For the next few months, in between long, patient hours of detailing our rhythmic dance with wood, our comradery grew, along with the three-dimensional forms under our hands. We commented; we quipped; we exerted gestural acts of reduction on our wood; we fell back into silent contemplation. We made a mess; we asserted order; we made a mess again. We were alone; and then we gravitated again towards each other, sharing food, cigarettes, stories and laughter; then we withdrew once again, into the isolated chaos of our individual imaginations. Dipping in and out of opposing realities became our way: relationship, aloneness; that which was inside us, and that which was outside us; that which "is," and that which "might be." Slowly we negotiated time and space to create form out of the formless mystery. It was a dance of duality—the twin banks on either side of our creative flow—as we carved ourselves into deeper consciousness of the great mystery.

As our self-assurance grew, we became more daring with the tools, and our gestures and cuts became more confident. We dove into the full torrent of our inspiration. As we learned to either sink or swim vigorously, in our own imaginations, we explored our capacities and limitations—and our ability, or not, to become creators of our own cedar stories.

Day by day, we entered this process with less hesitation. We touched fingertip to grain, adze to wooden groin, with more and more ease. We began to caress the totem curves with open abandon. We began to trust art-making as an erotic embrace of the unknown. We were learning how to stay utterly present while opening up to our pasts, as well as our futures. As our bodies and minds began to open to the flow of our existence, so did our hearts and voices, and we began to share our painful stories with each other.

With each cut, cut, cut of cold metal into warm wood, we slowly chip, chip, chipped through layers of our stored pain, into the deeper strata of ourselves, our memories, our subconscious, while at the same time accessing something deeper than our personal stories. Now and again, we would touch something omnipresent, dip into the universal questions. Why were we here? What was it all for? Where would we go next? In these intersecting layers and spaces we discovered surprises, agony, contentment and pleasure that we shared equally. Dangling vulnerably above the open space of conversation and silence, hovering somewhere between danger and safety, the old and the new, we began to trust ourselves again, as well as others. As we declared ourselves visually, we felt exposed, but also seen—perhaps for the first time. There was dignity in this declaration, of claiming ourselves to be enough in that moment, to take up space, to make a noise, to find our voice, to generate something audible and visible from deep in our souls.

As we alternated between stepping out as unique individuals, and then merging back into the shared sense of endeavor and community, we began to navigate the subtle dualities of separate self and community. We began to feel things that we had not allowed ourselves to feel in a long time. A new range of experience opened up sharply inside our ribs, like an umbrella. Where were we hiding from others? Where were we protecting ourselves? Was that pain we felt, or pleasure? Or simply intensity? Sometimes even peacefulness? Slowly, inch by inch, and stroke by stroke, we soothed our hearts and minds. Rhythmical hands began to unravel psychic knots and wipe our slates clean as we worked. The pain that we had caused others, and that which we had received, seemed to melt. The art began to heal our wounds through the extraordinary medicine of creating beauty in the world and space in our minds.

As totems and masks emerged, the powerful outlines of eyes, noses, mouths and teeth revealed themselves. Archetypal Coast Salish forms representing bear, wolf, salmon and beaver showed themselves in the work of the others, while I manifested my own forms—a totem of a woman in childbirth. This was my story in that moment: the agony and joy of giving birth to my own creative process, to my new self, through the medium of a tree. The mask that I had made earlier, and which gazed at me from a shelf, reflected my need for balance—the Yin-Yang of integrating the opposites within me, the dark, the light, the pain, the pleasure, the duality of life and death. In quiet communion with me, the mask affirmed who I was and what I needed. As I turned back to work on my pole, I felt the joy of manifestation coursing through my veins. I knew this would be my path. I was giving birth to my deeper identity—the archetype of the creator. Stroking the forms lovingly with my grinder and sander, I moved deeply into refining my life purpose.

As we stood back in awe to observe what was happening through us and despite us, I could see the students' hearts register a shift in internal chemistry. Beads of joy flowed through our blood, into our muscles, into our softening faces and relaxing shoulders, and out through our sweat—an alchemical biofeedback system that would keep us returning again and again to this rewarding process of connecting to our creativity, putting tool to wood, mind to body, heart to hands, soul to soul. This is a partnership that brings us each time out of a bleak landscape of depression, anxiety and isolation into meaning, belonging, and even ecstasy, through creativity.

It was not an easy process. Some days I struggled to show up, as the birthing process became intense and turbulent—my muscles ached, and there were inconvenient contractions in my mind, with many memories and feelings coursing through my immigrant, woman's heart. We each had our demons to face, our own grief, our own darkness. But we returned day after day to the studio to grapple once again with the biggest question: could we step up to the invitation to be all that we could be—both powerful and vulnerable—as we exerted ourselves into the world, in bold, generative acts? Could we show up and bare the intensity of this creative energy running through our veins, as we felt it shift us into greater dimensions of ourselves? Could we clean up our acts enough to be truly present to this experience and feel the growing pains, so that we could take our full potential out into the world? Could we allow ourselves to wake up to deeper levels of consciousness, as we first mimicked, and then aligned ourselves with, and then fully opened to, the creative process of the universe?

Like the sacred salmon, who, excited by pheromones, return each year to their birth river after a long journey out to sea, we chose to swim blindly upstream to our creative source. We began to respond instinctively as we felt close to home. Our minds became more focused, our imaginations began to awaken, our hearts became more ecstatic, as we followed the call... Not since childhood had we felt such freedom and joy as we surrendered to the currents playing through us. Instinctively, we remembered how to respond to the omnipresent invitation to relax and expand. A brief hesitation, perhaps, but then we jumped into the full flow of our rivers, and stroke by stroke, we writhed onwards, finding our way back to the fecund matrix, where art simply "happened" through us by opening to a well spring.

The ecstatic feeling of "oneness" began to visit us again and again. We began to drop our painful stories, and leave our past behind us. As we shaped our archetypal symbols, we simultaneously began to shape a more adaptive internal order. By creating our art over a year together, we begin to rewire ourselves, and create more integrated psychic patterning. Time stood still in the art-space, as past and future imploded into the present moment. We felt the collapse of linear time and space deep in our souls.

There was a new confidence in the tread of the artists. Our constricted and wounded hearts blossomed wide open. We had slowly become brave by shaping grain. Then, one day as our pole-totems took final shape, we turned to paint, coloring them in the traditional red, black and white, to reveal the full beauty of the ovoid and elliptical Coast Salish visual language. I chose a palette that reflected my own blended aesthetic, gathered from the influences within me of several cultures, including Africa, Britain, India and Canada. Our poles began to speak their own stories—of membership, history and connection to mythical creatures, of deeply spiritual and autobiographical significance. They could now be "read," vertically, from top to bottom. Cedar had become the narrative that healed our past, brought us into the present and indicated our future.

The day came when we were done. Totems must finally take up a life of their own. A sacred ceremony was planned by the community to celebrate and fully initiate the young men back into their own culture. Our mentors from the Simon Charlie Society joined us to honor this creative journey with us. Coast Salish friends and family assembled to witness the completion of our sacred process that had produced these healing totems. The elders, wearing traditional blankets, performed a community ceremony, with smudging and prayers, to bless the onward journeys of totems, stories and artists. There was drumming, and singing and feasting. The fires were lit and the salmon from the nearby delta were cooked in the traditional manner, in pits in the earth. There was laughter, pride and joy, and the faces of the young men shone with accomplishment and dignity.

After the ceremony, the young men returned to their various communities with their totems, which would be planted in the earth of their home towns, to stand tall under the rain and the sun, and then, like all living forms, to weather away, and eventually pass on into dust. The poles would be considered incomplete until they had returned once again from whence they had come—form returning to no-form.

By gathering Canadian Aboriginal artists together to teach them the traditional skills, Simon Charlie had hoped to reverse the loss of indigenous culture that has been slowly occurring in Canada and, indeed, around the world since colonization. Kamoji Wachiira (2009), an environmental activist from Kenya, explains indigenous knowledge and ways of being:

> Culture is coded wisdom, wisdom that has accumulated over thousands of years and generations. Some of that wisdom is coded in our ceremonies. It is coded in our values. It is coded in our songs, in our dances, in our plays. And because we as a society did not have a written culture, it is not something that we can go back to read about. When our elders died, they died with that culture. And so we are left with a vacuum. And we have tried to fill that vacuum with the values the missionaries have given us, based on the Bible. And as good as they are, they are not the coded wisdom of our people. There was something in our people that had helped them conserve the forests. They were not looking at trees and seeing timber. They were not

looking at elephants and seeing ivory or looking at the cheetah and seeing beautiful skin for sale. There was no such economic value to those things. So they let them be. It was in their culture to let them be. All people have their own culture. But when you remove that culture from them, then you kill them in a way. They may be alive physically, but you kill a very large part of them.

The Simon Charlie Society, an organization dedicated to cultural and language renewal among Coast Salish people, aimed to create a renaissance in local culture, heritage and traditions; they inaugurated several such gatherings over the years to teach heritage, culture and traditions to both Aboriginals and non-aboriginals (Turtle Island Magazine, 2003) in order to reverse the trend of cultural genocide. Caro (2005) says:

> Simon was very keen on preserving and creating pride in Hul'qumi'num art. He had a great respect for the art of his relations located on Vancouver Island but insisted that his art reflect his own culture and legends. Simon's dream was to establish a working cultural center where artists could learn about the culture and participate in the creation of Hul'qumi'num art.

Simon believed that after a year-long immersion in the art of mask and totem-pole carving, and supported by sacred ceremony, the young men would leave his studio and return back to their own communities to pass on their acquired cultural knowledge to others. He believed that in this way, he could assist the First Nations of Canada to heal from the trauma caused by colonization, and help their culture and visual language avoid extinction.

Once the program was over, I continued to visit with Simon and carve with him, on and off, for the following year. Our way was to sit in silence as our hands worked, Simon carving small winged creatures he was making for a mobile that represented the cultural stories he held. Sometimes he would tire. He could no longer carve the big trees, and he would nap on the studio sofa. I would place another log on the stove to keep him warm.

It had not always been easy between me and Simon. When I first approached him to join the program, Simon had made it clear I was not particularly welcome. Wood was traditionally a man's material in this culture, and I was female, and an immigrant to Canada. He accused me of many things, among them the deficiency of my not belonging to this land by birth, of my being "tribeless," as he called it. As an immigrant, he saw me somehow as not "whole"—being without a people to which to belong. But after a while, his angry outbursts stopped. Over our time together, Simon continued occasionally to test me, for my strength of character and determination, for my capacity to use tools and handle wood. I knew he accepted me when our silence became very deep. Interestingly, he never once asked me why I wanted to be part of this group of resilient young survivors. He didn't have to. He knew my commitment and motivation. He knew that I knew what he knew: that art has the power to transform people and their communities, and that I was passionate about this work.

My time with Simon was a great privilege, both as an artist and as a researcher. Because of his generosity, I was able to observe first hand how he and his organization reconnected young Aboriginal men to their indigenous culture through the traditional art-making practices and ceremonial, spiritual rituals. Simon saw that below the racial and gendered surface differences between me and the other artists in the group, I was simply a person also wishing to heal herself of cultural disconnection, pain and depression, someone who wished to deepen her spiritual practices of creativity. I had not struggled like some on the program, with issues of family abuse, or foetal alcohol syndrome. I had not been removed too early, and against my wishes, from my family, culture and language, to be sent to a residential school. I was not addicted, nor had I been to prison. But I knew I had to heal my own wounds. As an immigrant, I had experienced cultural dissociation and voicelessness; as a woman, my mind and body had been colonized by another gender to some extent; and as an artist I had been devalued as a creative worker by more left-brained thinkers in my culture. Simon was right. When I joined his studio, I had no tribe—but I did find one— through creativity.

The last time I saw Simon, he was standing in front of a massive log lying in the weeds outside his studio. The red cedar trunk was a truly spectacular old growth beauty, five feet in diameter, gifted by the people of Seattle to Simon, so that he could carve it as a "welcome figure" for their city. As he sipped his coffee, he contemplated what might one day become of this giant. Sadly, that same week, and in his mid-eighties, he passed away quietly. To this day, the log still lies outside his studio, waiting perhaps for one of his young apprentices to carve it.

The report in the local newspaper read:

> Simon Charlie had been a cultural ambassador. He took pleasure in teaching heritage, culture, and traditions as well as carving to both First Nations and non-First Nations. He was passionate about his Cowichan culture and heritage; he embraced learning from other cultures and was a strong advocate of sharing the creative process. (Caro, 2005)

Harvey Alphonse, Chief of Cowichan Tribes at the time, paid this tribute:

> Simon contributed to the community in so many ways. He honoured us by sharing so much of his life with us, as a teacher, as a leader, as a role model. He inspired us to each find our own unique gift we bring to the world. He challenged us to step forward and be proud of whom we are. He provoked us to set aside our differences and work together in harmony. (Caro, 2005)

During that year of learning about transmitting culture through an immersive art practice, I worked closely with the other young artists. As we built trust, we shared many stories as well as creative techniques. We taught each other how to sharpen carving knives with a whetstone; how to oil knife blades; how to translate a two-dimensional drawing onto a three-dimensional pole; how to apply paint to wood; how to service a chainsaw; how to carve a bear claw or eagle talon out of obsidian—a natural, volcanic glass traditionally believed to be protective, grounding and healing for the wearer. But more important than this shared knowledge was the experience of bridging our cultural divide with stories shared. One young man in particular, whom I will call George in order to respect his privacy, gifted me with his personal narrative, and charged me with sharing it when the time came. He wanted his story to be known, as an example of many other young people who had suffered. The two of us spent our Sundays outside of the project recording his story so that others might know what it was like to be impacted by cultural genocide, neo-colonial racism and the resulting inter-generational trauma. He wanted others to understand exactly what it was that he was trying to heal through art-making, and why he had committed to this program.

George told me that "Indians," as he called himself in a wry re-appropriation of a derogatory, colonizing term, should be thought of as "an endangered species." He said that if I read Charles Darwin, I would understand gene pool theory—that "reservations," or homelands created by white colonizers for indigenous people, were like shrinking pools of DNA. George explained that his own life was an example of the impact of reservations on First Nations people in Canada. As such, he felt strongly that people should know how his life had unfolded. It was important to him to note the historical context in which we found ourselves, so that the depth of trauma could be better understood.

Although the exact dates and routes of the peopling of the Americas are subject to ongoing debate, research (Dixon, 2007; Goebel, Waters and O'Rourke, 2008; Gugliotta, 2013) corroborates that approximately 50,000–17,000 years ago, falling sea levels allowed people to migrate from Siberia into north-western America, across the land bridge known as Beringia. George's ancestors, probably refugees following food and land resources, were at first confined by the Laurentide ice sheet to Alaska and the Yukon. However, following the glacial melt, his ancestors would have moved down into Canada, some 16,000 years before Caucasians arrived.

Until recently, this version of history, including the colonization of Aboriginal peoples, has not been widely taught. Rather, a biased interpretation of history has been preferred, which has been transmitted through the uncritical use of archival records, and which reflects a racist Western interpretation of Canadian history. Dr Emma LaRoque (2017) describes how this bias impacts indigenous people with ensuing trauma:

> Colonization can be defined as some form of invasion, dispossession and subjugation of a people. The invasion need not be military; it can begin—or continue—as geographical intrusion in the form of agricultural, urban or industrial encroachments. The result of such

incursion is the dispossession of vast amounts of lands from the original inhabitants. This is often legalized after the fact. Historically, First Nation peoples (defined as Status Indians by the Indian Act) lost some 98% of their original lands... The long-term result of such massive dispossession is institutionalized inequality.

She states that colonizers tend to turn to the belief, both personal and institutionalized, that their group is innately superior to another. Today, Aboriginal peoples continue to encounter forms of discrimination on a daily basis. LaRocque (2017) suggests that, as an inherent part of the colonial project:

> Europeans categorized themselves as the "civilized" and Indigenous peoples as the "savages" at the bottom of human development. From this institutionalized bias a complex set of images, terminology, policies and legislation has set Aboriginal peoples apart, both geographically (on reserves and residential schools), and as inferior peoples, even today...perpetuated through the media and the marketplace.

The net effect of institutionalized racism is extremely powerful and, consequently, can lead to racial shame and self-rejection. Stereotyping, mistrust and mistreatment of Aboriginal peoples can result in inter-generational strain and racial conflict. LaRocque (2017) says racism is political, as it facilitates and justifies the socio-economic access and mobility of one group, while disadvantaging another. She suggests that these policies have left Aboriginal peoples in Third World circumstances. She goes so far as to state that racism can also be deadly. Not only are Aboriginal youth committing suicide at six times the national average, but individuals have died from racially motivated killings. She suggests (2017) that racism affects all Canadians, yet many continue to deny that it exists, blaming Aboriginal peoples for their own socio-economic marginalization. This analysis, of how racism becomes institutionalized, and cultural genocide through shaming and isolation, can of course be applied to any colonized country.

George explained to me that he and his family had felt many effects of neo-colonial politics. He had grown up surrounded by political conversations on reservation land, as two of his grandfathers had been chiefs. However, he himself rejected the reservation system, or "Royal Culture," as he called it, for many reasons. George believed that chiefs ought to witness at least two-and-a-half generations before they could council others or calculate what was needed, and yet the current chief of his own people was a young man his own age. George had not liked what he viewed as nepotism, or the council system of favoritism that had resulted from the reservation system—designated homelands for indigenous people, created by white legislators. So he left the "rez," as he called it, and went to the city at a young age.

George shared with me how colonialism had impacted life for those who stayed on the reservation. He said many residents were frustrated. He explained that as a result of trauma, there was a lot of conflict, including family abuse. Fathers often drank and womanized, and mothers often played bingo and used sleeping pills called "Mother's Little Helpers." Some of the legacies of removing people from their culture and language include the loss of identity and the resulting addictions and inter-generational abuse that George went on to describe to me. Thurston (2012, p.4) says historical oppression and its negative consequences transmits across generations:

> There is evidence of the impact of intergenerational trauma on the health and well-being and on the health and social disparities facing Aboriginal peoples in Canada and other countries. The effects on children of survivors of the residential school system are documented.

As a child of four, George was often left alone, and had overdosed on his mother's pills. However, he survived and later went to school, but in kindergarten, he missed 43 days of school. Soon after, he learned to smoke, hitchhike and shoplift. By the time he was an adolescent, he had already decided that one ought to live fast and die young, as did many other teens on the rez. His cousin, for example, died in a heroin overdose. His brother died playing "chicken." He himself shoplifted his first soda-pop at the age of six, while his father sat in the bar and refused to come home. Although his father did beat his mother, his dad had got along well with most people, and consequently, George experienced a total of ten "mothers." His uncle, who grew dope illegally, accused George of stealing it, and so George ran away from his aunt, who at the time, was being paid to raise him.

At the age of 15, George did his first B and E (Break and Enter). He had fallen asleep after drinking a case of stolen liquor, and the cops had woken him up and taken him in. He was then jailed at the youth detention center.

George felt that residential schools had been partly responsible for the deliberate genocide of indigenous culture. Rice (2011) explains the residential school system in Canada:

> Beginning in the 1880s, Aboriginal children across Canada were removed, often forcibly, from their homes and placed in Indian Residential Schools. At the schools, students were forbidden to speak Native languages and practice their culture. Testimony from surviving former students presents overwhelming evidence of widespread neglect, starvation, extensive physical and sexual abuse, and many student deaths related to these crimes. As is so often the case...we only have survivor testimony to rely on. These estimates suggest that sexual abuse rates were as high as 75 percent in some schools, and rates of physical harms were higher still... These schools were designed and operated by the church and state with the purpose of destroying Native cultures and communities in every corner of Canada. This crime has caused incalculable harm.

As a survivor of the residential school system in the 1970s and 80s, George openly shared his traumatic experiences with me. He also explained that there were many things about residential school that were actually enjoyable, although it was much like "being in a minimum-security penitentiary for future criminals." Sometimes the Royal Canadian Mounted Police would come and get kids from their families and take them to the allocated residential school. George explained that this experience was different for everyone. Some kids cried to go to school, and others cried to leave. George himself did OK, as he got mostly As and Bs, but he understood that many did not fair so well. Rice (2011) explains the history of these schools:

> The government of Canada now identifies 136 institutions as former Indian Residential Schools that were established exclusively for Aboriginal children by the federal government in partnership with the country's four major churches. The schools operated for

approximately 100 years, with the final schools closing as recently as 1998. Canadian law made attendance at the schools mandatory for all Aboriginal children and made the school administration the legal guardians of the children who attended… There are no records accurately showing what proportion of Aboriginal children were taken from their families, but there is no question that every Aboriginal community in Canada today is affected by the experience of residential school. In addition to the untold suffering of direct survivors of the schools, the system continues to have devastating impacts on Aboriginal young people. The inter-generational experiences of a mass atrocity are felt when the damage done to one generation perpetuates in the lives of the next. Residential schools sought to interfere with the closest relationships in Aboriginal communities by taking children as young as four away from their parents, relatives, and community life. The consequences of this policy on family life are still felt across the country today.

George smiled as he told me that, ironically, at school he was cast in plays such as *Hiawatha,* and was sometimes made to wear a kilt in order to learn sword-dancing. But he also got to go to Disneyland, play in a band, carry the flag, and he had jogged every day. There was painting, pool and ping-pong, but there was violence too. He remembered that an older girl had once beaten him up. Mostly he remembered the smell of the school, and most of the other correctional institutions he had subsequently attended—"a mixture of PineSol and hate." He learned to carve his name very young, at the age of five, when he was dropped off at the boarding school. He always carved his name, he said. It helped him feel as if he belonged somewhere, that he existed. Later, in prison, he would recognize his name each time he was sent back. Once his friend had had his name carved on his own chest by some other prisoners. George laughed as he remembered that once he had had two charges against him at the same time, and he was expected to be in two courtrooms simultaneously—an impossible expectation.

Whenever he went to the big city, the first thing George would do was look for "skid row," because for him, this was "home from home." His nick-name in the city was the Doctor, because his friends came to him when they needed a needle to relieve them of their emotional pain. For a quick fix, he would administer the "medicine" straight into their jugulars. He himself would also go through periods of shooting up with the hookers downtown. Sometimes after he had been to the shooting galleries too often, he would get nightmares, and "see" chicken tendons in his arm. He had had some intense relationships with those girls, but never any commitment.

Sometimes, when George was lonely, he would hitchhike. One ride would result in a beer, another in a joint, another in some food. He liked to meet people like this, from all walks of life, from priests to politicians, and he would debate with them. His preferred car was a Lincoln Town Car. He had noticed on his travels that drivers of these cars seemed to be the most compassionate people. They could see he was hungry. However, other vehicles, like trucks, would dump him some place where he could not get another ride very easily.

Over our time carving together, I noticed that George could handle his knives with great skill. He patiently taught me how to use the chainsaw. He explained to me that when he was not in prison, he had worked in logging camps, or on archeological digs. George also liked to carve skulls in his spare time, and he would use road-kill that he found and would keep in his fridge, in order to study the exact form of the bones.

As we carved our totems, I noticed that George's figure was in the form of a male "provider," holding a salmon. He explained to me that he had two children somewhere—one even with his last name. But it was hard to provide for them. Some years, he had had full-time work roofing houses, which also paid for his weed, coke, crack, Ritalin, Talwin and Baby Ts (crack cocaine). But other times he had no work at all, and he might inject a cocktail of Valium, Tylenol 3 and whiskey. He explained that he never expected to live beyond 30, because of heroin. It was in prison that he discovered heroin. He had been addicted three times. George explained that heroin was like a woman—a safe harbor, very seductive. Although he was not "using" while he carved, he said he believed that relapse was probably inevitable.

George had noticed many things about himself over the years. For example, if he was in one place too long, he would feel the urge to move, which wasn't easy, as he had lost his driver's license, and he was no longer allowed to use public commuter transport, since he had seven charges against him for "lack of proof of ticket purchase." And because he needed to keep moving, George developed a problem—he liked to steal cars. When he was young and his father lost his car keys, George learned to hotwire the car, just for fun. He also learned to steal food, although he kept his thefts ethically under $20 per store. George explained that in fact he had a personal moral code. For example, he would never Break and Enter a house, and he would only do food-fraud in commercial places. He would "eat and run" from restaurants, but sometimes he would be too full of pizza, or too drunk to run, and then he would end up in jail for the night.

Once, he was caught for stealing meat that he could resell for half the price. The store-owner beat him to a pulp with an empty coke bottle. George knew what it was like to go hungry. Once he had gone "absent without leave" from prison, and spent three days without food. He had been cold and wet, running in difficult mountainous terrain, with rock faces to scale, and with fast creeks to cross. He only had two raw potatoes in all that time. It was not fun. Three times he had had to go up to the snowline just to get a view of the terrain, to see where he was. In those three days, he only traveled five miles before he decided to flag down a helicopter that was looking for him. George laughed wryly as he remembered that, on his return to prison, the guard commented, "Some Indian you are."

George knew most of the local correction centers well. As a child, he was fascinated by prisons, especially after he had visited his father in a correctional center. He wanted to walk in his father's footsteps. Once, both he and his father had been in prison at the same time. It wasn't that bad inside. Some days it was really helpful to be in prison. For example, George would make sure to get all his dental work done. And he could have sex all the time, as there were free condoms. But now, he added quietly, some of his good friends were dying of Acquired Immune Deficiency Syndrome (AIDS).

I asked George if he would mind sharing with me specifically how the arts had helped him. He said as an "outsider" of most societies, he had had mixed feelings about "learning culture." The first time he heard "pow-wow" music, for example (indigenous music for sacred ceremonies and dancing), he experienced uncomfortable chills. At that time, he was really biased against native sounds and images. He explained to me that they gave him "an awkward feeling," especially when indigenous people danced for tourists at the local lodge. But he had slowly changed. Now he really liked cultural practices instead of being ashamed by them. When everyone is dancing, he explained, testosterone levels go up and everyone radiates energy. He could feel the power and intensity of the group as they expressed themselves through this art form.

George said he loved carving. It encouraged him to fill his time creatively, instead of being on "self-destruct." Creating something out of nothing was such a surprise for him. He got into the "zone," where he got tunnel vision and could tune out his life. Even though he loved the three-dimensional challenge, he couldn't plan out his work. Rather, he had to work from instinct. He also had to work hard not to overwork his pieces. Sometimes, he could get obsessive and couldn't stop, cutting, cutting, cutting. However, he could never finish his pieces either. This confused him. Why could he never finish what he had started? He couldn't even sit still long enough through a sermon to get food afterwards at the soup kitchen. He couldn't sleep for more than two hours at a stretch and then only if he had his back to the wall. Neither could he stay in one place long enough to finish his art. He then asked me if I would make sure to finish his totem for him, because he suspected that he might be gone before it was done. He laughed then—he wasn't actually sure if he would leave this time, as he had really bad knees now, from walking so much in his life.

When I asked George about what he would do with his art, he thought about it for a while. He said that a year prior to the carving project, his house—which had been condemned by the council—had burned down, taking with it all his mother's letters, his carvings, his tools, his drawings. There were a lot of fires in his life, he explained, like the time when he was younger and had fallen asleep with the citronella candle burning under the couch to chase away the mosquitos: the couch caught fire. And the time he had been sniffing gas out of a bleach jug: he blacked out and fell over, and there was an explosion caused by the base-board heater. He consequently didn't have much art or many tools left.

But his dream? Yes, he would like to start a school, to sponsor people to carve and exercise his power to do something useful. He had no bank account but the bank kept sending him Visa cards. If he could buy a laptop, he would first of all download an apology from the Pope and the Prime Minister. But frankly, he would prefer money to do something more useful. There was only one catch—he was afraid of money. George explained that having money might suck him back into doing drugs. He was not afraid of sleeping outside and having no roof. He had survived periods of up to four months living outdoors. He was only afraid of two things—having money, and having people's disapproval, especially those who liked him. And he got most scared when he heard women shouting at their kids.

I asked George why he made art. He said that at first he carved to impress his mother and father, to try and get their approval. But his real drawing skills had started in juvie (juvenile detention), with fantasy art, underground comics, hazardous waste signs and, later, with tattoos. One day, he added, he would like to become an addictions counselor and use his art to help his people.

During our conversations, George left me with much food for thought. I could see the change in him over the year we carved next to each other. Lafrenière *et al.* (2005) corroborate the notion of specifically formulating "cultural identity" as a healing tool. They looked at two similar intervention projects with Aboriginal survivors of inter-generational trauma and the residential school system. They explain their approach:

> In the first program, individuals in the Aboriginal community learn about traditional knowledge and holistic well-being. The second deals with offenders (and others) to find alternatives to the criminal justice system, where these individuals are given referrals to experts and specific healing plans that integrate holistic healing. (cited by Thurston, 2012, p.35)

Thurston (2012, p.27) found that projects such as the Simon Charlie Society's project and others had done significant work to help Aboriginal survivors of trauma, which would include residential school, genocide, addictions, abuse, incarceration and inter-generational perpetuation. They concluded, however, that there is certainly more work to be done through such interventions. Thurston (2012) recommend that integrating Aboriginal world views and culture into existing programs, incorporating art-making programs that strengthen Aboriginal identity, and integrating such programs into mainstream health services would really help to heal the impact of colonialism and the resulting institutionalized racism and trauma.

George concluded our interviews by adding that there were no "bad times," only experiences. Ironically, due to attending a residential school run by a church, he had rebelled against all religion. And so he concluded that heaven and hell were just what you made out of life. With no heaven, he must therefore also be safe from hell. At the end of the day, he said, there was only the here and now. And sometimes there was art.

## Chapter 10

# CONCLUSIONS ABOUT HEALING TRAUMA AND LEARNING TO TRANSFORM THROUGH CREATIVITY

We are all refugees, moving from the known to the unknown. Creative practices help us transition, transform and transcend safely from one level of consciousness to another, whether we live in the concrete jungle or the Calais Jungle.

By gathering stories from pioneers facilitating art with refugees, I have begun to understand many things, about creativity and its power, although further questions are yet to be raised. There is a poetic irony within this book—by approaching facilitators to contribute a chapter of shared experience, I have also asked them to "do" what they "teach," to narrate their own story, in order to understand their own healing trajectories more deeply. They, too, needed to dive deeply into "memory work" in order to track a lifetime of pioneering perspectives. By doing this, they placed their life's work in a context of people, politics, geography, history, creativity, trauma and healing.

People who do this work often live in a painful field of resonance, and yet their lives are abundantly rich with meaning. Not one of our story-tellers set out to do this work with a clear-cut vision at age 18 of where they were headed; but through force of circumstances, by responding to their unique calling and by authentically following their own circuitous paths, their lives were drawn towards creative interactions with certain communities, and to do this healing work.

To voice their "own" stories, these facilitators turned to diverse genres, from factual ethnography, non-fiction, poetry, journaling, richly humorous metaphor and autobiographical memoir, in order to extrapolate meaning from their work, and to understand their own contribution to planetary health. By doing "narrative work" themselves they speak and write themselves into deeper meanings and identities. It is not easy to do this work, even for "facilitators": to become vulnerable and share personal narrative always takes courage.

By sharing their lives with those who have lived on the edge of what is only just humanly bearable, the facilitators have shown us how to extract depth from life around us, how to transform fragility into resilience, and how to forge community bonds and a sense of belonging through creative acts. This collection bears witness to the transformative creative process and its extraordinary capacity to heal trauma from the past, come deeply into the present and open up space for more adaptive futures.

The implications of this cutting-edge trajectory are both broad and deep—by placing creativity squarely at the center of public health, substantive transformation occurs. It is my hope that this presently marginalized work will become increasingly important over time. It is not the creation of masterpieces that counts here, although fine art "product" does have an important place in our cultures and can certainly be produced under this model. With transformational work, it is the magic of both the "process" and the "product" that is significant, and which become inseparable.

On the surface, each of these stories illustrates a different geographic location, context and medium, but underneath, each shares common core healing principles. The outcomes with each project are more joy, more resilience, more social intelligence through the telling of a healing visual narrative. It becomes evident that those carrying the brunt of the actual trauma, the vulnerable individuals caught up on the front lines of change, share inherent transformative capacities— an innate healing mechanism that can be tapped into like a well. All humans in fact share this mechanism, which can transform pain and pleasure into a measure of self-actualization.

We can conclude from the evidence here that creativity is carried within all people wherever they go, into prisons, into deserts and into jungle war zones, and this force cannot be dispossessed or dislocated. Illness or dispossession cannot take it from us, as long as we are still able to function. Creativity can only be repressed by our own thinking and self-doubt, beliefs that we need special "talent," "credentials" or "recognition" in order to do it. It is clear that creativity is blocked by the "left-brain chauvinism" (a playful metaphor I use for logic-dominance) within us, and around us, that might suggest that the doing of art is for others more talented, or more privileged with leisure, or that it is childish, "girly," unprofitable, valueless and useless for getting ahead. Creativity is more susceptible to our own self-destructive beliefs about it than it is to a tsunami, earthquake or virus. Wherever we go, creativity will be there also, simply waiting to be activated from within.

Creativity is a unique ability that we humans have evolved that can help us with our distinctly human challenges. It is clear from the multiple viewpoints expressed here that this simple but profound process of self-expression has some common structures and outcomes that I will now summarize.

There is some existing literature on exactly "what" changes within us as we transform. Ken Wilber (2000), for example, has written a meta-comparison of existing research on human development. He has drawn on the work of many great researchers to map "what changes" as we transform, which includes our needs, perspectives, identity and meaning. To these changes, I would like to add that when we transform through the arts in particular, we can also add changes in physiology, focus, mood, voice, aesthetic, outreach, activism, health, education, community, economies, problem solving and organization (Adnams Jones, 2016). In this way, art is associated with healing and learning, as well as self- and community-evolution. An art practice, either at home or on the front lines of trauma in a global hotspot, fosters the health assets defined by the World Health Organization (1948) as wisdom, creativity, talent and enthusiasm, qualities not previously acknowledged or valued by the left brain, or within existing literature on transformation.

Bessel Van der Kolk (2017), who has researched trauma for over 40 years, says that being traumatized is a failure of the imagination. When your imagination dies, you are stuck with what you have. Opening up the imagination is critical to healing. He suggests that healing from trauma includes finding new responses, interpretations and possibilities. To heal, one must find a way to:

- become calm and focused

- self-soothe through noticing one's autonomic nervous system, breath and heart rate variability

- notice one's internal world, feelings, thoughts, images, sensations

- find a way to become fully alive again

- synch and connect with people around one

- notice other people's distress, while remaining calm oneself

- no longer hold secrets about one's life

- release shame

- build self-esteem

- find joy and creativity

- reconstruct new identities and meanings.

Van der Kolk (2017) emphasizes that to heal, one must be seen, heard, met and known. One must attune to others, be interactive and "play." One must learn to feel the body, and also calm the mind. Art does this for people.

Psychotherapist Linda Graham (2017) says to heal we need conditioning, reconditioning and deconditioning through various tools, including:

- somatic tools, such as relaxing and moving

- emotional tools, such as cultivating different responses, compassion and wished-for outcomes

- intrapersonal tools, such as listening to various internal voices

- interpersonal tools, such as reaching out to community, engagement

- reflection tools such as an internal checklist of strengths and competencies

- positive reinforcement, such as being seen, heard and held through possible collapse, negativity

- the revisioning of narrow perspectives and old patterns.

Graham emphasizes (2017) that "relationships foster capacity," and that creating a safe container is vital: of self-awareness and self-acceptance, mindfulness and compassion, so that bodies and minds can be stabilized while tools and multiple intelligences are practiced. She says "space" heals—pause, notice, accept the moment as it is, choose a response. Art-making is nothing but a series of choices made by the participant—which tool, which color, which surface, which shape and so on. Choice-making is a practice that moves the practitioner towards agency. When we are temporarily suspended in a vacuum (or in a studio), we can also recalibrate and discover what really matters. This is the beginning of growth.

Graham suggests (2017) that "switching channels" through skillful distraction gives us a reprieve from the past and brings us into a space to regroup, relax and regulate. Through a conscious choice of healthy distraction (such as art-making) we can ground ourselves, shift out of contraction, reactivity and rumination. Group art work can be a particularly supportive container for survivors, who can share similar traumas and support each other. Telling our stories and hearing the stories of others without having to explain, justify or defend can be very regulating and normalizing. The experience of a "common" humanity becomes healing. Through the narration of a more adaptive identity, we can shift out of uncertainty and rejoin the world with new agency. Through reframing our stories, we include a more coherent narrative that includes the trauma, but that is much larger than the trauma. The trauma is finally seen in perspective: it is not the whole story. Through "re-storying" we notice that it is not the issue that is the issue, but rather it is our "response" to the issue that is the issue. When we find a redemptive moment in our stories, our healing begins.

As we have seen, art is well placed to do all these things, as a participatory methodology, in any learning space across the world, however makeshift or temporary. This democratic healing and learning approach is equally helpful in high-end studios, or in communities suffering from displacement, dispossession, ill-health, rurality and underemployment challenges; communities that may be non-reading and non writing; communities where participants speak several different languages from each other; or where the economics determine that practices be reasonably priced with materials that might be "re-purposed." Art is adaptable to any grassroots "salon," held spontaneously under any tree, anywhere in the world, with any gender, ethnicity or class. It is particularly useful in situations where patriarchy may have silenced people. Art can be a kind of subversive entry into empowerment when it is erroneously understood to be a leisure activity, or "women's work" by the men of a community.

Let's look now at a few of the major take-aways common to all the stories we have shared here. We can conclude that, most importantly, this kind of transformative practice needs a safe "container," with a structure designed for healing and learning, that can easily be put into place, and built with very little infrastructure. Central to this practice is the need for a sensitive and empathetic facilitator, who values respect, story, creativity, diversity, inclusion and voice, and who is prepared to witness and hold people as they transition. This requires becoming fully humane and open to others, with an appreciation for humanity's innate healing, imagination and creativity. It means helping people shift their awareness from the external world into their internal worlds, where the healing intrinsically begins. This is the process of helping people "rebuild," by accepting that bad things happen to good people. Tedeschi (quoted in Graham, 2017) suggests that:

> There is no returning to baseline for people whose lives have been upended. Trauma is not simply a hardship to overcome. The trauma becomes a dividing line in people's lives. It can catalyze deep transformation. People can do more than survive. They can become wise.

Rachel Yehuda, the Director for Traumatic Stress Studies at the Mount Sinai School of Medicine, says (Graham, 2017) that:

> Trauma causes changes… You don't stay the same. That is a really radical idea. You do recover in some ways but that recovery does not involve returning to base line. It involves recalibrating towards something new…bouncing forwards into a new sense of fulfillment and thriving. That's the growth.

Holding this kind of transformative growth space for others is privileged work, often transforming the facilitator too. We ourselves are never the same after we have done this work. We are certainly never separate, better than or above the participants. Van der Kolk (2017) suggests that there are several important factors for group facilitators to bear in mind. Most important is to remember that pathologizing participants is damaging to those already traumatized. It is not a matter of "fixing" any one else but rather activating already-present, self-arising, healing mechanisms. "Pacing" and "dosing" the projects is important, so tracking participants' progress and their responses is critical. Learn about their "edges," their range of tolerance, while paying attention to their physiological shifts. Allow for breaks and mistakes. Balance safety with some risk-taking, so that people can learn new things. In this way, facilitating is a matter of creating community engagement. Stress is released naturally as support is felt, allowing vitality and aliveness to return. Joy and playfulness become essential ingredients.

When inviting people to allow their defenses to come down, to become vulnerable, facilitators need to offer:

- creative experiences in safe places

- respectful consideration for the diversity of all involved

- a focus on local issues and personal narrative

- simple activities that have some logical task structure

- clear parameters

- the use of easily accessible materials

- democratic participation, voicing and ideation by all that is witnessed with authentic reflection and due consideration.

If these criteria are met, then it is possible that the following can occur for participants:

- The self and its predicament can be temporarily forgotten, even as its biography is being narrated—a paradox.

- Curiosity can be ignited.

- A sense of playfulness can be stimulated even within a very "adult" world of violence and pain, with a possible return to the innocence of childhood, which is a state of "being" rather than one of "surviving."

- A return to a pre-traumatic, pre-hyper-vigilant state of physiology can occur.

- A gentle focus can be offered, to help restore scattered or shattered minds.

- The imagination can be released, which can revitalize a repressed system that may have temporarily shut down due to traumatic experiences.

- Joy can return, however temporarily, through colorful acts of celebration, thereby rebalancing neurochemistry that might be depleted.

- Purpose can be restored—with the immediate emphasis on a project that can be mastered, organized and completed with a sense of accomplishment.

- The full brain can thus come back into play with balanced hemispheric activity—through both the "logic" of problem solving, and the creativity of "imagination."

- Community, collaboration and social bonding can be engendered—so necessary for our social species that so often feels alone.

- Old memories, as well as new futures, identities and meanings, can be explored.

- Needs, issues and perspectives can be "voiced," debated and constructed.

- A sense of dignity, agency and self-esteem can be restored, with some immediate sense of control experienced over a proximal environment.

This describes the trajectory from trauma to healing. As trauma can be, by nature, an event that is unspeakable and untranslateable (Van der Kolk, 2017) as it lies outside our recognition of any previous experience, the finding of images, words and voice becomes central to healing. Titrating emotional arousal and reframing our story is key. Transformation, or "transformance" as Diana Fosha (2017) of the Accelerated Experiential Dynamic Psychotherapy Institute calls it, is both a process and an outcome and is an innate drive that humans have towards growth, expansion, liberation and the dismantling of the false self. Diana calls it the "undoing of aloneness," and she suggests that co-created security puts transformance in motion. She points out, however, that transformance and resistance exist side by side, so change may not be a neat, progressive, "linear" unfolding. I would suggest that change can be messy, unpredictable and uneven, and can perhaps be considered to be a "rhizomatic" experience, or a "spiral" revisitation of the story, or a resonant field of group transformation (Adnams Jones, 2016).

The expressive arts allow us to "time travel"—a movement from past to present to future, for example, by revisiting the old story from a safer place, and then imagining a new story. When humans first marked their caves with images 35,000 years ago, the arts became a form of virtual reality, depicting our projections, fears, deities and desires. Today, we can still create virtual realities through images. We can move backward in time through memory, biography or family of origin work, or we can move into the present with meditative art work, or forward in time through futurizing "visualization." By doing this, we bridge into past and future aspects of ourselves, thus integrating several of our scattered and fragmented identities, left by the roadside along our journey. Awareness of our location in time and space through art is key. By creating visual "breadcrumbs," we mark our trajectory through life. No "app" can do this for us.

Our brain's natural healing mechanisms can be harnessed quite simply. As we tell our "story" we practice "authorship" of our own lives. Even if we cannot control the circumstances or trauma that life hands us, we can control our response to these things. Our response to life is in fact the only thing we can control. We can practice response-based resilience through the expressive arts. We "restore" through "re-storying."

Through this action of exploring our possible responses to life through artful ways, we can build empowered action. By moving from victim to survivor to activist to evolutionary (which is the transformative passage that reflects the movement from past wound to present awareness to future possibility), we begin to understand how to co-create self-actualization and the capacity to create change— not only "within" us but "without" us too, in our environment. By practicing our "visual voicing" skills in safe groups, we begin to build the necessary self-esteem to speak up about our needs, and speak out about our perspectives, performing acts that resist injustice and demand change. We break through culturally conditioned silencing and suppression that helps maintain the status quo. It is through reversing silence and acquiescence that we make evolutionary change in our culture. The expressive arts help us practice the sharing of trauma, the expression of pain and anger, and even disobedient discourse. This can move us forward into creating better futures.

Through respectful facilitation of bringing silenced discourses into dialogue, thereby disrupting the power of monologue that keeps "otherness" in its place on the margins of society, we can conduct "inquiries" about power and justice, called "conscientization" (Freire, 2006). By harvesting ideas, and shifting our passivity into safe action, we can create better worlds for ourselves and our children.

By doing this practice in groups, and reaching out to audiences, we build social bonds and discover mutuality of experience. We tap into the universal human experience that we all share, but which we sometimes struggle to express. We liberate each other through community and intimacy, as we discover an ecosystem of creativity for co-evolving ourselves into new, more adaptive psychic structures and perspectives. We learn how to reconcile difference and similarity. By mixing with those who are different from us, and those whom we discover are actually the same as us, we grow our tolerance and build mutuality. By joining together, learning together and co-creating together, we co-transform together.

As a by-product to making art, we also expand our cognitive and physical capacities. We develop skills such as hand-to-eye coordination, and aesthetic problem solving. We increase dexterity and kineasthetic learning through activity. Our health is improved on so many levels, as we move, commune and create, not only at the gross, muscular level, but also at the subtle levels of emotion, physiology and neurology, from hemispheric balance, to stress and traumatic memory release, to the stimulation of happy chemicals. And when we practice regularly over the long term, the deepest rewiring of neuronal pathways in our plastic brains is possible. Loneliness, anxiety, depression and stress can be relieved, factors that can be damaging not only to our own bodies but to our economies due to an overload on our healthcare systems. The arts can be used preventatively as well as homeopathically, as a self-soothing, safe release mechanism for accumulated stress, complex grief and patterns of anxiety, isolation and depression that are so prevalent today, and which medication cannot always cure (Vedantam, 2006). The arts help us build empathy and compassion, so desperately needed in our pressured, left-brained world.

By making art we also contribute to our environment by leaving civic gifts behind. Tangible artifacts track culture over time, leaving a rich historical record of our evolving perspectives as a species. We beautify as we go, and at the same time, we record our changing narratives and discourses. We humanize an otherwise barren landscape with our echo objects that document who we are, and who we are becoming. The expressive arts are not merely "decorations" and "commodities," they act as transformative mirrors for our identity as a species. They can be both profoundly "historical" as well as "prophetic," as we move backwards and forward in time and space. In this way, art becomes our global positioning system (GPS) that records the creative movements of our species' psyches.

I would like to close with what I would humbly suggest is the most important reason we might perform critical creative acts that are mutually transformative. The expressive arts align us with the underlying principles embedded within the universe itself. Not only do we mirror ourselves when we create, or mirror our societies; we also mirror the deepest creative drive there is. By accessing our innate creativity, we tap into the generative forces of evolution. Through acts of creativity we "realize" a powerful agency hidden within us, which we can release into what might at first appear to be a chaotic world full of entropy, but which is being organized by intelligent energy well beyond our understanding. As Paul Hogan states earlier:

"The universe in its emergence is neither determined nor random but creative. By aligning ourselves with this creativity through the gift of art we experience healing in our lives." By offering ourselves up to this innate force that is not only in the world around us, but which resides within us too, we allow ourselves to animate the great mystery of the universe—the "constant becoming" of all things, around and inside us, the coming into being of "something" from "nothing," moment by moment. By acts of creativity we move from entropy to playful centropy. We experience our own big bangs.

By aligning ourselves with creation rather than destruction, we confirm that we are alive, potent and part of an ecosystem of energy and intelligence that is self-organizing. By opening ourselves up to something larger than ourselves, something that wishes to express itself through us, we realize we are part of a much larger fractal pattern of "emergence," not just "emergency," both of which can co-exist in the same moment, as change-patterns. Creative acts align us with the larger impulses of the universe, reminding us that we are in fact never separated from the rest of life, however dislocated and dispossessed we may sometimes appear to be. This force of creativity, which is emergent evolution in action, cannot be destroyed, however traumatic our circumstances become (Adnams Jones, 2016).

Practicing creativity and self-expression is one way to align ourselves emotionally and biologically with the forces that create us, minute by minute. We are the result of millions of years of unfolding, and by being creative ourselves we continue to mimic and then fully realize our own coming into more complex orders of being. Whether quietly painting in a contemplative studio, or holding space for others in a desert on the front lines of a global emergency, we serve this evolutionary principle. Notwithstanding our geographic location, language, ethnicity, level of education, skill or talent, creativity only requires us to "do" it, in order to experience multiple, empowering transformations. This is the biofeedback mechanism built into the human body itself, for its survival and evolution. Just as pleasure guides the activities that help the human race survive, such as eating and procreating, we are guided by deepening pleasure that inspires us to create. We are rewarded with joy. When we feel our creativity to be an intelligent and innovative energy moving through us, then the expressive arts begin to serve as a meditative and spiritual practice for accessing depth and surrender to the moment, whatever the moment may look like.

I would like to suggest that creativity is an innate universal principle of joining energy, intelligence and openness to the present moment, in play. All we need to do is allow it to happen. Creativity is the bridge into new mindsets, new thinking and new futures. As Einstein suggested, we cannot solve our problems with the same levels of thinking we used to create them. As we learn how to be creative and understand the dynamics behind transformation, we can become truly generative. This is our power. May we move forward into ever-new thinking and problem solving, through creativity. This is how the transformation of our world will occur—not just through the healing of our own limited, individual experiences of trauma, but by deliberately stepping into our own expansion: through creating, re-creating and co-creating ever more adaptive selves in a universe that is fundamentally driven by change and emergence.

I would like to close with a quote from Howard Gardner (1993), who identifies visual-spatial intelligence as one of the innate intelligences within everyone, and who argues for art curricula that bridge all our multiple intelligences. He says:

> Perhaps if we can mobilize the full range of human intelligences and ally them to an ethical sense, we can help to increase the likelihood of our survival on this planet, and perhaps even contribute to our thriving. (p.12)

My deep gratitude goes to all those who added their wisdom, experience and conviction to this book, which points clearly to placing creativity at the center of our good health—not only for ourselves, but also for the future of our planet.

# CONTRIBUTORS

## Lily Yeh

Lily Yeh is an internationally celebrated artist whose work has taken her to communities throughout the world. As founder and executive director of the Village of Arts and Humanities in North Philadelphia from 1986 to 2004, she helped create a national model of community-building through the arts. In 2002, Yeh founded Barefoot Artists, Inc. in order to bring the transformative power of art to impoverished communities around the globe. In addition to the United States, she has carried out projects in many countries including Kenya, Ivory Coast, Ghana, Rwanda, China, Taiwan, Ecuador, Syria, Republic of Georgia, Haiti, Germany and Palestine. Her life and work are the subject of the feature-length documentary *The Barefoot Artist* (www.barefootartists.org).

## Dr. Carol Hofmeyr

Carol Hofmeyr was born in South Africa and qualified first as a medical doctor and then as an artist. Her husband, Dr Justus Hofmeyr, and their sons, Graeme, Robert and Nkululeko, are all variously involved in the Hamburg community. Carol formed the Keiskamma Trust, to support the citizens of Hamburg through art, healthcare and education. The Trust is run by professionals, volunteers and artists, including the key work of designer Noseti Makhubalo, healer Mavis Zita, educator-advocate Eunice Mangwane and many others. Carol has received an honorary doctorate for her work with HIV survivors (www.keiskamma.org).

## Max Levi Frieder

Max Levi Frieder is the co-founder and co-executive director of the international, community-based, public arts organization, Artolution. He graduated from the Rhode Island School of Design in the US with a degree in painting, and received his Ed.M and Ed.D (Candidate) in "Community Arts" from the Teachers College, Columbia University. His arts projects, which are around the world in refugee camps and hospitals, focus on education in emergencies, counseling through art, trauma relief, abuse, addiction, reconciliation and conflict resolution. His focus is on cultivating public engagement through creative facilitation and inspired community participation (www.artolution.org).

## Paul Hogan

Paul Hogan is a Canadian artist whose organization, Garden Path Serendipity, is dedicated to furthering ideals of community well-being and development through cultivation of the arts and the environment. Paul plays with image, story, myth and theater in collaboration with people from communities affected by civil disorder, natural disaster, poverty and social dislocation the world over. In 2003, he received an Ashoka Fellowship for his work in Sri Lanka. He has written several collections of stories based on his twenty years with the Butterfly Peace Garden of Batticaloa, and has developed a toy-based teaching syllabus called the Out-of-the-Box Curriculum (www.thegardenpath.ca).

## Dr. Sally Adnams Jones

Sally Adnams Jones is an expressive arts therapist and an award-winning artist and author. She is interested in exploring human potentials, reached through creative and meditative practices. She has a BA in Drama and English, an M.Ed in Yoga Education and a PhD in Art Education. She has taught Art and Design in Canada at the University of Victoria and the Pacific Design Academy. She has also been the director of a residential Yoga Education Community, and the director of a five-star Wellness Centre, at a Relais et Chateaux Hotel. When not in her studio, Sally counsels, teaches and researches the principles behind human transformation, creativity and well-being (www.sallyadnamsjones.com).

# REFERENCES

Adichie, C. (2009, July) "The danger of a single story" [video file]. Retrieved November, 2017 from www.ted.com/talks/chimamanda_adichie_the_ danger_of_a_single_story.

Adnams Jones, S. (2016) "Visual Art and Transformation: The Story of an African Village Living with HIV/AIDS." Unpublished dissertation, University of Victoria, British Columbia.

Ahmed, S. (2010) "Foreword." In R. Ryan-Flood and R. Gill (eds) *Secrecy and Silence in the Research Process: Feminist Reflections* (pp.xvi–xxi). New York, NY: Routledge.

AIDS.gov (2017) *Global Statistics*. Retrieved February, 2017 from www.hiv.gov/ hiv-basics/overview/data-and-trends/global-statistics.

Alcoff, L. and Potter. E. (eds) (1993) *Feminist Epistemologies*. London: Routledge.

Alexander, T. (1987) *John Dewey's Theory of Art, Experience, and Nature: The Horizons of Feeling*. Albany, NY: SUNY.

American Psychological Association (2017) *Trauma*. Retrieved February, 2017 from www.apa.org/topics/trauma.

Anda, R.F., Felitti, V.J., Bremner, J.D., Walker, J.D. *et al.* (2006) 'The enduring effects of abuse and related adverse experiences in childhood: A convergence of evidence from neurobiology and epidemiology.' *European Archives of Psychiatry and Clinical Neuroscience*, 256 (3), 174–186. Retrieved November, 2017 from https://link.springer.com/article/10.1007s00406-005-0624-4.

Andemicael, A. (2013) "The arts in refugee camps: Ten good reasons." *Forced Migration Review* (43), 69.

Anderson, A. and Roberts, B. (2005) "The Inter-Agency Network on Education in Emergencies." *Forced Migration Review*, 22, 8–10.

Arnheim, R. (1966) *Toward a Psychology of Art: Collected Essays*. Berkeley, CA: University of California Press.

Badenock, B. (2017) *Trauma and the Embodied Brain. Live Questions and Answers*. Louisville, CO: Sounds True.

Battersby, C. (1989) *Gender and Genius: Towards a Feminist Aesthetics*. Bloomington, IN: Indiana University Press.

Belenky, M.F., Clinchy, B.M., Goldberger, N.R. and Tarule, J.M. (1986) *Women's Ways of Knowing: The Development of Self, Voice and Mind.* New York, NY: Basic Books.

Belfiore, E. (2002) "Art as a means of alleviating social exclusion: Does it really work? A critique of instrumental cultural policies and social impact studies in the UK." *International Journal of Cultural Policy,* 8(1), 91–106.

Bishop, C. (2005) *The Social Turn: Collaboration and Its Discontents.* Artforum. Retrieved November, 2017 from www.gc.cuny.edu/CUNY_GC/media/CUNY-Graduate-Center/PDF/Art History/Claire Bishop/Social-Turn.pdf.

Bolin, P. (1999) "Teaching art as if the world mattered." *Art Education,* 52(4), 4–5.

Borwick, D. (2012) *Building Communities, Not Audiences: The Future of the Arts in the United States.* Winston-Salem, NC: ArtsEngaged.

Buber, M. (1958) *I and Thou.* New York, NY: Charles Scribner.

Cameron, M., Crane, N., Ings, R. and Taylor, K. (2013) "Promoting well-being through creativity: How arts and public health can learn from each other." *Perspectives in Public Health,* 133(1), 52–59.

Caro, J. (2005) *The Passing of a Master Carver and Cowichan Tribes Elder.* Retrieved May, 2017 from www.turtleisland.org/discussion/viewtopic.php?p=5618.

Cassou, M. (2008) *Point Zero: Creativity Without Limits.* San Raphael, CA: Point Zero Publishing.

Center for Nonviolence and Social Justice (2014) *What is Trauma?* Retrieved February, 2017 from www.tfec.org/wp-content/uploads/Murk_WhatisTrauma.pdf.

Chalmers, F.G. (1984) "Art and Ethnology." In R.N. McGregor (ed.) *Readings in Canadian Art Education* (pp.103–115). Vancouver, BC: WEDGE UBC.

Chase, R. (2000) *The Butterfly Garden, Batticaloa, Sri Lanka: Final Report of a Program Development and Research Project, 1998–2000.* Ratualana, Sri Lanka: Sarvodaya.

Coetzee, J.M. (1999) *Disgrace.* London: Secker & Warburg.

Coles, R. (1998) "The moral intelligence of children." *Family Court Review,* 36(1), 90–95.

Cornwall, A. (1998) "Gender Participation and the Politics of Difference." In I. Gujit and M. Kaul Shah (eds.) *The Myth of Community: Gender Issues in Participatory Development* (pp.46–57). London: Intermediate Technology Publications.

Csikszentmihalyi, M. (1990) *Flow: The Psychology of Optimal Experience.* New York, NY: Harper Perennial Modern Classics.

Csikszentmihalyi, M. (1996) *Creativity: Flow and Psychology of Discovery and Invention.* New York, NY: HarperCollins.

Csikszentmihalyi, M. (1997) *Finding Flow: The Psychology of Engagement with Everyday Life.* New York, NY: Basic Books.

Dawkins, R. (1989) *The Selfish Gene.* Oxford: Oxford University Press.

De Vault, M. and Cross, G. (2007) "Feminist Interviewing: Experience, Talk and Knowledge." In S.N. Hesse-Biber (ed.) *Handbook of Feminist Research: Theory and Praxis* (pp.173–197). Thousand Oaks, CA: Sage.

Deecke, M. (2013) *A Critical Assessment of Psychological Theories of Ecstasy: Towards an Integrative Model for Theorising Ecstasy.* Retrieved June, 2017 from www. wuj.pl/UserFiles/File/Studia Religiologica 46/1/FV/FirstView-4-Studia Religiologica46.pdf.

Denzin, N.K. and Lincoln, Y.S. (2008) *Collecting and Interpreting Qualitative Materials* (Vol. 3). Thousand Oaks, CA: Sage.

Dewey, J. (2005) *Art as Experience.* New York: Berkeley Publishing Group. (Original work published 1934.)

Dissanayake, E. (1992) *Homo Aestheticus: Where Art Comes From and Why.* Seattle, WA: University of Washington Press.

Dissanayake, E. (1999) "Making Special: An Undescribed Human Universal and the Core of a Behavior of Art." In B. Cooke and F. Turner (eds) *Biopoetics. Evolutionary Explorations in the Arts.* Lexington, KY: ICUS.

Dissanayake, E. (2008) "The Arts after Darwin: Does Art have an Origin and Adaptive Function?" In K. Zijlmans and W. van Damme (eds) *World Art Studies: Exploring Concepts and Approaches* (pp.241–263). Amsterdam: Valiz.

Dixon, E.J. (2007) "Archaeology and the First Americans." In B. Johansen and B.E. Pritzker (eds) *Encyclopedia of American Indian History* (vol. 1). Santa Barbara, CA: ABC-CLIO, pp.82–87.

Dryden-Peterson, S. (2006) "'I find myself as someone who is in the forest': Urban refugees as agents of social change in Kampala, Uganda." *Journal of Refugee Studies,* 19(3), 381–395.

Dutton, D. (2009) *The Art Instinct: Beauty, Pleasure and Human Evolution.* New York, NY: Bloomsbury Press.

Edwards, B. (1999) *The New Drawing on the Right Side of the Brain.* New York, NY: Tarcher.

Eisner, E. (2002) *The Arts and the Creation of Mind.* New Haven, CT: Yale University Press.

El-Bushra, J. (2000) "Transforming Conflict: Some Thoughts on Gendered Understanding of Conflict Processes." In S. Jacobs, R. Jacobson and J. Marchbank (eds) *States of Conflict: Gender, Violence and Resistance.* London and New York, NY: Zed Books.

Feige, D. (2010) "Art as reflexive practice." *Proceedings of the European Society for Aesthetics* (vol. 2). Retrieved December, 2013 from http://proceedings. eurosa.org/2/feige2010.pdf.

Fleming, M. (2010) *Arts in Education and Creativity: A Literature Review.* Newcastle upon Tyne: Great North House.

Fosha, D. (2017) *Transformation in ADP.* Sounds True Psychotherapy summit. Retrieved September, 2017.

Foucault, M. (1980) *Power/Knowledge: Selected Interviews and Other Writings.* New York, NY: Pantheon.

Frankl, V. (2006) *Man's Search for Meaning.* Boston, MA: Beacon Press.

Freire, P. (2006) *Pedagogy of the Oppressed.* New York, NY: Continuum. (Original work published 1970.)

Frost, J.L., Wortham, S.C. and Reifel, S.C. (2001) *Play and Child Development.* University of Texas, Austin, TX: Pearson.

Gablik, S. (1993) "The ecological imperative: Making art as if the world mattered." *Michigan Quarterly Review,* 32, 231.

Gal, S. (1991) "Between Speech and Silence." In M. di Leonardo (ed.) *Gender and the Crossroads of Knowledge.* Berkeley, CA: University of California Press.

Garavan, T. (1997) "The learning organization: A review and evaluation." *The Learning Organization,* 4(1), 18–29.

Gardner, H. (1993) *Multiple Intelligences: The Theory in Practice.* New York, NY: Basic Books.

Gargarella, E. (2007) *Landmarks for change: A case study examining the impact of community-based art education program on adolescents.* Available from ProQuest Dissertations & Theses Global. (304891333). Retrieved November, 2017 from https://etd.ohiolink.edu/pg_10?0::NO:10:P10_ACCESSION_NUM: akron1176391368.

Gaztambide-Fernandez, R.A. (2013) "Why the arts don't do anything: Towards a new vision of cultural production in education." *Harvard Educational Review,* 83(1), 211–236.

Gee, J.P. (2000) "Identity as an analytic lens for research in education." *Review of Research in Education,* 25(1), 99–125.

Gilligan, C. (1982) *In a Different Voice.* Cambridge, MA: Harvard University Press.

Goebel, T., Waters, M.R. and O'Rourke, D.H. (2008) "The Late Pleistocene Dispersal of Modern Humans in the Americas." *Science,* 319 (5869): 1497–1502.

Goldbard, A. (2006) *New Creative Community: The Art of Cultural Development.* Oakland, CA: New Village Press.

Goleman, D. (1996) *Emotional Intelligence: Why It Can Matter More Than IQ.* London: Bloomsbury Press.

Goleman, D. (2007) *Social Intelligence: Beyond IQ, Beyond Emotional Intelligence.* New York, NY: Bantam Books.

Goodman, A. (2002) "Transformative Learning and Cultures of Peace." In E.O'Sullivan, A. Morrell and M.A. O'Connor (eds) *Expanding the Boundaries of Transformative Learning: Essays on Theory and Praxis* (pp.185–198). New York, NY: Palgrave.

Graham, L. (2017) *Neuroscience for Psychotherapists.* Sounds True Psychotherapy summit. Retrieved September, 2017.

Greene, M. (1977) "Imagination and aesthetic literacy." *Art Education,* 30(6), 14–20.

Greene, M. (1995a) "Art and imagination: Reclaiming the sense of possibility." *Phi Delta Kappan,* 76(5), 378–382.

Greene, M. (1995b) *Releasing the Imagination: Essays on Education, the Arts, and Social Change.* San Francisco, CA: John Wiley and Sons.

Guetzkow, J. (2002) *How the Arts Impact Communities.* Princeton University, NJ: Center for Arts and Cultural Policy Studies.

Gugliotta, G. (2013) "When did humans come to the Americas?" *Smithsonian Magazine*. Washington, DC: Smithsonian Institution. Retrieved May, 2017 from www.smithsonianmag.com/sciencenature/when-did-humans-come-to-the-americas-4209273/?all&no-ist.

Hall, L. (2006) "The Transformative Potential of Visual Language with Special Reference to DWEBA's Use of Drawing as a Participatory Training Methodology in the Development Facilitation Context in KwaZulu-Natal." Unpublished Master's thesis in Fine Arts, KwaZulu-Natal University, Pietermaritzburg.

Hallmark, E.F. (2012) "Challenge: The arts as collaborative inquiry." *Arts Education Policy Review,* 113(3), 93–99.

Harding, S. (1993) "Rethinking Standpoint Epistemology: What is 'Strong Objectivity'?" In L. Alcoff and E. Potter (eds) *Feminist Epistemologies*. London: Routledge.

Havel, V. (1993) "Never Hope Against Hope." *Esquire*. Retrieved January, 2018 from http://www.esquire.com/news-politics/news/a12135/vaclav-havel-hope-6619552/.

Hement, J. (2007) "Public anthropology and the paradoxes of participation: Participatory action research and critical ethnography in provincial Russia." *Human Organization,* 66(3), 301–314.

Hesse-Biber, S.N. and Piatelli, D. (2007) "The Synergistic Praxis of Theory and Method." In S.N. Hesse-Biber (ed.) *Handbook of Feminist Research: Theory and Praxis* (pp.176–186). Thousand Oaks, CA: Sage.

Hicks, J.A. and King, L.A. (2007) "Meaning in life and seeing the big picture: Positive affect and global focus." *Cognition and Emotion,* 21(7), 1577–1584.

Hofmeyr, G., Georgiou, T. and Baker, C. (2009) "The Keiskamma AIDS Treatment Programme: Evaluation of a community-based antiretroviral programme in a rural setting." *SAJHIVMED,* 10(1), 38–41.

Holt, R.D. (1983) "Models for peripheral populations: The role of immigration." *Population Biology* (pp.25–32). Berlin/Heidelberg: Springer. (Original work published 1967.)

Horsefield, G. (2002) *The Slums: A Challenge to Evangelization*. Tangaza Occasional Papers, No. 14, p.26. Nairobi: Pauline's Publications Africa.

Hughes, L. (1931) *Dear Lovely Death*. New York, NY: Oxford University Press.

Huss, E. and Cwikel, J. (2005) "Researching creations: Applying arts-based research to Bedouin women's drawings." *International Journal of Qualitative Methods,* 4(4), 2–16.

Jenkins, H., Purushotma, R., Weigel, M., Clinton, K. and Robison, A.J. (2009) *Confronting the Challenges of Participatory Culture: Media Education for the 21st Century*. Cambridge, MA: MIT Press.

Jensen, E. (2001) *Arts with the Brain in Mind*. Alexandria, VA: ASCD (Association for Supervision and Curriculum Development).

Joseph, S. (2012) "What is trauma?" *Psychology Today*. Retrieved February, 2017 from www.psychologytoday.com/blog/what-doesnt-kill-us/201201/what-is-trauma.

Jung, C.G. (1959) *The Archetypes and the Collective Unconscious: The Collected Works of C.G. Jung (Vol. 9, Part 1).* H. Read, M. Fordham and G. Adler (eds) New York, NY: Bollingen Foundation and Pantheon Books.

Jung, C.G. (1966) *The Spirit in Man, Art, and Literature: The Collected Works of C.G. Jung (Vol. 15.).* H. Read, M. Fordham, G. Adler and W. McGuire (eds). New York, NY: Bollingen Foundation and Princeton University Press.

Jung, C.G. (1968) *Analytical Psychology: Its Theory and Practice (The Tavistock Lectures).* London: Routledge & Kegan Paul PLC.

Jung, C.G. (1971) *Collected Works by C.G. Jung. (Vol. 15, Spirit in Man, Art, and Literature).* (G. Adler and R.F.C. Hull, Trans.). H. Read, M. Fordham, and G. Adler (eds). Princeton, NJ: Princeton University Press.

Jung, C.G. (2009) *The Red Book: Liber Novus.* New York, NY: W.W. Norton.

Jung, C.G. (2014) *Collected Works of C.G. Jung. (Vol. 2, Psychology and Religion: West and East)* (2nd edn). H. Read and G. Adler (eds) (G. Adler and R.F.C. Hull, Trans.). Princeton, NJ: Princeton University Press.

Jung, C.G. and Read, H. (1968) *On the Psychology of the Trickster-Figure.* London: Routledge and Kegan Paul.

Kandel, E. (2012) *The Age of Insight: The Quest to Understand the Unconscious in Art, Mind, and Brain.* New York, NY: Random House.

Kelly, L. (2000) "Wars Against Women: Sexual Violence, Sexual Politics and the Militarized State." In S. Jacobs, R. Jacobson and J. Marchbank (eds) *States of Conflict: Gender, Violence and Resistance.* London and New York, NY: Zed Books.

Kesby, M. (2005) "Retheorizing empowerment-through-participation as a performance of space." *Signs,* 30(4), 2037–2065.

Kirmayer, L.J., Narasiah, L., Munoz, M., Rashid, M. *et al.* (2011) "Common mental health problems in immigrants and refugees: General approach in primary care." *Canadian Medical Association Journal,* 183(12), published for the Canadian Collaboration for Immigrant and Refugee Health. Retrieved February, 2017 from www.ncbi.nlm.nih.gov/pmc/articles/PMC3168672.

Korsmeyer, C. (2012) "Feminist aesthetics." *Stanford Encyclopaedia of Aesthetics.* Retrieved November, 2017 from https://plato.stanford.edu/entries/feminism-aesthetics.

Kovecses, Z., Benczes, R. and Csabi, S. (2009) *Metaphor: A Practical Introduction.* Oxford: Oxford University Press.

Krensky, B. (2009) *Engaging Classrooms and Communities through Art: A Guide to Designing and Implementing Community-Based Art Education.* Lanham, MA: AltaMira Press.

Lacy, S. (1994) *Mapping the Terrain: New Genre Public Art.* Seattle, WA: Bay Press.

Lafrenière, G., Diallo, P.L., Dubie, D. and Henry, L. (2005) "Can university/community collaboration create spaces for Aboriginal reconciliation? A case study of the healing of the seven generations and Four Directions community projects and Wilfrid Laurier University." *The First Peoples' Child & Family Review,* 2(1), 53–66. Cited in Thurston (2012).

Lakoff, G. and Johnson, M. (1980) *Metaphors We Live By*. Chicago, IL: University of Chicago Press.

Lao-Tze (1988) *Tao Te Ching*. Translated by Stephen Mitchell. New York, NY: HarperCollins.

LaRocque, E. (2017) *Aboriginal Perspectives*. Retrieved March 3, 2017 from www3.nfb.ca/enclasse/doclens/visau/index.php?mode=theme&language=english&theme= 30662&film=&excerpt=&submode=about&expmode=2.

Levine, P. (2010) *In an Unspoken Voice: How the Body Releases Trauma and Restores Goodness*. Berkeley, CA: North Atlantic Books.

London, P. (1989) *No More Second-Hand Art: Awakening the Artist Within*. Boston, MA: Shambhala.

London, P. (1992) "Art as transformation." *Art Education,* 45(3), 8–15.

Lowe, S. (2000) "Creating community: Art for community development." *Journal of Contemporary Ethnography,* 29(3), 357–386.

Lowenfeld, V. and Brittain, W.L. (1987) *Creative and Mental Growth*. Upper Saddle River, NJ: Prentice Hall.

Lynch, R.T. and Chosa, D. (1996) "Group-oriented communuty-based expressive arts programming for individuals with disabilities: Participant satisfaction and perceptions of psychosocial impact." *Journal of Rehabilitation,* 62(3), 75.

Majob, S. (2004) "No 'Safe Haven:' Violence Against Women in Iraqi Kurdistan." In W. Giles and J. Hyndman (eds) *Sites of Violence: Gender and Conflict Zones*. Berkeley, CA: University of California Press.

Mak, M. (2006) "Unwanted Images: Tackling Gender-Based Violence in a South African School through Youth Artwork." In F. Leach and C. Mitchell (eds) *Combatting Gender-Based Violence in and around Schools* (pp.113–123). London: Trentham Books.

Malchiodi, C. (2006/7) *Art Therapy Source Book*. New York, NY: McGraw-Hill Publishers.

Malchiodi, C. (ed.) (2012) *Handbook of Art Therapy*. New York, NY: Guilford Press.

Manji, A. (1999) "Feminism and methodology: Studying the impact of AIDS using participatory research." *Southern African Feminist Review,* 3(20), 1–18.

Maslow, A.H (1954) *Motivation and Personality*. New York, NY: Harper and Row.

Maslow, A.H. (1964) *Religions, Values, and Peak Experiences*. London: Penguin Books.

Maslow, A.H. (1968) *Toward a Psychology of Being*. New York, NY: Van Nostrand-Reinhold.

Maslow, A.H (1970/2014) *Religions, Values and Peak-experiences*. New York, NY: Important Books.

May, R. (1994) *The Courage to Create*. New York, NY: Norton. (Original work published 1978.)

McCarthy, K. and Kimberly, J. (2001) *A New Framework for Building Participation in the Arts*. Santa Monica, CA: RAND.

McGilchrist, I. (2009) *The Master and His Emissary: The Divided Brain and the Making of the Western World*. New Haven, CT: Yale University Press.

McNiff, S. (1992) *Art as Medicine: Creating a Therapy of the Imagination.* Boston, MA: Shambhala Publications.

McNiff, S. (1998) *Trust the Process: An Artist's Guide to Letting Go.* Boston, MA: Shambhala.

McNiff, S. (2004) *Art Heals: How Creativity Cures the Soul.* Boston, MA: Shambhala.

Merryfeather, L. (2014) "Stories of Women Who Support Trans Men: An Autoethnographic Voyage." Unpublished doctoral dissertation, University of Victoria, BC.

Mezirow, J. and Associates (1990) *Fostering Critical Reflection in Adulthood: A Guide to Transformative and Emancipatory Learning.* San Francisco, CA: Jossey-Bass.

Mezirow, J. and Associates (2010) *Learning as Transformation: Critical Perspectives on a Theory in Progress.* San Francisco, CA: Jossey-Bass. (Original work published 2000.)

Mienczakowski, J. (1995) "The theater of ethnography: The reconstruction of ethnography into theater with emancipatory potential." *Qualitative Inquiry,* 1(3), 360–375.

Mitchell, C. (2008) "Taking the picture, changing the picture: Visual methodologies in educational research in South Africa." *South African Journal of Educational Research,* 28(3), 365–383.

Mitchell, C. (2011) *Doing Visual Research.* Los Angeles, CA: Sage.

Mitchell, C., DeLange, N., Moletsane, R., Stuart, J. and Buthelezi, T. (2005) "Giving a face to HIV and AIDS: On the uses of photo-voice by teachers and community health care workers working with youth in rural South Africa." *Qualitative Research in Psychology,* 2(3), 257–270.

Moacanin, R. (2003) *The Essence of Jung's Psychology and Tibetan Buddhism.* Somerville, MA: Wisdom Publications.

Moletsane, R., Mitchell, C., De Lange, N., Stuart, J., Buthelezi, T. and Taylor, M. (2009) "What can a woman do with a camera? Turning the female gaze on poverty and HIV/AIDS in rural South Africa." *International Journal of Qualitative Studies in Education,* 22(3), 315–331.

Moskin, B. and Jackson, J. (2004) *Warrior Angel: The Work of Lily Yeh.* Retrieved October, 2017 from www.virtuevision.org/lily_yeh.pdf.

Naidus, B. (2009) *Arts for Change: Teaching Outside the Frame.* Oakland, CA: New Village Press.

*New York Times* (2015) "The global refugee crisis, region by region." Retrieved November, 2017 from www.nytimes.com/interactive/2015/06/09/world/migrants-global-refugee-crisis-mediterranean-ukraine-syria-rohingya-malaysia-iraq.html?_r=0.

O'Sullivan, E. (2002) "The Project and Vision of Transformative Education: Integral Transformative Learning." In E. O'Sullivan, A. Morrell and M.A. O'Connor (eds) (2002) *Expanding the Boundaries of Transformative Learning: Essays on Theory and Praxis* (pp.1–12). New York, NY: Palgrave.

Olsen, T. (2003) *Silences.* New York, NY: Feminist Press at CUNY. (Original work published 1978.)

Osho (1999) *Creativity: Unleashing the Forces Within*. New York, NY: St Martin's Griffin.

Parpart, J.L. (2010) "Choosing Silence: Rethinking Voice, Agency and Women's Empowerment." In R. Ryan-Flood and R. Gill (eds) *Secrecy and Silence in the Research Process: Feminist Reflections* (pp.15–29). New York, NY: Routledge.

Park-Fuller, L.M. (2003) "Audiencing the audience: Playback theatre, performative writing, and social activism." *Text and Performance Quarterly*, 23(3), 288–310.

Phoenix, A. (2004) "Extolling Eclecticism: Language, Psychoanalysis and Demographic Analysis, in the Study of 'Race' and 'Racism'." In M. Bulmer and J. Solomos (eds) *Researching Race and Racism* (pp. 37–51). London: Routledge.

Pillow, W. and Mayo, C. (2007) "Toward Understandings of Feminist Ethnography." In S.N. Hesse-Biber (ed.) *Handbook of Feminist Research: Theory and Praxis* (pp.155–171). Thousand Oaks, CA: Sage.

Pink, D.H. (2006) *A Whole New Mind: Why Right-brainers will Rule the World*. New York, NY: Riverhead Books, Penguin.

Provencal, A. and Gabora, L. (2007) "A compelling overview of art therapy techniques and outcomes: Review of 'Art Therapy has Many Faces'." *Psychology of Aesthetics, Creativity, and the Arts*, 1(4), 255–256.

Ramazonoglu, C. (with Holland, J.) (2002) *Feminist Methodology: Challenges and Choices*. London: Sage.

Read, H. (1943) *Education Through Art*. London: Faber and Faber.

Read, H. (1951) *Art and the Evolution of Man*. London: Freedom Press.

Read, H. (1960) *The Forms of Things Unknown: Towards an Aesthetic Philosophy*. New York, NY: Horizon Press.

Read, H. (1967) *Art and Alienation: The Role of the Artist in Society*. London: Thames and Hudson.

Rice, J. (2011) "Indian residential school truth and reconciliation Commission of Canada." *Cultural Survival Quarterly Magazine*. Retrieved May, 2017 from www.culturalsurvival.org/publications/cultural-survival-quarterly/indian-residential-school-truth-and-reconciliation.

Richardson, C. (2011) "The portable John Latham: Documents from the John Latham archive." *Visual Culture in Britain*, 12(3), 387–389.

Rogers, C.R. (1942) *Counseling and Psychotherapy: Newer Concepts in Practice*. Boston, MA: Houghton Mifflin Company.

Rosenthal, M. (2015) *The Science Behind PTSD Symptoms: How Trauma Changes the Brain*. Psych Central. Retrieved October 9, 2017 from https://psychcentral.com/blog/archives/2015/09/16/the-science-behind-ptsd-symptoms-how-trauma-changes-the-brain.

Rothschild, B. (with Rand, M.L.) (2006) *Help for the Helper: The Psychophysiology of Compassion Fatigue and Vicarious Trauma*. New York, NY: Norton.

Ryan, A.B. (2001) *Feminist Ways of Knowing: Towards Theorizing the Person for Radical Adult Education*. Leicester: National Institute of Adult Continuing Education.

Ryan-Flood, R. and Gill, R. (eds) (2010) *Secrecy and Silence in the Research Process: Feminist Reflections.* New York, NY: Routledge.

Santa Barbara, J. (2004) "The Butterfly Peace Garden." *Croatian Medical Journal,* 45(2), 232–233.

Schneider Adams, L. (1994) *Art and Psychoanalysis.* Boulder, CO: Westview Press.

Schugurensky, D. (2002) "Transformative Learning and Transformative Politics: The Pedagogical Dimension of Participatory Democracy and Social Action." In E. O'Sullivan, A. Morrell and M.A. O'Connor (eds) *Expanding the Boundaries of Transformative Learning: Essays on Theory and Praxis* (pp.59–76). New York, NY: Palgrave.

Seham, J.C. (1997) "The effects on at-risk children of an in-school dance program." Unpublished doctoral dissertation, Adelphi University, New York.

Shamay-Tsoory, S.G. (2011) "The neural bases for empathy." *The Neuroscientist,* 17(1), 18–24.

Shephard, G. (2014) *Community Art for Change: Architects of Change.* Knowledge Network TV documentary, Canada. April 2014.

Shuman, A. (2005) *Other People's Stories: Entitlement Claims and the Critique of Empathy.* Urbana, IL: University of Illinois Press.

Shusterman, R. (2008) *Body Consciousness: A Philosophy of Mindfulness and Somaesthetics.* Cambridge: Cambridge University Press.

Silber, I.C. (2005) "Mothers, Fighters, Citizens: Violence and Disillusionment in Post-War El Salvador." In S.D. Cruze and A. Rao (eds) *Violence, Vulnerability and Embodiment.* Oxford: Blackwell.

Simon Fraser University Museum (2008) *A Journey into Time Immemorial: Bark Stripping.* Retrieved May, 2017 from www.sfu.museum/time/en/panoramas/beach/bark-stripping.

Smilan, C. (2009) "Building resiliency to childhood trauma through arts-based learning." *Childhood Education,* 85(6), 380–384.

Smilan, C. (2011) *Art Education: Annotated Bibliography.* Oxford Bibliography Online, Oxford Publications. Retrieved January, 2018 from http://www.oxfordbibliographies.com/view/document/obo-9780199756810/obo-9780199756810004.xml?rskey=vAZL8s&result=1&q=cathy+smilan #firstMatch

Smith, H. (1976) *Forgotten Truth.* New York, NY: Harper.

Stafford, M.B. (1994) *Artful Science: Enlightenment, Entertainment, and the Eclipse of Visual Education.* Cambridge, MA: MIT Press.

Stafford, M.B. (2007) *Echo Objects: The Cognitive Work of Images.* Chicago, IL: University of Chicago Press.

Stanley, L. and Wise, S. (1993) *Breaking Out Again: Feminist Ontology and Epistemology.* London: Routledge.

Steif, A. (2010) "Endless Resurrection: Art and Ritual in the Upper Paleolithic." Unpublished honors thesis, University of Michigan, Ann Arbor.

Stephens, P.G. (2006) "A real community bridge: informing community-based learning through a model of participatory public art." *Art Education,* 59(2), 40–46.

Stockett, K. (2009) *The Help.* New York, NY: Penguin.

Stuckey, H.L. and Nobel, J. (2010) "The connection between art, healing, and public health: A review of current literature." *American Journal of Public Health,* 100(2), 254–263.

Talbot, C. (2013) *Education in Conflict: Emergencies in Light of the Post-2015 MDGs and EFA Agendas.* Network for International Policies and Cooperation in Education and Training (NORRAG), Working Paper #3.

Tedeschi, R. and Calhoun, L. (2004) "Posttraumatic Growth: A New Perspective on Psychotraumatology." *Psychiatric Times,* 21 (4). Retrieved January, 2018 from http://www.psychiatrictimes.com/ptsd/posttraumatic-growth-new-perspective-psychotraumatology-0.

Thurston, W.E. (2012) *Intervention to Address Intergenerational Trauma: Overcoming, Resisting and Preventing Structural Violence. Intergenerationl Trauma and Aboriginal Youth.* Retrieved May, 2017 from www.ucalgary.ca/wethurston/files/wethurston/Report_InterventionToAddressIntergenerationalTrauma.pdf.

Tolstoy, L. (1942) *War and Peace.* New York, NY: Simon and Schuster.

Turtle Island Magazine (2003) Retrieved May, 2017 from www.turtleisland.org/discussion/viewtopic.php?t=1041.

United Nations (2015) *International Migration Report, 2015, Highlights.* New York, NY: United Nations, Department of Social and Economic Affairs. Retrieved November 17, 2016 from www.un.org/en/development/desa/population/migration/publications/migrationreport/docs/MigrationReport2015_Highlights.pdf.

United Nations Educational, Scientific and Cultural Organization (UNESCO) (2011) *The Quantitative Impact of Conflict on Education.* Retrieved November, 2017 from http://unesdoc.unesco.org/images/0019/001913/191304e.pdf.

United Nations Educational, Scientific and Cultural Organization (UNESCO) (2012) "Twenty percent of young people in developing countries fail to complete primary school and lack skills for work." Retrieved November, 2017 from http://en.unesco.org/gem-report/sites/gem-report/files/gmr2012-pressrelease.pdf.

United Nations Educational, Scientific and Cultural Organization (UNESCO) (2016) *UNESCO Report 2016.* Retrieved November, 2017 from http://en.unesco.kz/unesco-report-2016.

United Nations High Commissioner for Refugees (2015) *Global Trends Report 2014: World at War.* Geneva: UNHCR.

United Nations Refugee Agency (2016) *Worldwide Displacement Hits All-time High as War and Persecution Increase.* Retrieved November 25, 2016 from www.unhcr.org/558193896.html.

Van der Kolk, B. (2014) *The Body Keeps the Score: Brain, Mind, and Body in the Healing of Trauma.* New York, NY: Viking Publishers.

Van der Kolk, B. (2017) *PTSD.* Sounds True. Trauma summit. Retrieved November, 2017 from www.goodreads.com/work/quotes/26542319-the-body-keeps-the-score-brain-mind-and-body-in-the-healing-of-trauma.

Vedantam, S. (2006) *Drugs Cure Depression in Half of Patients.* Retrieved September, 2017 from www.washingtonpost.com/wp-dyn/content/article/2006/03/22/AR2006032202450.html.

Wachiira, K. (2009) *Taking Root: Vision of Wangari Maathai.* Retrieved May, 2017 from www.popmatters.com/review/73023-independent-lens-taking-root-the-vision-of-wangari-maathai.

Ward, J. and Winstanley, D. (2003) "The absent presence: Negative space within discourse and the construction of minority sexual identity in the workplace." *Human Relations,* 56(10), 1255–1280.

Weitz, J. (1996) *Coming Up Taller: Arts and Humanities Programs for Children and Youth at Risk.* Darby, PA: Diane Publishing.

White, M. (2009) *Arts Development in Community Health: A Social Tonic.* Oxford: Radcliffe Publishing.

Wilber, K. (1996) *A Brief History of Everything.* Boston, MA: Shambhala.

Wilber, K. (2000) *Integral Psychology: Consciousness, Spirit, Psychology, Therapy.* Boston, MA and London: Shambhala.

Williams, D. (1995) *Creating Social Capital: A Study of the Long-Term Benefits from Community Based Arts Funding.* Adelaide: Community Arts Network of South Australia.

World Health Organization (1948) *Preamble to the Constitution of the World Health Organization.* Official Records of the WHO 2. Geneva: World Health Organization.

World Health Organization (2016) *Refugees.* Retrieved November 25, 2016 from www.who.int/topics/refugees/en.

Wurman, R.S. (ed.) (1986) *What Will Be Has Always Been: The Words of Louis I. Kahn.* New York, NY: Access Press and Rizzoli International.

Yeats, W.B. (2015) *Adam's Curse.* Retrieved November, 2017 from www.poetryfoundation.org/poem/172057.

# SUBJECT INDEX

# AUTHOR INDEX

Printed in Great Britain
by Amazon

64546329R00185